PAUL THE MARTYR

Society of Biblical Literature

Writings from the Greco-Roman World Supplement Series

John T. Fitzgerald, Editor

Number 4

PAUL THE MARTYR

The Cult of the Apostle in the Latin West

PAUL THE MARTYR

THE CULT OF THE APOSTLE IN THE LATIN WEST

By

David L. Eastman

Society of Biblical Literature
Atlanta

PAUL THE MARTYR
The Cult of the Apostle in the Latin West

Library of Congress Cataloging-in-Publication Data

Eastman, David L.
    Paul the martyr : the cult of the apostle in the latin west / by David L. Eastman.
        p. cm. — (Society of Biblical Literature. Writings from the Greco-Roman
        World. Supplements ; 4)
    Includes bibliographical references and index.
    ISBN 978-1-58983-515-3 (paper binding : alk. paper) — ISBN 978-1-58983-516-0
    (electronic format)
    1. Paul, the Apostle, Saint—Cult—Rome. I. Title.
    BS2506.3.E27 2011
    225.9' 2—dc22   2011000223

19 18 17 16 15 14 13 12 11   5 4 3 2 1
Printed on acid-free, recycled paper conforming to
ANSI/NISO Z39.48-1992 (R1997) and ISO 9706:1994
standards for paper permanence.

CONTENTS

ACKNOWLEDGMENTS

Writing this book has been possible only because of the generous support of my family and many other people in my life. First and foremost, I wish to thank my wife, Natalie, who has been a constant source of encouragement throughout this process and a wonderful companion on the many adventures that research travel can bring.

My research has been greatly aided by the feedback of a number of colleagues. Bentley Layton, Stephen Davis, Robert S. Nelson, Harold Attridge, and John Matthews read this manuscript in dissertation form and offered insightful critiques that sparked my thinking in fruitful directions as I began revisions. John T. Fitzgerald has done exemplary work as the editor of this volume, always prompting greater clarity in the development of my arguments. A number of other colleagues have read portions of this manuscript or have brought to my attention important comparative materials, including Candida Moss, Nicola Camerlenghi, Ryan Stokes, Brent Nongbri, Timothy Luckritz Marquis, Paul Dilley, Tudor Sala, Michael Peppard, Joshua Garroway, Jeremy Hultin, Joshua Burns, Adela Yarbro Collins, Dale Martin, Robert Gregg, Raymond Van Dam, Danny Praet, Robin Jensen, Marcia Colish, Kevin Wilkinson, and Wolfgang Wischmeyer. I am also indebted to the many great teacher-scholars who have invested in me and fueled my enthusiasm for historical exploration, especially Timothy Gregory, Paul Magdalino, Ruth Macrides, Jean-Pierre Arrignon, and Helmut Koester.

Special assistance during my research in Rome was provided by Giorgio Filippi, Director of Excavations at the Basilica of St. Paul Outside the Walls, who has graciously allowed me access to photographs and other materials related to his ongoing research at the basilica. Umberto Utro, Curator of the Museo Pio Cristiano of the Vatican Museums, spent an afternoon discussing with me the museum's rich collection of sarcophagi and has since provided me with other research support. Financial support for research travel came from Yale University, the Stavros S. Niarchos Research Fellowship, and the Berkeley, Biddle, and Woolsey Travel Fellowship of the Yale Department of Classics.

Finally, I wish to extend sincere thanks to my parents, John and Beulah Eastman. Over the years they have made numerous sacrifices—too many to count, in fact—to enable me to pursue my academic dreams. This book is dedicated to them.

ABBREVIATIONS

PRIMARY SOURCES

1 Apol.	Justin Martyr, *Apologia I*
1 Clem.	*1 Clement* (Πρὸς Κορινθίους)
Act. apost.	Arator, *De actibus apostolorum*
Acta Cypr.	*Acta Cypriani*
Acta mart. Scillit.	*Acta martyrum Scillitanorum*
Acta Pet.	*Acta Petri*
Acta Pet. Paul.	*Acta Petri et Pauli*
Acta Phil.	*Acta Phileae*
Acta Thom.	*Acta Thomae*
Acta Xanth. Pol. Reb.	*Acta Xanthippae et Polyxenae et Rebeccae*
Adv. Donat.	Optatus of Milev, *Adversus Donatistas*
Adv. Jud.	Tertullian, *Adversus Judaeos*
Aen.	Virgil, *Aeneid*
Ann.	Tacitus, *Annales*
Apol.	Tertullian, *Apologeticus*
Apos. Con.	*Constitutiones apostolicae*
Bibl. hist.	Diodorus of Sicily, *Bibliotheca historica*
Brev. vit.	Seneca, *De brevitate vitae* (*Epistulae morales*)
C. Const.	Hilary of Poitiers, *Liber contra Constantium*
C. Galil.	Julian, *Contra Galileos*
C. litt. Petil.	Augustine of Hippo, *Contra litteras Petiliani*
Carm.	*Carmina* (various authors)
Catech.	Cyril of Jerusalem, *Catecheses*
Chron.	Jerome, *Chronicon*
Cod. Theod.	*Codex Theodosianus*
Comm. Ezech.	Jerome, *Commentariorum in Ezechielem libri XVI*
Comm. Gal.	Jerome, *Commentariorum in Epistulam ad Gatatas libri III*
Conf.	Augustine of Hippo, *Confessionum libri XIII*
Cur.	Augustine of Hippo, *De cura pro mortuis gerenda*

Dep. mart.	*Depositio martyrum*
Dial.	Sulpicius Severus, *Dialogi*
Dies nat. Pet. Paul.	Augustine of Hippo, *Sermo in die natalico apostolorum sanctorum Petri et Pauli*
Div.	Cicero, *De divinatione*
Ep.	*Epistulae* (various authors)
Ep. Tars.	Pseudo-Ignatius, *Epistula ad Tarsenses*
Ep. Tra.	Pliny the Younger, *Epistulae ad Trajanum*
Epigr.	*Epigrammata* (various authors)
Epit. chron.	Prosper of Aquitaine, *Epitoma chronicon*
Exc.	Ambrose of Milan, *De excessu fratris sui Satyri*
Fast.	Ovid, *Fasti*
Flod. hist. rem. eccl.	Flodard of Reims, *Flodoardi historia remensis ecclesiae*
Fr. hist.	Hilary of Poitiers, *Fragmenta historica*
FSI	Fonti per la storia d'Italia
Geogr.	Strabo, *Geographica*
Glor. mart.	Gregory of Tours, *De gloria martyrum*
Glor. martyr.	Pseudo-Cyprian, *De gloria martyrii*
Goth.	Procopius of Caesarea, *Bellum gothicum*
Haer.	Irenaeus of Lyon, *Adversus haereses*
Herm. *Vis.*	Shepherd of Hermas, *Vision(s)*
Hist. eccl.	*Historia ecclesiastica* (various authors)
Hist. franc.	Gregory of Tours, *Historia francorum*
Hist. persec.	Victor of Vita, *Historia persecutionis Africanae provinciae*
Hist. Rom.	Velleius Paterculus, *Historiae Romanae*
Hom.	*Homiliae* (various authors)
Hom. Act.	John Chrysostom, *Homiliae in Acta apostolorum*
Hom. Eph.	John Chrysostom, *Homiliae in epistulam ad Ephesios*
Hom. Gen.	John Chrysostom, *Homiliae in Genesim*
Hom. Rom.	John Chrysostom, *Homiliae in epistulam ad Romanos*
Hymn.	Ambrose of Milan, *Hymni*
Ign. *Rom.*	Ignatius of Antioch, *To the Romans*
Itiner.	Egeria, *Itinerarium*
Jud. gent.	John Chrysostom, *Contra Judaeos et gentiles quod Christus sit deus*
Laud. Paul.	John Chrysostom, *De laudibus sancti Pauli apostoli*
Laud. sanct.	Victricius of Rouen, *De laude sanctorum*
Leg.	Cicero, *De legibus*
Lib. pontif.	*Liber pontificalis*
Loc. sanct.	*De locis sanctis martyrum quae sunt foris civitatis Romae*
Luct.	Lucian of Samosata, *De luctu*

Mart.	John Chrysostom, *Homilia in martyres*
Mart. Ascen. Isa.	*Martyrdom and Ascension of Isaiah*
Mart. Hier.	*Martyrologium Hieronymianum*
Mart. Ign.	*Martyrium Ignatii*
Mart. Paul.	*Martyrium sancti Pauli apostoli (Acta Pauli)*
Mart. Perp. Felic.	*Martyrium Perpetuae et Felicitatis*
Mart. Pol.	*Martyrium Polycarpi*
Mirabil.	*Mirabiliana*
Mirac. Anast.	*Miraculum sancti Anastasii martyris*
Mirac. Theclae	Basil of Seleucia, *Miracula Theclae*
Mort.	Lactantius, *De mortibus persecutorum*
Nero	Suetonius, *Vita neronis (De vita caesarum)*
Oboed.	Augustine of Hippo, *De oboedientia*
Or. 4 (C. Jul.)	Gregory of Nazianzus, *Oratio 4 (Contra Julianum)*
Pass. Dat. Saturn.	*Passio ss. Dativi, Saturnini presb. et aliorum (Acts of the Abitinian Martyrs)*
Pass. Paul.	*Passio sancti Pauli apostoli*
Pass. Pet. Paul.	*Passio sanctorum apostolorum Petri et Pauli*
Pass. Sebast.	*Passio Sebastiani*
Paul. ep. comm.	Theodoret of Cyrus, *In quatuordecim sancti Pauli epistolas commentarius*
Perist.	Prudentius, *Peristephanon (De coronis martyrum)*
Praescr.	Tertullian, *De praescriptione haereticorum*
Profut.	Vigilius of Rome, *Epistula Vigilii papae ad Profuturum episcopum*
Relat.	Symmachus, *Relationes*
Rom.	Plutarch, *Vita Romuli (Vitae parallelae)*
Sacrum. Leon.	*Sacramentarium Leonianum (Sacramentarium Veronense)*
Sanct. Eph. Alex.	Eusebius "Gallicanus," *Hom. 55: De sanctis martyribus Ephypodio et Alexandro*
Sanct. Maxim.	Faustus of Riez, *De sancte Maxime*
Scorp.	Tertullian, *Scorpiace*
Serm.	*Sermones* (various authors)
Temp. rat.	Bede, *De temporum ratione (Chronica maiora)*
Theoph.	Eusebius of Caesarea, *Theophania*
Tract. Ps.	Jerome, *Tractatus sive homiliae in psalmos*
Urb. cond.	Livy, *Ab urbe condita*
Vero Aug.	Marcus Cornelius Fronto, *Vero Augusto Domino meo*
Vigil.	Jerome, *Adversus Vigilantium*
Vir. ill.	Jerome, *De viris illustribus*
Virginit.	Ambrose of Milan, *De virginitate*

Vit. Ambr.	Paulinus of Milan, *Vita Ambrosii*
Vit. Apoll.	Philostratus, *Vita Apollonii*
Vit. Const.	Eusebius of Caesarea, *Vita Constantini*
Vit. Cypr.	Pontius of Carthage, *Vita Cypriani*
Vit. Epiph.	*Vita sancti Epiphanii*
Vit. Fulg.	Ferrandus of Carthage, *Vita sancti Fulgentii*
Vit. Leon.	*Vita sancti Leonis papae*
Vit. Mart.	*Vita Martini* (various authors)
Vit. Maxim.	Dinamius Patricius, *Vita Maximi*
Vit. patrum	Gregory of Tours, *Vita patrum*
Vit. patrum Iur. Eug.	*Vita patrum Iurensium* (*Eugendii*)
Vit. sanct. Mart.	Sulpicius Severus, *Vita sancti Martini*

SECONDARY SOURCES

AASS	*Acta sanctorum quotquot toto orbe coluntur.* 68 vols. Antwerp and Brussels: Societé des Bollandistes, 1643–1940.
AcAr	*Acta archaeologica* (Copenhagen)
AcBern	Acta Bernensia
ACW	Ancient Christian Writers
AEAA	*Archivo Español de Arte y Arqueología*
AEAr	*Archivo Español de Arqueología*
AevumAnt	*Aevum Antiquum*
AfRG	*Archiv für Religionsgeschichte*
AJA	*American Journal of Archaeology*
AJP	*American Journal of Philology*
AJT	*American Journal of Theology*
AKG	Arbeiten zur Kirchengeschichte
AlOm.A	Alpha-Omega. Lexika, Indizes, Konkordanzen zur klassischen Philologie. Reihe A
Ambr	*Ambrosius*
AMidi	*Annales du Midi*
AnBib	Analecta Biblica
AnBoll	*Analecta Bollandiana*
ANRW	*Aufstieg und Niedergang der römischen Welt: Geschichte und Kultur Roms im Spiegel der neueren Forschung.* Part 2, *Principat.* Edited by Hildegard Temporini and Wolfgang Haase. Berlin: de Gruyter, 1972–.
AnTard	*Antiquité tardive*
APARA.D	*Atti della Pontificia Accademia Romana di Archeologia, Dissertazioni*

APARA.R	*Atti della Pontificia Accademia Romana di Archeologia, Rendiconti*
ARID	*Analecta Romana Instituti Danici*
ArtB	*The Art Bulletin*
ASEs	*Annali di storia dell'esegesi*
Aug	*Augustinianum*
AUU.HR	Acta Universitatis Upsaliensis. Historia Religionum
BA	*Biblical Archaeologist*
BAA	*Bulletin d'Archéologie algérienne*
BAC	Biblioteca de autores cristianos
BAH	Bibliothèque archéologique et historique. Institut français d'archéologie de Beyrouth
BAnT	Bibliothèque de l'Antiquité tardive
BArC	*Bullettino di Archeologia Cristiana*
BARIS	British Archaeological Reports International Series
BBR	*Bulletin for Biblical Research*
BEFAR	Bibliothèque des Écoles françaises d'Athènes et de Rome
BEHEc	Bibliothèque de l'enseignement de l'histoire ecclésiastique
BEL.H	Bibliotheca "Ephemerides liturgicae." Sectio historica
BETL	Bibliotheca ephemeridum theologicarum Lovaniensium
BHBB	Biblioteca histórica de la Biblioteca Balmes
BibS(F)	Biblische Studien (Freiburg)
BMusPont	*Bollettino dei Monumenti, Musei e Gallerie Pontificie*
BRAH	*Boletín de la Real Academia de la Historia*
BTGran	Biblioteca teológica Granadina
BWeid	Bibliotheca Weidmanniana
BZNW	Beihefte zur Zeitschrift für die neutestamentliche Wissenschaft
CACat	Collezione "Amici delle catacombe"
CAr	*Cahiers archéologiques*
CArch	Christliche Archäologie
CatRI	Catacombe di Roma e d'Italia
CCSA	Corpus Christianorum. Series Apocryphorum
CCSL	Corpus Christianorum. Series latina
CCommChr	Cahiers de Communauté chrétienne
CEFR	Collection de l'École française de Rome
CIL	*Corpus inscriptionum Latinarum.* Berlin: Akademie der Wissenschaften, 1863–.

CMSBAV	Catalogo del Museo sacro della Biblioteca Apostolica Vaticana
CP	*Classical Philology*
CRAI	Comptes rendus de l'Académie des inscriptions et belles-lettres
CrArte	*Critica d'Arte*
CRoI	Le chiese di Roma illustrate
CSEL	Corpus scriptorum ecclesiasticorum latinorum
CUFr	Collection des universités de France
CUFr.L	Collection des universités de France. Série latine
DACL	*Dictionnaire d'archéologie chrétienne et de liturgie.* Edited by Fernand Cabrol and Henri Leclercq. 15 vols. Paris: Letouzey et Ané, 1913–1953.
EBib	Études bibliques
Eccl. occ. mon. iur.	*Ecclesiae occidentalis monumenta iuris antiquissima.* Edited by Cuthbert H. Turner. 2 vols. Oxford: Clarendon: 1899–1939.
EC	*Early Christianity*
ECF	The Early Church Fathers
EHS.A	Europäische Hochschulschriften. Reihe 38, Archäologie
EHS.K	Europäische Hochschulschriften. Reihe 28, Kunstgeschichte
EMEur	*Early Medieval Europe*
Epig	*Epigraphica*
EPros	Études prosopographiques
EUJaca	Edizioni Universitarie Jaca
FC	Fathers of the Church
FKDG	Forschungen zur Kirchen- und Dogmengeschichte
FoiVie	*Foi et Vie*
FontC	Fontes christiani
HAnt	*Hispania Antiqua*
HNT	Handbuch zum Neuen Testament
HRF	Histoire religieuse de la France
HTR	*Harvard Theological Review*
HTS	Harvard Theological Studies
ICC	International Critical Commentary
ICUR	*Inscriptiones christianae urbis Romae septimo saeculo antiquiores.* Edited by Giovanni Battista de Rossi. 2 vols. Rome: Roma Officina Libraria Pontificia, 1861–1888. New series edited by Angelo Silvagni, Rome: Befani, 1922–.

ILCV	*Inscriptiones latinae christianae veteres.* Edited by E. Diehl. 2 vols. Berlin: Weidmann, 1925–1927.
Int	*Interpretation*
IP	*Instrumenta Patristica*
ISLL	Illinois Studies in Language and Literature
ISS	Inscriptiones Sanctae Sedis
JBL	*Journal of Biblical Literature*
JECS	*Journal of Early Christian Studies*
JEH	*Journal of Ecclesiastical History*
JJS	*Journal of Jewish Studies*
JMEMS	*Journal of Medieval and Early Modern Studies*
JOUHS	*Journal of the Oxford University History Society*
JRS	*Journal of Roman Studies*
JSAH	*Journal of the Society of Architectural Historians*
JSNTSup	Journal for the Study of the New Testament Supplement Series
JTS	*Journal of Theological Studies*
KAV	Kommentar zu den apostolischen Vätern
KLIO.BAG	*KLIO: Beiträge zur alten Geschichte*
LNSAS	Leicester-Nottingham Studies in Ancient Society
MAC	Monumenti dell'antichità cristiana
MD	*La Maison-Dieu*
MDAI(R)	*Mitteilungen des Deutschen Archäologischen Instituts, Römische Abteilung*
MEFR	*Mélanges d'archéologie et d'histoire de l'école française de Rome*
MEFRA	*Mélanges de l'Ecole française de Rome, Antiquité*
MGH.AA	Monumenta Germaniae Historica. Auctores antiquissimi
MGH.Ep	Monumenta Germaniae Historica. Epistolae
MIÖG	*Mitteilungen des Instituts für österreichische Geschichtsforschung*
MNHIR	*Mededelingen van het Nederlands Instituut te Rome*
MPAIBL	*Mémoires présentés par divers savants à l'Académie des Inscriptions et Belles-Lettres de l'Institut de France*
MST	Mediaeval Sources in Translation
NAWG.PHK	*Nachrichten der Akademie der Wissenschaften in Göttingen. Philologisch-Historische Klasse*
NBArC	*Nuovo Bullettino di Archeologia Cristiana*
NC	La Nouvelle Clio
NICNT	New International Commentary on the New Testament

NovT	*Novum Testamentum*
NovTSup	Supplements to Novum Testamentum
NS	new series
NSS	Nuovi Studi Storici
OCT	Oxford Classical Texts/Scriptorum classicorum bibliotheca oxoniensis
OECS	Oxford Early Christian Studies
OHM	Oxford Historical Monographs
OS	old series
PaP	*Past and Present*
Par.	Paradosis. Études de littérature et de théologie ancienne.
PG	Patrologia graeca. Edited by J.-P. Migne. 161 vols. Paris: Migne, 1857–1866.
PIAUP	Publications de l'Institut d'Art et d'Archéologie de l'Université de Paris
PL	Patrologia latina. Edited by J.-P. Migne. 217 vols. Paris: Migne, 1844–1864.
RAfr	*Revue africaine*
RAr	*Revue archéologique*
RBén	*Revue bénédictine*
REAug	*Revue des études augustiniennes*
RechAug	*Recherches augustiniennes*
RED.F	Rerum ecclesiasticarum documenta. Series maior, Fontes
RevScRel	*Revue des sciences religieuses*
RHEF	*Revue d'histoire de l'Église de France*
RHPR	*Revue d'Histoire et de Philosophie religieuses*
RhWAW.G	Rheinisch-Westfälische Akademie der Wissenschaften: Vorträge G
RivAC	*Rivista di Archeologia Cristiana*
RLLTC	Recentiores: Later Latin Texts and Contexts
RQ	*Römische Quartalschrift für christliche Altertumskunde und Kirchengeschichte*
RQ.S	Römische Quartalschrift für christliche Altertumskunde und Kirchengeschichte. Supplement
RSCr	Roma sotterranea cristiana
RSR	*Recherches de science religieuse*
SAC	Studi di antichità cristiana
SAC(B)	Studi di antichità cristiane (Bologna)
SacEr	*Sacris Erudiri*
SAEB	Studia archaeologica ("Erma" di Bretschneider)

SBLMS	Society of Biblical Literature Monograph Series
SBLRBS	Society of Biblical Literature Resources for Biblical Study
SBLWGRW	Society of Biblical Literature Writings from the Greco-Roman World
SBLWGRWSup	Society of Biblical Literature Writings from the Greco-Roman World Supplement Series
SC	Sources chrétiennes
SEAug	Studia ephemeridis Augustinianum
SGL	Scriptores Graeci et Latini
SHG	Subsidia Hagiographica
SSAC	Sussidi allo studio delle antichità Cristiana
StPatr	*Studia Patristica*
StRicNS	Studi e ricerche (Bologna). New Series
StSKG	Studien zur spätantiken Kunstgeschichte
TCH	The Transformation of the Classical Heritage
TCU	Testi e commenti. Università di Urbino. Istituto di filologia classica
TEsp	Temas Españoles
ThH	Théologie historique
TS	Texts and Studies
TTH	Translated Texts for Historians
TTHLS	Translated Texts for Historians. Latin Series
TUGAL	Texte und Untersuchungen zur Geschichte der altchristlichen Literatur
VC	*Vigiliae Christianae*
VCSup	Supplements to Vigiliae Christianae
VetChr	*Vetera Christianorum*
WBC	Word Biblical Commentary
WKRGMK	Wissenschaftliche Kataloge des Römisch-Germanisches Museums Köln
WTJ	*Westminster Theological Journal*
WUNT	Wissenschaftliche Untersuchungen zum Neuen Testament
ZKG	*Zeitschrift für Kirchengeschichte*
ZNW	*Zeitschrift für die Neutestamentliche Wissenschaft und die Kunde der älteren Kirche*

FIGURES

Introduction

On June 28, 2007, Pope Benedict XVI proclaimed June 2008 to June 2009 the Year of Paul. This special celebration honored the two thousandth anniversary of the apostle's traditional date of birth. The pontiff announced that the year would include "a series of liturgical, cultural and ecumenical events, as well as various pastoral and social initiatives, all inspired by Pauline spirituality." In addition to these programmatic aspects of the year, the pope placed a strong emphasis on pilgrimage to the Basilica of St. Paul Outside the Walls in Rome: "This 'Pauline Year' will take place in a special way in Rome, where for 2000 years under the papal altar of this basilica, lies the tomb that according to experts and undisputed tradition has conserved the remains of the apostle Paul." To encourage participation, the pontiff offered a special indulgence to those who made a pilgrimage to Rome to pray at the tomb. While Rome was the center of activity for the Year of Paul, the festivities were not confined to that city. The pope also encouraged Christians everywhere to follow the example of Rome: "In all parts of the world, similar initiatives can be organised in dioceses, shrines and places of worship by religious institutions, by social or educational institutes bearing the name of St Paul or inspired by his character and teaching."[1] The indulgence was equally available to those who made a pilgrimage or participated in sacred exercises anywhere else in the world "in holy places dedicated to St Paul."[2]

Liturgy, pilgrimage, prayer at holy sites, the proliferation of sacred shrines to Paul, the promise of spiritual benefits—these were prominent aspects of the year-long festival in his honor. These were also important components of an ancient Pauline cult that began in the first century and grew dramatically

---

1. Pope Benedict XVI, "Pauline Year Proclamation," *Basilica Papale San Paolo Fuori le Mura Press Office*, 28 June 2007, online: http://www.annopaolino.org/interno.asp?id=2&lang=eng.

2. Cardinal James Francis Stafford, "Decree of Special Indulgences," *Basilica Papale San Paolo Fuori le Mura Press Office*, 10 May 2008, online: http://www.annopaolino.org/Indulgenza%20ING.pdf.

in the fourth century. This book tells the story of this ancient cult of Paul as martyr in the Latin West.

The Cults of Martyrs and Saints

The cult of the martyrs was one of the focal points of Christian piety in late antiquity. The basis of the cult was the belief that the martyrs (those who chose to die rather than recant their Christian faith) occupy a particularly elevated position in the spiritual hierarchy. Having voluntarily followed the example of Christ to the point of death, they reside in the presence of God and enjoy God's special favor.[3] Although they are physically dead, they remain alive and accessible to Christians who seek their intercession and assistance.

Many of Christianity's most famous martyrs died during the movement's first three centuries, when Christians were victims of various persecutions. In some cases they were attacked by mobs, but in other instances they were put to death by order of the imperial government.[4] Within the Roman Empire, the earliest imperial persecution took place under the emperor Nero (ca. 64 C.E.), and the last and worst persecution occurred between 303 and 311 under the emperor Diocletian. The century that followed Diocletian's death brought a dramatic change in the status of Christianity. The emperors Licinius and Constantine issued the Edict of Milan in 313, which granted religious freedom to Christians (Lactantius, *Mort.* 48; Eusebius, *Hist. eccl.* 10.5), and by the end of Constantine's reign in 337, Christianity had become the favored religion of the Roman Empire. Finally, in 380, the emperors Theodosius I, Gratian, and Valentinian II issued the Edict of Thessaloniki, making Christianity the official religion of the empire (*Cod. Theod.* 16.1.2).

Legal freedom and a growing number of wealthy, influential converts allowed Christians to expand the scope of practices through which they honored the martyrs. This process was both creative and circular, for as veneration practices increased and expanded, so did the perceived extent of a martyr's influence. All these practices, when taken together, constituted a martyr's *cult.* As cults grew in popularity and exposure in this period of relative safety, Christians began also to venerate confessors (those who had professed their faith but had not died as martyrs) and others who had been considered particularly holy while alive. The distinction between these different types of holy

---

3. On the elevated status of martyrs—to a level that some even found problematic—see Candida R. Moss, *The Other Christs: Imitating Jesus in Ancient Christian Ideologies of Martyrdom* (New York: Oxford University Press, 2010), 149–72.

4. G. E. M. de Ste. Croix, *Christian Persecution, Martyrdom, and Orthodoxy* (ed. Michael Whitby and Joseph Streeter; Oxford: Oxford University Press, 2006), 105–52.

people became blurred, and Christians commonly referred to all of them as *saints*. We therefore often speak about the "cult of the saints" rather than specifically the cult of the martyrs.[5]

The Nature of the Evidence

The Pauline cult was composed of a number of practices through which Christians created and re-created an image of Paul as a martyr worthy of veneration.[6] These practices can be grouped under four broad headings to which I will make reference throughout the book: places, stories, objects and rituals, and patronage relationships. By way of setting the context for my overall study, I will introduce these categories here accompanied by examples from other prominent saints' cults. However, this presentation in distinct categories should not obscure the fact that many practices overlapped and interacted with each other, as we will see in the case of the Pauline cult.

---

5. The study of these cults has led to a substantial bibliography. I will not rehearse the entire history of scholarship here, because this has been ably done by Stephen Wilson, "Annotated Bibliography," in *Saints and Their Cults: Studies in Religious Sociology, Folklore and History* (ed. Stephen Wilson; Cambridge: Cambridge University Press, 1983), 309–417; and Lucy Grig, *Making Martyrs in Late Antiquity* (London: Duckworth, 2004), 146–51. To these summaries I must add several important studies on the cults of particular saints. Raymond Van Dam, *Saints and Their Miracles in Late Antique Gaul* (Princeton: Princeton University Press, 1993) is a work primarily (although not exclusively) on the cult of Martin of Tours, particularly through the lens of the writings of the sixth-century bishop Gregory of Tours. In *Saint Demetrios of Thessaloniki: Civic Patron and Divine Protector, 4th–7th Centuries CE* (HTS 47; Harrisburg, Pa.: Trinity Press International, 1999), James C. Skedros illustrates how text and architecture were woven together to produce a saint whose cult exerted considerable social and political influence in this Macedonian city. Finally, Stephen J. Davis's *The Cult of Saint Thecla: A Tradition of Women's Piety in Late Antiquity* (OECS; Oxford: Oxford University Press, 2001) provides an analysis of the cult of the martyred virgin in Asia Minor and Egypt. Davis integrates text, art, and archaeology into his study of women's piety and the social practices that emerged around the Thecla cult. My own study of the Pauline cult is in part inspired by the work of Van Dam, Skedros, and Davis.

6. On the development of martyr cults within the broader social context of late antiquity, see three essays in Ellen Bradshaw Aitken and Jennifer K. Berenson Maclean, eds., *Philostratus's Heroikos: Religion and Cultural Identity in the Third Century C.E.* (SBLWGRW 6; Atlanta: Society of Biblical Literature, 2004): Hans Dieter Betz, "Hero Worship and Christian Beliefs: Observations from the History of Religion on Philostratus's *Heroikos*," 25–47; Jackson P. Hershbell, "Philostratus's *Heroikos* and Early Christianity: Heroes, Saints, and Martyrs," 169–79; James C. Skedros, "The *Heroikos* and Popular Christianity in the Third Century c.e.," 181–93.

PLACES

The first of these practices was the *designation of particular locations as holy places*. Certain locations were ascribed special importance for the commemoration of the martyrs. Christians tended to favor birth places, sites of preaching or miracles, martyrdom locations, and tombs. One of the earliest recorded examples of this comes from the *Martyrdom of Polycarp*. Probably written in the latter half of the second century, it recounts the trial and violent death of the bishop of Smyrna in Asia Minor (modern Izmir, Turkey[7]) between 155 and 170 C.E.[8] After Polycarp's execution and cremation by a Roman soldier, the Christians of Smyrna collected his bones and laid them in "a suitable place" (*Mart. Pol.* 18.2–3). This place became the center of commemoration and veneration of the martyred bishop in the years following his death.[9]

---

7. I will identify places in this book by their most recognizable names, whether those be the ancient or modern names. In each case the corresponding names will also be given in parentheses.

8. Both the date of Polycarp's death and the date of composition of the *Martyrdom* continue to be disputed. The most likely date of death is 155 or 167. For a summary of the arguments, see Jan Den Boeft and Jan Bremmer, "Notiunculae Martyrologicae IV" (review of A. A. R. Bastiaensen, ed., *Atti e Passioni dei Martiri*), *VC* 45.2 (1991): 107–8. On the composition date, the majority of scholars still favor the late second century, e.g., Boudewijn Dehandschutter, "The Martyrium Polycarpi: A Century of Research," *ANRW* 27.1:497–502; idem, "Research on the Martyrdom of Polycarp: 1990–2005," in *Polycarpiana: Studies on Martyrdom and Persecution in Early Christianity: Collected Essays* (ed. J. Leemans; BETL 205; Leuven: Peeters, 2007), 85–92; Gerd Buschmann, *Das Martyrium des Polykarp* (KAV 6; Göttingen: Vandenhoeck & Ruprecht, 1998), 39–40; Paul A. Hartog, *Polycarp and the New Testament* (WUNT 2/134; Tübingen: Mohr Siebeck, 2002), 17–32. Proponents of a third-century date for part or all of the text have included Hans von Campenhausen, "Bearbeitungen und Interpolationen des Polykarpmartyriums," in *Aus der Frühzeit des Christentums: Studien zur Kirchengeschichte des ersten und zweiten Jahrhunderts* (Tübingen: Mohr Siebeck, 1963), 253–301; Candida R. Moss, "On the Dating of Polycarp: Rethinking the Place of the Martyrdom of Polycarp in the History of Christianity," *EC* 1 (2010): 539–74.

9. Cf. R. A. Markus, "How on Earth Could Places Become Holy? Origins of the Christian Idea of Holy Places," *JECS* 2 (1994): 257–71. Markus argues that, prior to the fourth century, Christians were opposed to the notions of sacred space and sacred time. His argument does not account for texts such as the *Martyrdom of Polycarp*, Eusebius's reference to the tombs of Peter and Paul around the turn of the third century, third-century liturgical calendars from both Rome and North Africa, and other evidence of popular practices that will be discussed in this book. Markus's argument does hold true for the earliest period, however. An important example is the tomb of Jesus, which was not a place of veneration prior to the time of Constantine, as shown by Helmut Koester, "On Heroes, Tombs, and Early Christianity: An Epilogue," in *Flavius Philostratus: Heroikos* (trans. Jennifer K.

In many cases, Christians *marked these holy places with some kind of shrine or monument.*[10] These could be simple or elaborate, depending on the context and resources of those constructing it. In the year 384, the female pilgrim Egeria visited a shrine of the martyr Thecla on a hill just south of Seleucia (modern Silifke, Turkey). This is the traditional location of the martyr's death, and the shrine itself was attached to a church and surrounded by a wall (*Itiner.* 23.2–4). In the middle of the fifth century, the center of the local cult moved to a small church built over a cave at the foot of the hill. Soon after, the emperor Zeno constructed an enormous basilica that engulfed both the cave and the smaller church, thereby employing architecture to mark this entire area as holy space.[11]

STORIES

The *production of literary accounts of a martyr's great deeds and death* was a prominent aspect of many martyr cults. Cyprian was a third-century bishop in Carthage (near modern Tunis, Tunisia). He was arrested in 258 and executed by order of the Roman consul. A deacon of Carthage named Pontius wrote the *Life of Cyprian* in the years immediately following the martyr's death. In the introduction to his work, Pontius comments, "Since … it is right that [Cyprian's] example should be recorded in writing, I have thought it appropriate to prepare this brief and concise narrative … that this incomparable and lofty pattern may be prolonged for posterity into immortal remembrance" (*Vit. Cypr.* 1). What follows is a flattering account of Cyprian's life in which every decision, even in the midst of controversy, was made with infallible wisdom. His model death was preceded by a model life. Pontius was not attempting to produce an objective, historical account of Cyprian's life and martyrdom. Rather, he was sculpting an image of the bishop that would be perpetuated by the reading and circulation of his narrative.[12]

Berenson Maclean and Ellen Bradshaw Aitken; SBLWGRW 1; Atlanta: Society of Biblical Literature, 2001), 257–64.

10. This practice was, of course, not unique to Christians. On the Jewish practice of constructing and honoring tombs of the prophets, see, e.g., Matt 23:29; Luke 11:47–48.

11. Davis, *Cult of Saint Thecla*, 36–39. Theodore of Mopsuestia is said to have made regular pilgrimages to Thecla's shrine at Seleucia. According to a legend in the Chronicle of Seert, on one occasion he had a dream in which he saw Thecla alongside an old man (Paul?) who gave him fourteen keys to unlock the fourteen Pauline epistles. See John T. Fitzgerald, "Theodore of Mopsuestia on Paul's Letter to Philemon," in *Philemon in Perspective: Interpreting a Pauline Letter* (ed. D. Francois Tolmie; BZNW 169; Berlin: de Gruyter, 2010), 342–43.

12. "One might even go so far as to argue that [early Christian historians] did not simply preserve the story of persecution and martyrdom but, in fact, created it" (Elizabeth

The *publishing of the alleged trial transcripts* was another means of circulating stories. Texts of this type, in fact, represent a significant percentage of the surviving stories about martyrs.[13] They often consist primarily of back-and-forth debates between determined Christians and exasperated government officials. The *Acts of Phileas* is a fourth-century text recounting the trial and execution of the bishop of Thmuis (Egypt). The text focuses on the futile attempts by the proconsul Culcianus to convince Phileas to offer sacrifice in honor of the emperor:

> Culcianus said to him, "Now sacrifice." [Phileas] replied, "I will not sacrifice; I never learned how." Culcianus said to him, "Paul sacrificed, did he not?" He replied, "No." Culcianus said, "Surely Moses sacrificed." He replied, "Solely for the Jews it was prescribed to sacrifice in Jerusalem to God alone...." Culcianus said to him, "Now sacrifice." Phileas replied, "I will not sacrifice." (*Acta Phil.* 2–3)[14]

The climax of these texts is often the martyr's bold pronouncement of unwavering faith ("I am a Christian"), even when faced with death. In some cases, these trial transcripts were later incorporated into larger narratives of the martyrs' lives (e.g., *Mart. Perp. Felic.* 6).

Sermons were also a way of telling stories about a martyr. These were often given on a martyr's "birthday," a term Christians used for the anniversary of his or her death. Augustine is a rich source of such sermons, including several in honor of Cyprian. He opens the first of these with the following declaration:

> Such a happy and religious occasion as this, on which we are celebrating the blessed martyr's passion, requires me to pay the debt of the sermon I owe to your ears and hearts.... And now at this time we recall all that happened then by reading about it and appreciating it, not only without any sadness at all, but even with immense gladness. (*Serm.* 309.1, Hill)

This day had been set aside to commemorate Cyprian's death, and Augustine proceeded to tell his own version of the events leading up to the former bishop's martyrdom. He creatively interpreted and applied the story as moral exhortation for the audience in his basilica.

A. Castelli, *Martyrdom and Memory: Early Christian Culture Making* [New York: Columbia University Press, 2004], 25).

13. The importance of trial manuscripts is clearly seen in the extensive list of martyrdom accounts summarized by Moss, *Other Christs*, 177–201 (appendix).

14. There are some differences between the Latin and Greek versions of this text, but this passage appears in both surviving versions.

Stories about martyrs circulated as well through *oral tradition*. The particular holy places associated with martyrs provided fertile settings for visitors to hear and exchange stories. Egeria recounts that monks and other people told her stories about the places she was visiting and the holy people associated with those places (*Itiner.* 20.12). As with all storytelling, these interactions represented a creative process through which new elements and perspectives entered into the tradition. The images of martyrs, therefore, were constantly in flux, being shaped and reshaped by those telling stories about their lives and deaths.

OBJECTS AND RITUALS

The *collection and veneration of relics* were central to many cults. Relics were the most important physical objects for a cult, and we may distinguish them into two categories. Primary relics were the martyr's actual physical remains. As early as the second century, Christians were treating relics with special care. Polycarp's cremation did not deter the local Christians from gathering the bones for special veneration: "Thus we later took up his bones, which are more valuable than precious stones and more refined than gold" (*Mart. Pol.* 18.2). Even pieces of bone were desirable, for "wherever a drop of dew has fallen on men in the shape of a particle of bone, the tiny gift from a consecrated body, holy grace has brought forth fountains in that place, and the drops of ashes have begotten rivers of life" (Paulinus of Nola, *Carm.* 19.359–362). Blood or other bodily fluids were also considered equal to the bones themselves. As Vincent of Saragossa lay on his death bed after being tortured, the faithful were drawn to the martyr's open wounds: "One covers with kisses the double cuts made by the claws, another eagerly licks the red gore on the body. Many wet a linen garment with drops of blood, to lay it up at home as a holy safeguard for their descendants" (Prudentius, *Perist.* 5.337–344, Thomson).

Secondary relics (*brandea* or *sanctuaria*) were objects that had come into contact with primary relics and then carried spiritual power that had been transferred to them. At the traditional tomb of Peter in Rome,

> If someone wishes to take away a blessed relic, he weighs a little piece of cloth on a pair of scales and lowers it into [the tomb]; then he keeps vigils, fasts and earnestly prays that the power of the apostle will assist his piety. [What happens next] is extraordinary to report! If the man's faith is strong, when the piece of cloth is raised from the tomb it will be so soaked with divine power that it will weigh much more than it weighed previously. (Gregory of Tours, *Glor. mart.* 27, Van Dam)

Both primary and secondary relics, even if only in fragmentary form, were seen as conduits and access points of the spiritual power that a martyr could wield. As Bishop Paulinus of Nola once wrote, "Wherever there is part of a saint's body, there, too, his power emerges" (Paulinus of Nola, *Carm.* 27.445, Walsh).

Producing and procuring items bearing the name and/or image of the martyr were two related practices. Portable objects of this type were often produced and distributed as mementos of a visit to a holy place. Visitors to a shrine of the martyr Menas in Egypt could take home ceramic flasks featuring the image of Menas on one side and Thecla on the other.[15] Some of these flasks probably contained holy oil taken from the site. Sarcophagi represent another class of object that could bear images of a martyr, particularly iconographical representations of his or her death. They were far more expensive and less mobile than ceramic flasks, but in some cases they were transported a considerable distance, as we will see in the case of Paul.

The practice of *pilgrimage* was adapted from Greco-Roman religions. Christians traveled to designated holy places in order to honor the saints, venerate their relics, and secure secondary relics or other mementos. Some early Christian pilgrims traveled great distances. Egeria's journey took her from western Europe (probably Spain) as far east as Egypt and Syria. Constantine's mother, Helena, went from Rome to Palestine in the early fourth century, where she established Christian churches at holy sites (Eusebius of Caesarea, *Vit. Const.* 3.42–46). Other Christians visited shrines in their own regions. According to the *Miracles of St. Thecla*, the residents of Seleucia and Tarsus regularly engaged in mutual pilgrimage along the Cilician coast between their sites for Thecla and Paul, respectively (Basil of Seleucia, *Mirac. Theclae* 4, 29).

The installation of *privileged burial sites near a martyr's tomb* was linked closely to relics. Ancient Christians displayed a clear desire to be interred "near the saints" (*ad sanctos*). Relics were believed to carry the saint's full power, so it was desirable to be buried as close as possible. Those lying "near the saints" would benefit at the final judgment and resurrection on account of their proximity to these special tombs.[16] Bishop Ambrose of Milan had

---

15. Davis, *Cult of Saint Thecla*, 114–26. For other examples of such mementos, see Cynthia Hahn, "Loca Sancta Souvenirs: Sealing the Pilgrim's Experience," in *The Blessings of Pilgrimage* (ed. Robert Ousterhout; Urbana: University of Illinois Press, 1990), 85–96; Maggie Duncan-Flowers, "A Pilgrim's Ampulla from the Shrine of St. John the Evangelist at Ephesus," in Ousterhout, *The Blessings of Pilgrimage*, 125–39; Charalambos Bakirtzis, "Byzantine Ampullae from Thessaloniki," in Ousterhout, *The Blessings of Pilgrimage*, 140–50; Blake Leyerle, "Pilgrim Eulogiae and Domestic Rituals," *AfRG* 10 (2008): 223–37.

16. André Grabar, *Martyrium: Recherches sur le culte des reliques et l'art chrétien antique* (2 vols.; Paris: Collège de France, 1946), esp. 1:487–532; Yvette Duval, *Auprès des*

greater confidence in his eternal fate because he was to be buried over the bodies of the martyrs Gervasius and Protasius in a basilica that he had built: "I believe that I will be more commendable to God, because I will rest over the bones of the body of a saint" (*Exc.* 1.18).[17] His (supposed) body is visible even today in the Basilica di Sant'Ambrogio in Milan, where Ambrose is still flanked by the bodies of the two martyrs.

The *celebration of annual feast days* was a well-attested part of a martyr's cult. The *Martyrdom of Polycarp* provides the earliest recorded example of this practice. After burying the bones of Polycarp, the Christians of Smyrna continued to commemorate the day of his death: "As we are able, we gather together there with joy and gladness, and the Lord will permit us to celebrate the birthday of his martyrdom in memory of those who have gone before and for the training and preparation of those who will do so in the future" (*Mart. Pol.* 18.3). They held an annual gathering on Polycarp's "birthday" to remember his death and example, mindful that their own day of testing could be coming soon. The growth in the number of such feast days contributed to the eventual development of liturgical calendars.[18]

A practice closely associated with feast days was the *celebration of meals in honor of a martyr*. These special banquets, inspired by Roman meals in honor of departed ancestors, took place at the tombs or shrines of the saints. Augustine says that his mother regularly partook in these meals in North Africa: "It had been my mother's custom in Africa to take meal-cakes and bread and wine to the shrines of the saints on their memorial days" (*Conf.* 6.2, Pine-Coffin). Ambrose of Milan forbade this practice in his city. Augustine followed him in condemning it in Africa, because these unsupervised gatherings had been the occasion for immoral activity. The bishops were in a distinct minority, however, for most Christians eagerly participated in these special meals honoring the martyrs.[19]

---

saints corps et âme: L'inhumation "ad sanctos" dans la chrétienté d'Orient et d'Occident du IIIe au VIIe siècle (Paris: Études Augustiniennes, 1988).

17. Ambrose was credited with having found the relics of these previously unknown martyrs (Ambrose, *Ep.* 22; Paulinus of Nola, *Vit. Ambr.* 14).

18. The other primary contributing factor to the development of liturgical calendars was the Roman civil calendar, which listed public holidays and festivals for particular deities. Natascia Donati and Patrizia Stefanetti, *Dies natalis: I calendari romani e gli anniversari dei culti* (Rome: Quasar, 2006); Denis Feeney, *Caesar's Calendar: Ancient Times and the Beginnings of History* (Berkeley: University of California Press, 2007), 138–211.

19. Ramsay MacMullen, *The Second Church: Popular Christianity A.D. 200–400* (SBLWGRWSup 1; Atlanta: Society of Biblical Literature; Leiden: Brill, 2009), 57–62; Ann Marie Yasin, "Funerary Monuments and Collective Identity: From Roman Family to Christian Community," *ArtB* 87.3 (2005): 433–57.

PATRONAGE RELATIONSHIPS

Another practice in many cults was *claiming a personal relationship with a martyr using the model and language of patronage.* Patronage was a foundational concept in the social structure of the Roman world and involved an agreement between two parties of unequal standing. The more powerful patron provided favors to the less powerful client, who would render service in return.[20] The parties involved were sometimes described as friends, suggesting more comparable standing, but in reality these relationships still frequently involved social unequals.[21] As far as Christianity is concerned, patronage appears to have played a key role in its various social networks from the first century onward, sometimes invoking the language of both kinship and friendship.[22] This role was maintained and even expanded within the cults of martyrs, where patronage may be seen in the association between martyrs and local bishops, particular cities, or even entire regions. Prudentius speaks of Cyprian as a patron not only for his native North Africa but also for the regions of Britain, Gaul (France), Italy, and Spain: "He has attained to the realms of heaven, yet nonetheless he moves over the earth and does not leave this world. He still discourses, still holds forth, expounding, teaching, instructing, prophesying.... Indeed he is both teacher on earth and martyr too in heaven; here he instructs men, from there as their patron gives them gifts in love" (*Perist.* 13.99–101, 105–106, Thomson). Cyprian had become a figure who could intercede in the heavenly realms on behalf of the faithful on earth, and in return his clients "raised up a tomb and consecrated his ashes" (13.98, Thomson).

---

20. Richard P. Saller, *Personal Patronage under the Early Empire* (Cambridge: Cambridge University Press, 1982); Andrew Wallace-Hadrill, *Patronage in Ancient Society* (LNSAS 1; London: Routledge, 1989); Elizabeth Deniaux, *Clientèles et pouvoir à l'époque de Cicéron* (CEFR 182; Rome: École française de Rome, 1993).

21. David Konstan, *Friendship in the Classical World* (Cambridge: Cambridge University Press, 1997); John T. Fitzgerald, ed., *Greco-Roman Perspectives on Friendship* (SBLRBS 34; Atlanta: Scholars Press, 1997). On inequality among *friends*, see Saller, *Personal Patronage*, 11–13; Konstan, *Friendship*, 93–98, 105–6, 135–37; idem, "Patrons and Friends," *CP* 90 (1995): 328–42.

22. E.g., John T. Fitzgerald, "Christian Friendship: John, Paul, and the Philippians," *Int* 61.3 (2007): 284–96; L. Michael White, "Paul and *Pater Familias*," in *Paul in the Graeco-Roman World: A Handbook* (ed. J. Paul Sampley; Harrisburg, Pa.: Trinity Press International, 2003), 457–87; Peter Lampe, "Paul, Patrons, and Clients," in Sampley, *Paul in the Graeco-Roman World*, 488–523.

Taken together, these practices contributed to the cult of a martyr,[23] and this study integrates these various forms of evidence to create a thick description of the cult of the apostle Paul in late antiquity. I have limited the scope of my inquiry to Rome and the Latin West, from the earliest vestiges of the cult to the death of bishop Gregory I of Rome (604 C.E.).

The first part of the book focuses on the two primary locations in Rome where Paul was venerated as a martyr: the site of the current Basilica of St. Paul Outside the Walls on the Ostian Road, and the Catacombs of St. Sebastian on the Appian Road. The Ostian Road site had ties to Paul's martyrdom and burial, while the Appian Road location preserves the earliest archaeological evidence of the Pauline cult. The designation of these places as holy places—or sacred spaces—led to substantial architectural and cultic development at both locations. Equally interesting are the sites outside Rome where the Pauline cult was established. The second part of the book focuses on these locations in the rest of Latin Europe and North Africa. A major theme in these chapters is the way in which the Pauline cult served to connect these other regions to Rome. Christians appropriated Roman models of sacred space and created cultic centers as a means of asserting association with—or intentional separation from—the spiritual capital of the West. In this book I will seek to demonstrate that the identification and architectural development of sacred places provided the primary framework for the Pauline cult. The complex interplay of practices that occurred in these spaces both reflected and generated popular conceptions of Paul the martyr.

thesis

23. Another expression of some cults was the practice of naming children after a particular saint. I do not discuss it at length here because I am unaware of evidence for this in the Pauline cult in the West. In Egypt, however, Christians did name their children for the apostle. See Willy Clarysse, "The Coptic Martyr Cult," in *Martyrium in Multidisciplinary Perspective* (ed. M. Lamberigts and P. Van Deun; BETL 117; Leuven: Peeters, 1995), 386–87.

Part 1
The Cult of Paul in Rome

1

THE CULT OF PAUL ON THE OSTIAN ROAD

Then standing up Paul turned toward the east, raised his hands to heaven and prayed for a long time. And after he had conversed in Hebrew with the fathers through prayer, he stretched out his neck and spoke no more. As the executioner cut off his head, milk splashed on the tunic of the soldier. And the soldier and all who were standing nearby were amazed at this sight and glorified the God who had given such honor to Paul. And they went away and reported to Caesar what had happened.

This account of Paul's death comes from a late second-century Greek work known as the *Martyrdom of the Holy Apostle Paul* (*Mart. Paul.* 5).[1] This was one of earliest accounts of Paul's demise and proved to be foundational for all later traditions about Paul's life and legacy as a martyr. Because Christians believed that Paul had died in Rome, the city became the center of the Pauline martyr cult. More specifically, the faithful focused their veneration of the apostle on two particular locations. Both were on major roads leading south out of the city: the Ostian Road and the Appian Road (fig. 1.1).

This chapter focuses on the first of these locations. The Ostian Road ran southwest from Rome to the city's principal port at Ostia, 30 kilometers away at the mouth of the Tiber River. In Paul's time the Ostian Road was a busy thoroughfare of people and goods flowing to and from the capital city of the Roman Empire. Christians placed Paul's death at a particular point along this route, thus declaring the site Christian sacred space. In this chapter I will trace the history of this location in late antiquity, focusing on the textual traditions concerning Paul's death at the site, the architectural development of the site, the practices centered on the alleged apostolic tomb, and the critical role of relic veneration. I will close the chapter with an analysis of a sixth-century

---

1. This work is the third part of the larger *Acts of Paul*, which contains three major divisions: *The Acts of Paul and Thecla*, *3 Corinthians*, and the *Martyrdom of the Holy Apostle Paul*. These components may have originally circulated independently before being edited into one text.

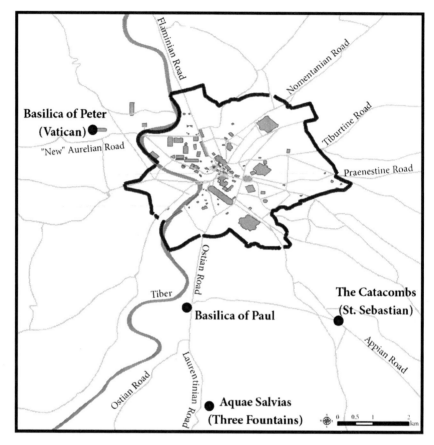

Fig. 1.1. Apostolic cult sites in Rome.

text that placed Paul's martyrdom at another place in Rome and created a rival location for commemorating the apostle's death. For all the traditions that we encounter, the designation of sacred space was foundational to the development and expansion of cultic practices.

1.1. TEXTUAL AND LITURGICAL ORIGINS OF THE CULT

A study of the literary sources of the first few centuries reveals an increasing level of precision about the details of Paul's martyrdom. We will examine the sources in chronological order and will see how each text contributed to the creation of the Pauline cult.[2] Particular attention will be given to the authors'

---

2. I will not provide here an exhaustive list of all the patristic references to the death of

attempts to clarify where Paul died, when Paul died, and who was responsible for his death.

The texts of the New Testament include hints about the death of the apostle but no particular account of the event.[3] Paul's letter to the Philippians, traditionally understood to have been written from Roman imprisonment, suggests that he believes his demise could be imminent (Phil 1:20–23). According to 2 Tim 4:6, the apostle is "already being poured out as a drink offering, and the time of my departure has come." The closest we get to Paul's death is in the Acts of the Apostles. Here Luke tells us that, after his arrest in Jerusalem, Paul appeals his case to Caesar and is sent to Rome to stand trial before the imperial court. The apostle spends two years there under house arrest but remains free to evangelize. Luke does not tell us how this incarceration ends, and scholars have spilled considerable ink speculating on whether or not it resulted in Paul's death.[4]

Paul. My focus is on the most substantial sources dealing with the subject. For a collection of the minor references, see H. W. Tajra, *The Martyrdom of St. Paul: Historical and Judicial Context, Traditions, and Legends* (Tübingen: Mohr Siebeck, 1994), 166–97.

3. Cf. Johannes Munck, *Petrus und Paulus in der Offenbarung Johannis* (Copenhagen: Rosenkilde & Bagger, 1950). Munck argues that the account of the two lampstands in Rev 11:3–13 is the story of Peter and Paul in Rome. The context of the passage suggests, however, that these events were to take place in Jerusalem, the location of the "temple of God" (11:1) and "where their Lord was crucified" (11:8). On other critiques of Munck, see David E. Aune, *Revelation 6–16* (WBC 52B; Nashville: Thomas Nelson, 1998), 601.

4. This question is intimately tied to that of why Luke seemingly ends Acts so abruptly. The primary theories have generally followed these lines of thought: (1) Paul died at the end of the two years, but Luke suppressed this fact in order to end the narrative on a positive note. (2) Paul died at the end of Acts, but Luke either did not know Paul had died or had died himself before he could finish the story. (3) Paul was released after two years, either by outright acquittal or because his accusers failed to come to Rome, and his later evangelistic activities are reflected in texts such as the Pastoral Epistles. (4) Luke knew what happened to Paul but did not consider it necessary to note, either because it was not critical to his project in Acts or because he could assume that all his readers already knew the apostle's fate. Clear synopses of these arguments and the substantial bibliography can be found in Colin J. Hemer, *The Book of Acts in the Setting of Hellenistic History* (ed. Conrad H. Gempf; WUNT 49; Tübingen: Mohr Siebeck, 1989), 383–87; Charles K. Barrett, "The End of Acts," in *Geschichte-Tradition-Reflexion: Festschrift für Martin Hengel zum 70. Geburtstag* (ed. Hubert Cancik, Hermann Lichtenberger, and Peter Schäfer; 3 vols.; Tübingen: Mohr Siebeck, 1996), 3:547–50. These summaries do not include the latest works written on the topic, but a survey of the recent literature reveals a series of reprisals and rejoinders that continue to cover the same ground. None of these theories enjoys the scholarly consensus, and in the absence of new evidence, the same debates are likely to continue. See Richard I. Pervo, *Acts: A Commentary* (ed. Harold W. Attridge; Hermeneia; Minneapolis: Fortress, 2009), 688–90.

Although Luke does not specify in the narrative what eventually happens to Paul, he does include textual clues that point toward the apostle's death. In Acts 20, Paul calls the elders from Ephesus to meet him at Miletus. He warns them that wolves will come in among the flock after his "departure" (20:29). At the end of this address, the elders weep and embrace Paul, "grieving most of all because of the word that he had spoken, that they would never again see his face" (20:38). In addition to these foreshadowings in the dialogue, Luke also structures his account of Paul's trials in a way that highlights parallels between the fate of Paul in Acts and that of Jesus in the Lukan Gospel. Both Jesus and Paul go to Jerusalem despite a triple prediction that they will suffer there. Both receive a warm welcome and subsequently enter the temple, where they are seized. Both then endure a series of four trials, during which they are handed over to Gentiles, slapped, declared innocent three times, and subjected to a mob's cry of "Away with him." They submit themselves to God's will and are treated kindly or praised by a Roman centurion (Luke 9:51–23:47; Acts 20:1–27:43). By the end of the accounts, both have fulfilled the preaching ministry given to them.[5] It is striking that Luke does not complete the parallel by recounting the death of Paul. Nonetheless, an audience familiar with Jesus' fate in Luke's Gospel might infer that Paul was headed down a similar road in Acts.

A letter from the church of Rome to the church of Corinth (commonly known as *1 Clement*) includes the earliest specific mention of Paul's martyrdom.[6] Written at the end of the first century or in the early decades of the second century C.E.,[7] the letter states the following:

---

5. Wayne Meeks and John T. Fitzgerald, eds., *The Writings of St. Paul* (2nd ed.; New York: Norton, 2007), 171–72; Pervo, *Acts*, 533–34, 592–93; Ben Witherington III, *The Acts of the Apostles: A Socio-rhetorical Commentary* (Grand Rapids: Eerdmans, 1998), 627–28; Charles H. Talbert, *Literary Patterns, Theological Themes, and the Genre of Luke-Acts* (SBLMS 20; Missoula, Mont.: Scholars Press, 1974), 17–18; Jerome Neyrey, *The Passion according to Luke: A Redaction Study of Luke's Soteriology* (New York: Paulist, 1985), 98–107; Richard N. Longenecker, "The Acts of the Apostles," in *The Expositor's Bible Commentary* (ed. F. E. Gabelein; 12 vols.; Grand Rapids: Zondervan, 1976–1992), 9:515.

6. Eusebius of Caesarea ascribes this letter to Clement, whom he calls Rome's third bishop (*Hist. eccl.* 3.15–16; 4.23.11; cf. Irenaeus, *Haer.* 3.3.3, where Clement is the fourth bishop). However, the author is never identified, and the letter is written in the first person plural ("we"). It is possible that Clement was the secretary for the group of presbyters in Rome (Herm. *Vis.* 2.4.3).

7. The traditional dating of *1 Clement* assigns the letter to the reign of the emperor Domitian, ca. 95 C.E. This date has been supported by, among others, Adolf von Harnack, *Einführung in die alte Kirchengeschichte: Das Schreiben der römischen Kirche an die Korinthische aus der Zeit Domitians (I. Clemensbrief)* (Leipzig: Hinrich, 1929); Elio Peretto, *Clemente Romano: Lettera ai Corinzi* (Bologna: Dehoniane, 1999), 34–36; Andreas Lindemann, *Die Clemensbriefe* (HNT 17; Tübingen: Mohr Siebeck, 1992), 12–13; Horacio E. Lona, *Der*

On account of jealousy and envy the greatest and most righteous pillars
were persecuted and fought to the death. Let us place before our eyes the
noble apostles.... On account of jealousy and conflict Paul pointed the way
to the prize for perseverance. After he had been bound in chains seven times,
driven into exile, stoned, and had preached in both the East and the West,
he received the noble glory for his faith, having taught righteousness to the
whole world and having gone even to the limit of the West. When he had
borne witness [μαρτυρήσας][8] before the rulers, he was thus set free from the
world and was taken up to the holy place, having become the greatest example of perseverance. (*1 Clem.* 5.3.5–7)

The Roman author (or group of authors) provides few details about the circumstances of Paul's martyrdom. Having preached and traveled widely,
including "to the limit of the West" (τὸ τέρμα τῆς δύσεως),[9] Paul stood "before
the rulers" (ἐπὶ τῶν ἡγουμένων) one final time. The identity and location of
these rulers are not given. The author(s) of the letter may have assumed that
the Christians of Corinth already knew this information, or this passage could
be an allusion to the tradition reflected in Acts 9:15, where the Lord describes
Paul as "my chosen instrument for carrying my name before the Gentiles [or
nations] and kings and the sons of Israel." After fulfilling this charge, Paul
was "persecuted and fought to the death," allowing him to go to "the holy
place." Many have inferred from *1 Clement* that Paul's death took place in
Rome "before the rulers" of the empire, yet the text does not specify where or
when the apostle met his demise.[10]

---

erste Clemensbrief (KAV 2; Göttingen: Vandenhoeck & Ruprecht, 1998), 75–78. Laurence
L. Welborn has critiqued the historical connection with Domitian in "The Preface to 1
Clement: The Rhetorical Situation and the Traditional Date," in *Encounters with Hellenism:
Studies on the First Letter of Clement* (ed. Cilliers Breytenbach and Laurence L. Welborn;
Leiden: Brill, 2004), 197–216. He suggests a broader range of possible dates, 80–140 C.E.,
and describes other attempts at precise redating as "based upon faulty premises" (at 201–2
nn. 22–24). Most recently, Otto Zwierlein has argued for a date of 120–125 C.E. in *Petrus
in Rom: Die literarischen Zeugnisse* (Berlin: de Gruyter, 2009), 245–333. He asserts that the
author of the letter knows much of the New Testament, including some of the later epistles,
thus pushing the date into the third decade of the second century. The alleged parallels that
Zwierlein puts forth, however, are often strained and ultimately unconvincing.

   8. By the end of the first century C.E., there is no evidence that the verb μαρτυρέω had
taken on the technical meaning of "dying as a martyr." See Boudewijn Dehandschutter,
"Some Notes on 1 Clement 5, 4–7," *IP* 19 (1989): 83–89.

   9. The question of Paul's alleged journey to Spain will be addressed in chapter 3.

   10. Other second-century sources that connect Peter and Paul with Rome but do not
mention their martyrdoms there include Ign. *Rom.* 4.3 and Irenaeus of Lyon, *Haer.* 3.3.2–3.
The Ignatius passage is of particular note, for he contrasts their position as apostles with his
own as "a condemned man." Given that Ignatius was on his way to be martyred in Rome,

The *Martyrdom of the Holy Apostle Paul* (the third major section in the *Acts of Paul*) contains the first detailed description of Paul's death. Scholarly consensus dates it to 180–190 C.E., although parts of the text could date much earlier.[11] According to this text, Paul died in Rome by the order of the emperor Nero. The apostle's conflict with Nero initially centered on the person of Patroclus, the imperial cup-bearer. While listening to Paul's preaching in a building outside Rome, the young man nodded off and fell out a window to his death.[12] He was raised from the dead through the prayer of Paul and returned to Nero's service. The emperor soon learned that Patroclus was now in the service of another king, "Christ Jesus, the king of the ages." Threatened by this rival king, who "destroys all kingdoms under heaven, and … alone shall remain in all eternity," Nero ordered the execution of all "enemy" soldiers (*Mart. Paul.* 2).

Paul was brought before him as the champion of the armies of Christ. Although Nero threatened death, Paul declared that he would claim ultimate victory by returning from the dead to visit the emperor. The guards then took Paul outside the city to kill him. As we saw at the opening of this chapter, Paul turned toward the east, raised his hands to heaven, and prayed. He then presented his neck to the executioner. Milk from his severed head splattered onto the soldier. At the end of the account, the apostle paid a posthumous visit to Nero and pronounced his victory as "the soldier of God" (*Mart. Paul.* 6). In this text we find expansion and clarification of the more general account in *1 Clement*. The author of the *Martyrdom of Paul* specifies that Rome was the location of Paul's death. He also introduces Nero as the primary antagonist and provides a background story explaining why Paul had fallen afoul of the emperor.

Similar details appear at the beginning of the *Acts of Peter*. While most of this text predates the *Martyrdom of the Holy Apostle Paul*, most scholars believe that the opening scene of Paul's departure from Rome was a third-

---

we might expect a comparison to Peter and Paul, not a contrast. Only in the pseudonymous *Epistle to the Tarsians* does "Ignatius" reflect an awareness of the traditional deaths of the apostles (*Ep. Tars.* 3.3). In the spurious *Martyrdom of Ignatius*, the arrested bishop thanks the Lord for binding him in chains "like your apostle Paul" (2.8) and rejoices when they land at Puteoli on the way to Rome, because he desires to follow in the footsteps of Paul (5.3).

11. An important recent study on the composition of the *Acts of Paul* is Glenn E. Snyder, "Remembering the *Acts of Paul*" (PhD diss., Harvard University, 2010). Snyder argues (at 60–64), for example, that the martyrdom account may have been composed as early as the reign of Trajan.

12. The story of Patroclus seems to reflect a common tradition with the story of Eutyches in Acts 20:7–12.

century addition.[13] The story begins with an account of Paul's successful preaching in the city.[14] After a period of time, Paul began fasting and waiting for his next assignment from God. At last he received a vision instructing him to go to Spain. The believers in Rome were deeply saddened and feared that they would never see him again. They begged him to return to Rome, and at that point a voice from heaven interjected, "Paul, the servant of God, is chosen for ministry for the rest of his life. In the hands of Nero, the impious and wicked man, he will be perfected before your eyes." After preaching several days of rousing sermons, Paul boarded a ship and left Rome for Spain (*Acta Pet.* 1–3). At the end of the *Acts of Peter*, there is an expectation of Paul's return to Rome to meet his demise (*Acta Pet.* 40),[15] but these events are never recounted.

Another author of the early third century, the ecclesiastical writer Caius, was the first to associate Paul specifically with the Ostian Road. Caius's comments are preserved in the *Ecclesiastical History* of the church historian Eusebius of Caesaria, who wrote during the reign of Constantine (306–337). According to Eusebius, Caius had claimed, "I can show ... the trophies of the apostles. For if you will go to the Vatican, or to the Ostian Road, you will find the trophies of those who have laid the foundation of this church" (Eusebius, *Hist. eccl.* 2.25.7, Cruse). The Greek term "trophy" (τρόπαιον) typically referred to a commemorative monument raised after the defeat of an enemy. In this case, these monuments at the Vatican and on the Ostian Road were seen as heralding the victory by God's illustrious martyrs.

But what exactly were these "trophies"? According to Eusebius, Caius made his statement in the context of a debate over "the places where the

---

13. Gérard Poupon, "Les 'Actes de Pierre' et leur remaniement," *ANRW* 25.6:4372–81; Willy Rordorf, "The Relation between the *Acts of Peter* and the *Acts of Paul*: State of the Question," in *The Apocryphal Acts of Peter: Magic, Miracles and Gnosticism* (ed. Jan N. Bremmer; Leuven: Peeters, 1998), 178–91.

14. The prominence of Paul in this text is an indication of his continuing influence in and through the second century. On the ongoing importance of the apostle in this period, see Richard I. Pervo, *The Making of Paul: Constructions of the Apostle in Early Christianity* (Minneapolis: Fortress, 2010); Andreas Lindemann, *Paulus im ältesten Christentum: Das Bild des Apostels und die Rezeption der paulinischen Theologie in der frühchristlichen Literatur bis Marcion* (Tübingen: Mohr Siebeck, 1979); David K. Rensberger, "As the Apostle Teaches: The Development of the Use of Paul's Letters in Second-Century Christianity" (PhD diss., Yale University, 1981); Benjamin L. White, "'Imago Pauli': Memory, Tradition, and Discourses on the 'Real' Paul in the Second Century" (PhD diss., University of North Carolina at Chapel Hill, 2010).

15. There is also a passing reference to Paul in *Acta Pet.* 6, but here we learn only that Paul has been absent from Rome for some time.

earthly tabernacles of the aforesaid apostles are laid" (*Hist. eccl.* 2.25.6, Cruse). The "earthly tabernacles" of Peter and Paul were the places where their bodies lay. Their "trophies," therefore, were their tombs that sat within large Roman burial grounds on the Ostian Road and the Vatican hill.[16] Eusebius confirms that "the names of Peter and Paul still remain in the cemeteries of that city [Rome] even to this day" (2.25.5, Cruse).[17] In another work he specifies with reference to Paul, "The martyrdom of his death and the sepulcher which (is erected) over him are, even to this day, greatly and abundantly honored in the city of Rome" (Eusebius, *Theoph.* 4.7, Lee). In Caius's mind, the presence of the tomb of Paul on the Ostian Road justified the importance of this location in Rome as a spiritual center and as a focal point of the apostolic cult. Archaeologists have sought evidence of this early tomb or of a shrine that may have enclosed the tomb. To this point, however, excavations at the site have revealed only traces of a structure that may predate the fourth century. These scant remnants are impossible to identify and date accurately, so the size and form of Caius's trophy remain a mystery.[18]

The final source among these early literary traditions is a Roman liturgical calendar that places the cult of Paul on the Ostian Road. The *Burying of*

16. This interpretation has been widely accepted, e.g., Giorgio Filippi, "La basilica di San Paolo fuori le mura," in *Pietro e Paolo: La storia, il culto, la memoria nei primi secoli* (ed. Angela Donati; Milan: Electa, 2000), 59; Paolo Liverani, "La basilica di San Pietro in Vaticano," in Donati, *Pietro e Paolo*, 55; Christine Mohrmann, "Á propos de deux mots controversés de la latinité chrétienne: Tropaeum-Nomen," *VC* 8.1 (1954): 163. Cf. Charles Guignebert, *La primauté de Pierre et la venue de Pierre à Rome* (Paris: Nourry, 1909), 304–11. Guignebert's arguments against the association of the trophies with the tombs are not convincing.

17. As part of his famous critique of the Christian cult of the saints, the emperor Julian (ca. 362 C.E.) charged that from an early date "the memorials [μνήματα] of Peter and Paul … were being worshipped in secret" (*C. Galil.* 327C).

18. The most concerted effort to interpret the evidence is in Richard Krautheimer, *Corpus basilicarum christianarum Romae* (5 vols.; Vatican City: Pontificio Istituto di Archeologia Cristiana, 1977), 5:112–16, 147–48, 160–61. He relied heavily upon the sketches made by Italian architect Virginio Vespignani in the 1830s. These drawings have proved notoriously difficult to interpret, because Vespignani did not include elevations, directional markers, or other details that would have allowed a more precise reconstruction. Recent excavations by the Vatican Museums have yielded no new information on this earlier monument to this point, but further investigations may occur in the future. Engelbert Kirschbaum has suggested, without much support, that an earlier shrine may date back to the second or even the first century. See *The Tombs of St Peter and St Paul* (trans. John Murray; New York: St. Martin's, 1957), 176. One attempt at reconstructing the monument is B. M. Apollonj-Ghetti, "Le basiliche cimiteriali degli apostoli Pietro e Paolo a Roma," in *Saecularia Petri et Pauli* (SAC 28; Vatican City: Pontificio Istituto di Archeologia Cristiana, 1969), 26, fig. 15.

the Martyrs is a list of dates and sites of feasts held at Rome in honor of certain martyrs, particularly Roman martyrs. In its surviving form, it probably dates from 336 C.E. and is the earliest extant Christian festival calendar of its type. The entry for June 29,[19] the traditional feast day of Peter and Paul in the West,[20] reads as follows: "[Feast of] Peter in the Catacombs, of Paul on the Ostian Road, when Tuscus and Bassus were consuls" (*Dep. mart.*).[21] Tuscus and Bassus were consuls in the year 258. The editor does not specify if this festival for Paul began in 258 or was already occurring by 258. Scholars have long debated this point, and I will return to this question in detail in chapter 2. For the moment, what is important is that the fourth-century editor of the *Burying of the Martyrs* connects the Ostian Road with a special feast in honor

---

19. The reason for the choice of June 29 is unknown. Beginning in the late fourth century, authors began to claim that both the apostles had been martyred on June 29, but there was not agreement on whether or not they had died in the same year. Ambrose (*Virginit.* 19.124), Augustine (*Serm.* 295.7; 381.1), Prudentius (*Perist.* 12.5, 21–22), Gregory of Tours (*Glor. mart.* 28), and Arator (*Act. apost.* 2.1247–49) believed that they had died a year apart. Others held that they had died on the exact same day: Jerome (*Vir. ill.* 5; *Tract. Ps.* 96.10) and Maximus of Turin (*Serm.* 1.2; 2.1; 9.1). A corroborating passage credited to Damasus of Rome is spurious (in *Eccl. occ. mon. iur.* 1.2, p. 157). The second-century author Dionysius of Corinth had stated that the apostles died "at the same time," but there is no mention of a particular date either by Dionysius or by Eusebius, who quotes him (Eusebius, *Hist. eccl.* 2.25.8). Scholars have generally viewed June 29 as a purely liturgical date with no historical connection to the martyrdoms, e.g., Hippolyte Delehaye, *Les origines du culte des martyrs* (2nd ed.; SHG 20; Brussels: Société des Bollandistes, 1933), 264. Based on a reference in Ovid (*Fast.* 6.795–796), some have argued that the Christian festival day was an attempt to take over the traditional date of the foundation of Rome by Romulus. See Carl Erbes, *Die Todestage der Apostel Paulus und Petrus und ihre römischen Denkmäler* (Leipzig: Hinrichs, 1899), 39–40; Oscar Cullmann, *Peter: Disciple, Apostle, Martyr* (2nd ed.; trans. Floyd V. Filson; London: SCM, 1962), 129–30; J. M. Huskinson, *Concordia Apostolorum: Christian Propaganda at Rome in the Fourth and Fifth Centuries* (BARIS 148; Oxford: British Archaeological Reports, 1982), 82. The identification of June 29 as the founding date of Rome has been incisively critiqued by Gitte Lønstrup, "Constructing Myths: The Foundation of *Roma Christiana* on 29 June," *ARID* 33 (2008): 27–64. Lønstrup does note that June 29 might be associated with the foundation of a temple by Augustus in honor of Quirinus (the god with whom Romulus was equated after his death), but even this possible connection lacks sufficient support in the sources.

20. Hans Lietzmann, *Petrus und Paulus in Rom* (2nd ed.; Berlin: de Gruyter, 1927), 127–28, has shown that December 28 was the festival date in the East, as attested by Gregory of Nyssa and a Syriac martyrology dated to 411.

21. "III kal. iul. Petri in Catacumbas et Pauli Ostense Tusco et Basso consulibus." The text has survived because it was attached to the 354 *Filocalian Calendar*, a Roman civil calendar. The approximate dating of the *Burying of the Martyrs* is calculated based on information in the *Burying of the Bishops* (*Depositio episcoporum*), a related calendar that was also transmitted by the *Filocalian Calendar*.

of Paul within the context of his cult. This celebration was taking place by the middle of the third century at or near the "trophy" of Paul.

The earliest literature on Paul's death reflects an increasing precision concerning the details and location of the martyrdom. The specificity of Caius and the *Burying of the Martyrs* replaced the ambiguity of the New Testament, *1 Clement*, the *Acts of Paul*, and the *Acts of Peter*. The later authors identified a particular place on the Ostian Road as a sacred site for the Pauline cult. In the fourth century, the construction of imperial basilicas reinforced the importance and prominence of the site and provided an architectural context for the veneration of the apostle.

1.2. The Creation of a "Holy Place": Architectural Development of the Site

Imperial Rome was a city of religious monuments. From the Julian Basilica in the Forum to the Altar of Peace in the Field of Mars, shrines to the gods and heroes permeated the civic space. They reminded the Romans that their welfare in part depended on these divine figures. After the emperors Constantine I and Licinius issued the Edict of Milan in 313, making Christianity a legal religion, monuments for Christian heroes also began to appear. Because these monuments were usually founded at or near gravesites, by Roman law they had to be outside the city walls.[22] By the late fourth century, a cluster of Christian shrines surrounded Rome. These monuments included two imperially sponsored basilicas on the Ostian Road: a modest basilica in the early fourth century, and a grand basilica near the end of that same century. These buildings memorialized the place at which the apostle Paul had, according to tradition, died and been buried. They evoked the stories of Paul's ultimate victory over Nero, yet they also invited new interpretations of the relationship between Rome and Christianity.

1.2.1. The Constantinian Basilica

The emperor Constantine erected the first basilica in honor of Paul on the Ostian Road. According to a later ecclesiastical chronicle, the *Book of Pontiffs* (*Liber Pontificalis*), "Then the emperor Constantine built a basilica to St. Paul the apostle at the suggestion of bishop Silvester; and he buried and sealed his body in bronze just like St. Peter's." The source provides a list of the financial resources that Constantine dedicated to this basilica, including a large, gold

---

22. This prohibition goes back to the earliest Roman law code, the Twelve Tables, compiled in the fifth century B.C.E. (Cicero, *Leg.* 2.23.58).

Fig. 1.2. Remains of Constantinian apse with "tomb of Paul" in the background. Courtesy of Giorgio Filippi.

cross to hang over Paul's sepulcher (*Lib. pontif.* 34, Davis).[23] Unfortunately, the details in this account can not be verified archaeologically, because the building was dismantled in the later fourth century. Excavations have revealed only parts of the apse and perhaps fragments of the exterior walls of the church (fig. 1.2).[24] Based on these scant remains, we are able to calculate the diameter of the church's apse at about 7.5 meters. The overall length and width of the basilica are impossible to establish, although some have estimated the size at approximately 21 meters long by 12 meters wide.[25] If this is at all accurate, then the dimensions of the structure were quite modest compared with other fourth-century

---

23. This work claims to record significant events from the time of each bishop of Rome, beginning with Peter. Krautheimer believed that this entry in the *Book of Pontiffs*, and particularly the reference to Silvester, was a later interpolation. See Krautheimer, *Corpus basilicarum*, 97. The archaeological evidence supports a Constantinian date, but to this point not the other details in the *Book of Pontiffs*.

24. Giorgio Filippi, "La tomba di San Paolo: I dati archeologici del 2006 e il taccuino Moreschi del 1850," *BMusPont* 26 (2007–2008): 323. The apse is now visible through a glass cover placed in the floor of the current basilica.

25. This estimate is based upon the drawings in Paolo Belloni, *Sulla grandezza e disposizione della primitiva basilica ostiense stabilita dalla sua absida rinvenuta nell'anno* (Rome: Tip. Forense, 1853). Belloni's plan took into account the boundaries provided by adjacent roads and has been widely accepted and reproduced, e.g., Jean-Charles Picard, "Le Quadriportique de Saint-Paul-hors-les-murs à Rome," *MEFRA* 87.1 (1975): 378; Hugo Brandenburg, *Ancient Churches of Rome from the Fourth to the Seventh Century: The Dawn of Christian Architecture in the West* (trans. Andreas Kropp; BAnT 8; Turnhout: Brepols, 2005), 103.

churches built by Constantine in Rome. For example, St. Peter's was 123 by 65 meters, while the Lateran Basilica measured 100 by 55 meters.

How might we explain the relatively small size of this church? The answer seems to lie in the layout of the neighborhood. The emperor made this building as large as possible without interrupting the streets in the surrounding area (fig. 1.3). It was limited by the Ostian Road on the eastern side, and another street marked the western boundary of the basilica. The more limited scale of this basilica did not mean limited exposure, however. Entrance to this church came directly from the Ostian Road on the eastern side. Because the church fronted on this major thoroughfare, a large number of people would have passed the basilica on a daily basis.

The Constantinian church became a landmark along this principal road, and its prominent location would have symbolized the growing influence of Christianity in Rome. The emperor endowed the construction of this basilica, in order to aggrandize the memorial that stood over Paul's traditional burial site. As a result, the veneration of Paul was no longer restricted to a marginalized group of Christians gathered at a small, roadside shrine. This church bore witness to an endorsement of the cult of Paul under the sponsorship of the emperor himself.

This positive connection between the basilica and the emperor marked a radical shift in the site's symbolic value concerning the relation-

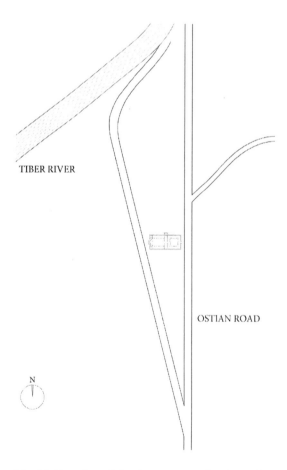

Fig. 1.3. Location of the Constantinian basilica. After Krautheimer; drawing by John Capen Brough.

ship between the Roman government and Christianity. Paul had traditionally died at this location at the hands of Nero. His "trophy" stood as a monument to the conflict between Rome and Christianity. After the construction of the Constantinian basilica, Christians came to venerate the apostle in a building that communicated a message exactly opposite from that of the original "trophy." No longer did the shrine commemorate the martyr's victory over the corrupt Roman emperor—Paul's defeat of Nero. Instead, the basilica celebrated *cooperation* between Paul and the imperial order. The cult of the apostle became an instrument of propaganda instead of a sign of resistance. The faithful still traveled here in order to honor Paul, but in doing so they were now being exposed to a new political ideology. In Constantine's vision, the apostle and the emperor worked together as victorious champions of the army of Christ and protectors of this great city.[26]

1.2.2. THE THEODOSIAN BASILICA AND THE CHRISTIAN FOUNDING OF ROME

In the last quarter of the fourth century, imperial intervention led to the demolition of Constantine's basilica in favor of a much grander edifice on the site. In 383/384 C.E., the emperors Theodosius I, Valentinian II, and Arcadius wrote to Sallustius, the prefect of Rome. They offered to fund the construction of a larger basilica over the tomb of Paul, but the road that ran behind the apse on the western side of the Constantinian church presented an obstacle. If the city officials would grant permission to eliminate this road, then the emperors would pay to build an entirely new (*ex novo*) structure.[27]

Several motivations lay behind this undertaking. First of all, according to the letter, Sallustius had reported that the Constantinian basilica could not accommodate the large number of pilgrims to the site. The late fourth century saw a resurgence in Paul's popularity in Rome,[28] and the current structure was

---

26. The churches built by Constantine "were informed by clear social, political, and religious agendas. Constantine's churches were symbols of both religious and imperial power" (Jeanne Halgren Kilde, *Sacred Power, Sacred Space: An Introduction to Christian Architecture and Worship* [New York: Oxford University Press, 2008], 40).

27. Otto Günther, *Epistulae imperatorum pontificum aliorum inde ab a. CCCLX-VII usque ad a. DLIII datae: Inde ab a. CCCLXVII usqve ad a. DLIII datae* (CSEL 35.1.2; Leipzig: Tempsky, 1895), 46ff., no. 3; reprinted in André Chastagnol, "Sur quelques documents relatifs à la basilique de Saint-Paul-hors-les-murs," in *Mélanges d'archéologie et d'histoire offerts à André Piganiol* (ed. Raymond Chevallier; Paris: SEVPEN, 1966), 436–37. The letter itself does not provide a precise date, but 383/384 is favored by Chastagnol (at 426); Krautheimer, *Corpus basilicarum*, 5:97; and Brandenburg, *Ancient Churches*, 114. Cf. *ILCV* 1763, where the date is given as 386.

28. Richard Krautheimer, "Intorno alla fondazione di SPFLM," *APARA.R* 53–54

not sufficient to meet the demand. Second, the discrepancy in size between the basilica of Paul and that of Peter on the Vatican hill may have been a cause of concern. The two greatest apostles and founders of the Roman church were worthy of comparable monuments. Constantine had limited his efforts on the Ostian Road so as not to disrupt the area around the basilica. The emperors now decided that the popularity of Paul justified a significant alteration to the layout of the roads. Finally, Bishop Damasus of Rome (366–384) probably played a part. During his tenure Damasus undertook an extensive program of construction and enlargement of Christian martyr shrines around Rome.[29] It is possible that he encouraged the emperors to pursue this project to honor Paul.[30] Whether or not Damasus had a hand in this endeavor, he certainly would have received the news enthusiastically and given his full support.

The new basilica was dedicated in November 390 or 391,[31] although it

---

(1980–1982): 213–20; Huskinson, *Concordia Apostolorum*, 2, 61–62. One indication of the renewed interest in Paul in the fourth century was the production of extensive commentaries on the Pauline epistles in Rome by Marius Victorinus and Ambrosiaster; see Hans von Campenhausen, *The Fathers of the Latin Church* (trans. Manfred Hoffman; London: Black, 1964), 184–85. Von Campenhausen also places the work of Augustine in the light of this "new interest in Paul's theology" in the West. For Victorinus, see Stephen A. Cooper, *Marius Victorinus' Commentary on Galatians: Introduction, Translation, and Notes* (Oxford: Oxford University Press, 2005), esp. 41–87, where he discusses the importance of artistic presentations of Paul; Bernhard Lohse, "Beobachtungen zum Paulus-Kommentar des Marius Victorinus und zur Wiederentdeckung des Paulus in der lateinischen Theologie des vierten Jahrhunderts," in *Kerygma und Logos* (ed. A. M. Ritter; Göttingen: Vandenhoeck & Ruprecht, 1979), 351–66. On Ambrosiaster, Sophie Lunn-Rockliffe, *Ambrosiaster's Political Theology* (Oxford: Oxford University Press, 2007); W. Geerlings, "Untersuchung zum Paulusverständnis des Ambrosisaster" (PhD diss., University of Tübingen, 1980); A. A. R. Bastiaensen, "Augustin commentateur de saint Paul et l'Ambrosiaster," *SacEr* 36 (1996): 37–65.

29. Danilo Mazzoleni, "Papa Damaso e l'archeologia cristiana," in *Saecularia Damasiana: Atti del Convegno internazionale per il XVI centenario della morte di papa Damaso I (1984)* (Vatican City: Pontificio Istituto di Archeologia Cristiana, 1986), 5–14; Fabrizio Bisconti and Danilo Mazzoleni, *The Christian Catacombs of Rome: History, Decoration, Inscriptions* (Regensburg: Schnell & Steiner, 1999), 49–59.

30. Richard Krautheimer, *Rome: Profile of a City, 312–1308* (Princeton: Princeton University Press, 1980), 42–43.

31. To this same period belongs the earliest known painting of Paul, found in 2009 as part of a larger complex of images in the cemetery of Saint Thecla, less than 1 kilometer south of the Theodosian basilica on the Ostian Road ("Roman Archaeologists Find Oldest Images of Apostles in a Catacomb," June 22, 2010, online: http://blogs.reuters .com/faithworld/2010/06/22/roman-archaeologists-find-oldest-images-of-apostles-in-a-catacomb). As of the completion of this book, the scientific publication of these paintings has not yet appeared, and access to the site is still restricted.

How prevalent is Rome w/ Xtinity before this?

was not completed until the time of the emperor Honorius (395–423).[32] It stood largely intact until 1823, when a devastating fire destroyed most of the building. (The current basilica on the site was dedicated in 1854.) A fifth-century dedicatory mosaic survived the fire and runs above the main arch in the interior of the modern church: "Theodosius began this hall, which is sanctified by the body of Paul, the teacher of the world, and Honorius completed it."[33] Much larger than its predecessor, the basilica measured over 128 meters in length and 65 meters in width across the nave. The transept stretched 71 meters across (fig. 1.4). It was a five-aisle basilica like St. Peter's but surpassed it in both size and grandeur. While the builders of St. Peter's had reused materials taken from other structures, the new Pauline basilica featured white marble quarried near Constantinople specifically for this church.[34]

The architects moved the apse from the western end of the building to the eastern end. At the western end of the new basilica was a large courtyard surrounded by porticoes. This magnificent church now extended from the Ostian Road on the east to the marshland of the Tiber River on the west. A bronze tablet from 391/392 identified it as the "Basilica of the Apostle Paul and the Three Emperors."[35] These three emperors, like Constantine before them, desired to lay claim to a connection to Paul by marking this holy place with a monument, but on a grand scale. As patrons of this basilica, they had in turn become clients of the apostle.

The earliest surviving description of this new edifice comes from the Spanish Christian poet Prudentius, who visited Rome between 401 and 405:

> Elsewhere the Ostian Road keeps the memorial church of Paul, where the river grazes the land on its left bank. The splendour of the place is princely,

---

32. The construction of this church was part of a larger project that included the building of a bridge farther up the Tiber. This project became surrounded by intrigue and controversy when money ran short, the bridge collapsed, and the two architects, Cyriades and Auxentius, levied accusations of mismanagement against each other. A formal inquiry was held, and oversight of the project was handed over to a lawyer named Aphrodisias (Symmachus, *Relat.* 25–26). Joan Barclay Lloyd has suggested that Damasus was behind the entire project, but the evidence does not support this assertion. See "Krautheimer and S. Paolo fuori le mura: Architectural, Urban, and Liturgical Planning in Late Fourth-Century Rome," in *Ecclesiae urbis: Atti del Congresso internazionale di studi sulle Chiese di Roma (IV-X secolo), Roma, 4–10 settembre 2000* (ed. Federico Guidobaldi and Alessandra Guiglia Guidobaldi; 3 vols.; Vatican City: Pontificio Istituto di Archeologia Cristiana, 2002), 1:24.

33. *ICUR* 2:4780; *ILCV* 1761a.

34. Brandenburg, *Ancient Churches*, 115–16.

35. *CIL* 6:33895 and 15:7138; *ILCV* 1763.

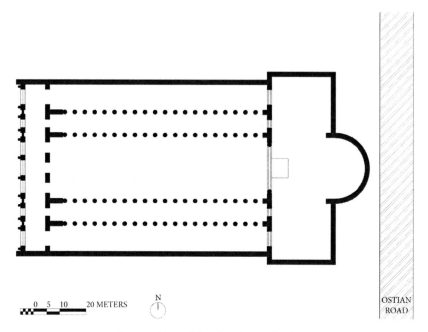

Fig. 1.4. Plan of the Theodosian basilica.
After Brandenburg; drawing by John Capen Brough.

for our good emperor[36] dedicated this seat and decorated its whole extent
with great wealth. He laid plates on the beams so as to make all the light
within golden like the sun's radiance at its rising, and supported the gold-
panelled ceiling on pillars of Parian marble set out there in four rows. Then
he covered the curves of the arches with splendid glass of different hues,
like meadows that are bright with flowers in the spring. (Prudentius, *Perist.*
12.45–54, Thomson)

In the eyes of Prudentius, the extravagant use of gold, white marble, and mul-
ticolored glass created an overwhelming visual effect in honoring the apostle
to the Gentiles. The significance of the church went far beyond appearance,
however. The location and orientation of this new Theodosian basilica inspired

---

36. Prudentius probably has in mind Theodosius I, who reigned as sole emperor from
392 to 395. Later tradition also remembered Theodosius as the primary agent in building this church, so it is often referred to as the Theodosian basilica. Theodosius probably
visited the basilica in progress during his visit to Rome in 389 (John F. Matthews, *Western
Aristocracies and Imperial Court, A.D. 364–425* [Oxford: Clarendon, 1975], 227–28).

Prudentius to reimagine the sacred topography of Rome and the very origins of the city.

In place of the traditional foundation accounts, the poet crafted a new story in which Paul, Peter, and the Christian God played the central roles along the banks of the Tiber River. According to Prudentius, "The marshland of Tiber, washed by the near-by river, knows that its turf was hallowed by two victories, for it was witness both of cross and sword,[37] by which a rain of blood twice flowed over the same grass and soaked it" (Prudentius, *Perist.* 12.7–10, Thomson). The western entrance to the new basilica of Paul faced the Tiber River, as did the eastern entrance to the Vatican basilica across town on the opposite side of the river. The poet was careful to highlight that the Tiber linked the two buildings geographically.[38] More importantly for Prudentius, however, it formed the conceptual bridge between the major cult sites for Paul and Peter: "Tiber separates the bones of the two and both its banks are consecrated as it flows between the hallowed tombs" (12.29–30). Prudentius did not ignore the fact that Paul had died along the Ostian Road—in fact, Prudentius provides the earliest literary reference to the Ostian Road as the site of Paul's death. He emphasized, however, that the proximity of the Tiber gave special meaning to the shedding of Paul's blood, as if his blood had mixed with Peter's. The two greatest apostles shared this common ground. The very soil was now made holy by their martyrdoms, and the new basilica to Paul adorned the place appropriately.

Prudentius's focus on the Tiber had wider implications. By sanctifying the river, the poet metaphorically declared the refounding of Rome as a Christian city. According to tradition, the Tiber had played a central role in the founding of Rome. In the *Aeneid*, a discouraged Aeneas lies down next to the river to sleep. Father Tiber, the river god, visits him in a dream and promises that Aeneas's offspring will found a mighty city: "When thirty years have circled from this time, Ascanius will found Alba—glorious name. I prophesy the truth.... I am the brimming river grazing these banks and cutting through these rich fields, the azure Tiber, favorite streams of heaven" (Virgil, *Aen.* 8.46–48, 62–64, Ruden). Aeneas awakes, encouraged by this visitation, and calls upon the gods to bring this promise to fruition: "Nymphs of Laurentum, who give birth to rivers, and Father Tiber with your holy stream, take me and keep me safe—at last—from danger.... Only stay with me: prove your holy

---

37. A reference to Peter's traditional death by inverted crucifixion (*Acta Pet.* 37–40) and Paul's death by decapitation.

38. Michael J. Roberts, *Poetry and the Cult of the Martyrs: The* Liber Peristephanon *of Prudentius* (RLLTC; Ann Arbor: University of Michigan Press, 1993), 170–71.

favor" (8.71–73, 78). The promise of Father Tiber proves true when Aeneas's son founds Alba Longa, the mother city of Rome.

In Virgil's pagan[39] epic, the river lay behind the inception of Rome by the pronouncement of the god. In Prudentius's Christian poem, the river marks the foundation point. Here the Lord's apostles had gained the crown of martyrdom and ushered in a new era: "It was witness both of cross and sword." In addition, Prudentius gives Rome a new divine, founding "Father." While Father Tiber had given his promise to Aeneas, the Christian God, the "supreme Father," gave Paul and Peter to Rome as "the two dowers of the faith" (Prudentius, *Perist.* 12.55–56, Thomson).[40]

Prudentius's creative reinterpretation of the Tiber allowed him to replace the Roman foundation account in the *Aeneid*. It also permitted him to play with Rome's other primary foundation myth, the story of Romulus and Remus. Livy and Plutarch are our primary sources for this myth, which runs as follows: Before the founding of Rome, Amulius was king of the settlement of Alba Longa. He feared that his niece, Rhea Silvia, might have sons who would one day seize his throne, so he forced her to become a Vestal Virgin. Amulius believed that this would solidify his position, but the god Mars fell in love with Rhea and seduced her. As a result of their union, she bore Romulus and Remus, the twin sons of the god. Amulius was furious and ordered that the boys be thrown into the Tiber. The swelling river did not drown the boys, however. Instead, it carried them safely to shore, where a she-wolf found and suckled them. As the king had feared, the twins later returned to overthrow him (Livy, *Urb. cond.* 1.4–5; Plutarch, *Rom.* 3–8).

For Prudentius, the Tiber had again witnessed the apparent deaths of Rome's founding figures in the martyrdoms of Paul and Peter. Just as Amulius believed that he had secured his rule by killing Romulus and Remus, so did Nero assume that he had eliminated the threat posed by the apostles. Like the mythological twins, the apostolic pair lived on (spiritually, at least) and brought about the demise of the evil ruler who had attempted to assassinate them. This image of a defeated Nero is prominent at the end of the *Acts of Paul*. After his death, Paul appears to Nero and declares, "Caesar, behold Paul, the soldier of God. I have not died but live in my God. But many evil things and a great punishment will come upon you, you miserable man, because you

---

39. I recognize that "pagan" is a problematic term, but we have yet to settle on another term that covers the same range of meaning without polemical overtones.

40. Pierre-Yves Fux has noted that the verb *stringo* appears in *Aen.* 8.62–64 and in *Perist.* 12.46, another indication of the epic, literary echoes in Prudentius. See *Les sept passions de Prudence: Peristephanon 2, 5, 9, 11–14* (Par. 46; Fribourg: Editions Universitaires, 2003), 427 n. 46.

unjustly spilled the blood of the righteous just a few days ago" (*Mart. Paul.* 6). The lofty destiny of the two apostles, like that of Romulus and Remus, could not be thwarted by the stratagems of a paranoid and malicious king.[41]

Prudentius connected the apostles with the Romulus and Remus story at yet another point.[42] According to the myth, Romulus eventually killed Remus, and Rome took its name from Romulus. The Romans were the "people of Romulus." In Prudentius's poem, this same group was dedicated to the commemoration of Peter and Paul on their June 29 joint feast day: "The people of Romulus [*plebs Romula*] goes pouring through the streets two separate ways, for the same day is busy with two festivals" (*Perist.* 12.57–58, Thomson). In this Christianized city, the Romans still bore the name of Romulus; however, they now venerated Paul and Peter as their founding pair.[43]

The Roman stories concerning Father Tiber and Romulus and Remus converged on a marble altar dedicated to Mars (fig. 1.5) from the time of Trajan (98–117).[44] This representation of the Roman Lupercalia, an annual festival that recalled the story of Romulus and Remus (Ovid, *Fast.* 2.411–420), shows two large figures moving from the viewer's left to right and looking back at the personification of the Palatine Hill. Below their feet is a she-wolf suckling the infants Romulus and Remus. Father Tiber reclines in the lower right corner and observes the entirety of the scene. This collage of mythic imagery merges the Tiber and Romulus and Remus traditions into a coherent picture of the foundation of the city. In a similar way, Prudentius sculpted literary imagery into a coherent scene of his new foundation account for Rome. In his poem, Father Tiber and Romulus and Remus were replaced by those who had superseded them, the Christian God and the apostles Paul and Peter. The Tiber became a symbol of the origins of a Christian Rome. The river flowed through the ancient capital, sanctifying its banks and giving it a new identity.

The fourth-century imperial basilicas on the Ostian Road served several functions in the development and promotion of the Pauline cult. On one level,

---

41. For an insightful treatment of Nero's reign, including his presentation by Roman historians, see Edward Champlin, *Nero* (Cambridge: Harvard University Press, 2005).

42. Later in the fifth century, Leo I famously compared Paul and Peter to Romulus and Remus (*Serm.* 82.1), but Prudentius preceded Leo by over half a century.

43. Romulus and Remus were not the only Roman pair with which Peter and Paul could be compared. The twins Castor and Pollux (the Dioscuri) were guardians of Rome, a role that the apostles also later took over. See Charles Pietri, "Concordia Apostolorum et renovatio urbis (Culte des martyrs et propagande pontificale)," *MEFR* 73 (1961): 316; Dennis Trout, "Damasus and the Invention of Early Christian Rome," *JMEMS* 33.3 (2003): 521–23.

44. This altar was unearthed in Ostia and is currently housed in the Palazzo Massimo alle Terme in Rome.

Fig. 1.5. Altar of Mars showing the Lupercalia. Discovered at Ostia and
now in the Museo Nazionale Romano /Palazzo Massimo, Rome.
Photograph by Marie-Lan Nguyen.

they were physical markers of Christian sacred space and provided venues
in which the faithful could focus their veneration on Paul. The Constantinian basilica replaced Caius's "trophy" monument, while the Theodosian
basilica created more room for the increasing number of visitors to the site.
On another level, these Pauline churches prompted a reconsideration of the
relationship between Rome and Christianity. In the case of Constantine, his
basilica declared that the emperor was now an ally of the martyred apostle
and of the faith for which he had died. Paul and Constantine carried the same
banner. They did not oppose one another, as Paul and Nero had done. When
Prudentius saw the Theodosian basilica and its relationship to the Tiber, he
reimagined the very origins of Rome. The Christian God and the apostles,
rather than Father Tiber and Romulus and Remus, had laid the foundations
for the city along the Tiber's banks. The significance of the basilicas on both
levels points to the importance of the Pauline cult for the Christians of Rome.
Roman Christian identity was tied closely to the legacy of its great martyr, and
this connection was celebrated on the Ostian Road. At this point we shift our

focus to a cluster of other practices through which bishops and pilgrims alike contributed to the perpetuation and expansion of the cult.

1.3. APOSTOLIC POWER FROM THE GRAVE: VENERATION PRACTICES AT PAUL'S TOMB

In poem 2 of *On the Crowns of Martyrdom,* Prudentius bemoans the plight of his fellow Spaniards, who live so far from the tomb of the martyr Lawrence and the other sacred sites of Rome:

> O thrice and four times, yea seven times blessed the dweller of Rome, who pays honor to thee and the abode of thy bones in presence, who can kneel by them, who sprinkles the spot with his tears, bowing his breast to the ground and in a low voice pouring out his prayers. Us the Vascon Ebro separates from thee, we are far removed beyond two mountain ranges, across the Cottian heights and the snowy Pyrenees. Scarcely even have we heard report how full Rome is of buried saints, how richly her city's soil blossoms with holy tombs. (*Perist.* 2.529–548, Thomson)[45]

The faithful in Rome had a spiritual advantage, simply because they lived near the sepulchers of holy men and women. Proximity to the sacred brought certain advantages that those in Spain could not enjoy.

Paul's tomb in the Theodosian basilica was one such place where the "soil blossoms" in Rome. As a result, it became the focal point for a variety of devotional practices in late antiquity.[46] In the pages that follow, I will begin by discussing two important artifacts from the sepulcher area: a sarcophagus that some claim contains Paul's body, and an inscription slab that once covered this sarcophagus. I will then turn to the specific practices of privileged burials, pilgrimage, and relic veneration and will explain how each related to the tomb. As the evidence shows, the grave of the apostle attracted both living and dead Christians who sought the blessings of Paul's presence in this sacred space.

---

45. Prudentius was by no means the only Spanish example of interest in the cult of saints. Bishop Damasus of Rome, one of the greatest patrons of the Roman cult, was of Spanish origin, as probably was the pilgrim Egeria.

46. Relics were not the only focal points for worship within Christian basilicas in this period, as shown by Ann Marie Yasin, *Saints and Church Spaces in the Late Antique Mediterranean: Architecture, Cult, and Community* (Cambridge: Cambridge University Press, 2009), 151–208. In the case of the Ostian Road, however, the significance of the tomb and its alleged relics is undeniable.

1.3.1. Important Archaeological Discoveries at the Tomb Site

The most significant artifact from the Theodosian basilica is a sarcophagus that the Vatican claims contains the bones of Paul. Scholars have long assumed that such a coffin had existed, for the arch inscription specifically states that the basilica was "sanctified by the body of Paul." Until recently, however, the evidence for it was lacking. Several nineteenth-century sources state that witnesses saw an ancient-looking sarcophagus beneath the high altar during the reconstruction work that followed the fire of 1823. Strangely, the notes and sketches that architect Virginio Vespignani made at that time included no mention of this. Vespignani recorded a number of other sarcophagi, but this important find received no attention.[47] When the nineteenth-century builders constructed the high altar for the current basilica, they filled in the crypt with cement and made access to the ancient levels impossible. This prevented any verification of the existence of the coffin.[48]

In 2002 the Vatican Museums launched a new excavation in search of this sarcophagus. Under the leadership of Giorgio Filippi, the archaeological team broke through the thick layer of nineteenth-century cement. The Vatican announced in 2006 the discovery of a marble sarcophagus 2.55 meters long, 1.25 meters wide, and 0.97 meters high. It has a rough, plain front with a barrel-vaulted lid (fig. 1.6). Archaeologists have dated the coffin to the late fourth century, meaning it was most likely placed here at the time of the construction of the Theodosian basilica. The date suggests that the three emperors would have moved Paul's body from a previous sarcophagus to this one, and Filippi has expressed confidence that this is the very sarcophagus that was the focus of Pauline veneration in the ancient church.[49]

---

47. The chronicle of the Benedictine monastery on the site records the sarcophagus sighting. Hartmann Grisar, *Analecta romana* (Rome: Desclée Lefebvre, 1899), 290–91 n. 2, reported that the abbot of St. Paul's had also seen a tomb and the remains of iron grating. Vespignani was definitely aware of the sarcophagus. Giorgio Filippi of the Vatican Museums showed me a copy of a coin of Pope Gregory XVI (1831–1846) that Vespignani had placed beneath this coffin, but the architect did not otherwise draw attention to it.

48. Filippi, "La tomba di San Paolo: I dati archeologici," 321–24.

49. Ibid., 324; idem, "Un decennio di ricerche e studi nella basilica Ostiense," in *San Paolo in Vaticano: La figura e la parola dell'Apostolo delle Genti nelle raccolte pontificie* (ed. Umberto Utro; Todi: Tau Editrice, 2009), 37–40. As early as 2004, Filippi published some initial results of the excavation. He made references to Paul's grave and even identified the side of the coffin in an image as "sarcofago di S. Paolo." See "La tomba di San Paolo e le fasi della basilica tra il IV e VII secolo: Primi risultati di indagini archeologiche e ricerche d'archivio," *BMusPont* 24 (2004): 200, fig. 11c. However, no information about the sarcophagus per se (description, dimensions, etc.) came out until a news release from

Fig. 1.6. Close-up of the "sarcophagus of Paul." Photograph by Annewies van den Hoek.

Archaeologists were hesitant to speculate about the contents of the coffin, however. This reservation was understandable after the embarrassing incident surrounding the alleged tomb of Peter. Excavations in the 1940s beneath the altar of St. Peter's basilica in Rome unearthed a grave believed to be that of the apostle Peter. The archaeologists found bones inside, and the Vatican announced that they had discovered the relics of Peter himself. Further investigation revealed that these bones came from male and female humans and several animals.[50] Only later did scientists rediscover in storage another set of bones unearthed in the excavation and now considered by some to be Peter's. In light of this debacle surrounding Peter's alleged tomb, restraint in the case

the Vatican in December 2006: Catholic News Agency, "Tomb of St. Paul to be Visible for Pilgrims," December 12, 2006, online: http://www.catholicnewsagency.com/showarchive .php?date=2006-12-12.
    50. Margherita Guarducci, *Pietro ritrovato: Il martirio, la tomba, le reliquie* (2nd ed.; Milan: Mondadori, 1970); Venerando Correnti, "Relazione dello studio compiuto su tre gruppi di resti scheletrici umani già rinvenuti sotto la confessione della Basilica Vaticana," in *Le reliquie di Pietro sotto la Confessione della Basilica vaticana: Una messa a punto* (ed. Margherita Guarducci; Rome: Coletti, 1967), 83–160; J. E. Walsh, *The Bones of St. Peter* (New York: Doubleday, 1982), 99–107.

of the Pauline sarcophagus was certainly in order, and the contents remained unknown.

In June 2009, Pope Benedict XVI made a surprise announcement at the close of the Pauline Year (the jubilee year in honor of the two thousandth anniversary of the apostle's traditional birth date). He reported that archaeologists had inserted a probe into the sarcophagus and found bone fragments accompanied by traces of incense, purple linen, and a blue fabric with linen filaments. Carbon 14 testing on the bones revealed that they probably dated from the first or second century C.E. The pope stated that the result of the testing "seems to confirm the unanimous and uncontested tradition that they are the mortal remains of the Apostle Paul."[51] A complete, scientific publication of these tests and the results has yet to appear, so it is impossible at this point to make an assessment of the Vatican's claims. Ultimately, there is no way to establish whether or not the bones in the coffin actually belong to Paul, so questions will remain. These questions about the contents, however, do not undermine the significance of this sarcophagus as a cultic object.

An earlier sarcophagus probably rested within the small apse of the Constantinian basilica at the building's western end. The Theodosian builders placed this new coffin in the same location, apart from raising its elevation slightly, possibly on account of the humidity in the ground.[52] Because the orientation and size of the Theodosian basilica changed, the grave's relative location within the structure was also altered. It now occupied a more central position beneath the main arch, where the nave and the transept met (fig. 1.7). In the Theodosian phase, therefore, this coffin was front and center for those gathered for worship in the nave.

The other major find from the tomb area tells us about the presentation and accessibility of this sarcophagus. During renovations to the altar following the fire of 1823, two marble slabs (fig. 1.8) came to light that bear the inscription, "To Paul the apostle and martyr" (*Paulo apostolomart[yri]*). Early assessments dated the inscription to the time of Constantine. More recent scholarly opinion has favored a date in the late fourth or early fifth century,

---

51. Catholic News Agency, "Test 'Seems to Confirm' Bone Fragments are St. Paul's, Pope Benedict Says," June 29, 2009, online: http://www.catholicnewsagency.com/showarchive .php?date=2009-06-29. Presumably, he means "the mortal remains" except for the head, which is supposedly housed in the Lateran Basilica with the head of Peter.

52. Filippi describes the area in antiquity as "waterlogged" (*acquitrinosa*). See "La tomba di San Paolo alla luce delle recent ricerche," in *Il culto di San Paolo nelle chiese cristiane e nella tradizione Maltese* (ed. J. Azzopardi; Rabat, Malta: Wignacourt Museum, 2006), 6.

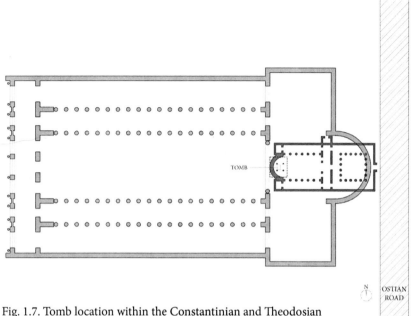

Fig. 1.7. Tomb location within the Constantinian and Theodosian
basilicas. After Belloni; drawing by John Capen Brough.

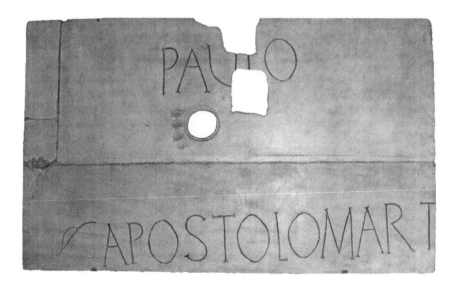

Fig. 1.8. *Paulo apostolomart* slabs. In the Abbazia di San Paolo fuori le Mura, Rome.
Photograph by Brent Nongbri.

that is to say, from the period of the Theodosian construction.[53] One round and two square holes were cut into the upper slab at a later date, and I will return in due course to explain these modifications to the stone.

These slabs originally stood upright on the sides of a structure that surrounded and identified the sarcophagus (fig. 1.9).[54] Paul received two titles here, apostle and martyr. Tradition had well established Paul's importance as the "apostle to the Gentiles," the one called by Christ himself in a vision to preach the gospel to non-Jews (Gal 1:16; Acts 9:15). He had spread the message far and wide across the Mediterranean, including to the Romans through an epistle and a visit to the city. On the Ostian Road, however, his identity was incomplete without the addition of "martyr." He had not only preached at Rome but had also died there, perhaps near the very spot where he now lay. For this reason throngs of Christians came to this place to venerate him, necessitating this larger basilica.

Filippi has suggested that the structure over the coffin served as both a memorial shrine and the site for the celebration of the Eucharist in the Theodosian basilica.[55] As a memorial shrine for Paul, it permitted the pouring of libation offerings in honor of the apostle. A libation consisted of pouring a liquid at a sacred place, often the tomb of a god or an esteemed ancestor.[56] Some believed that wine libations provided nourishment for the dead (Lucian of Samosata, *Luct.* 9), while others honored the dead by pouring perfumes or other precious liquids. The custom was widely practiced in antiquity, and Prudentius attests that libations were part of the Roman cult of the martyrs.[57] In his poem honoring Hippolytus, he notes that at the tomb of the martyr on the Tiburtine Road, "They print kisses on the clear metal, *they pour down*

53. The Constantinian date was espoused by G. B. de Rossi, "I monumenti antichi cristiani," *BArC* 2 (1863): 153, and then picked up by *ICUR* 2:4775; Kirschbaum, *Tombs*, 179–81. On the more recent dating, see Filippi, "La basilica," 61; Hugo Brandenburg, "Die Architektur der Basilika San Paolo fuori le mura: Das Apostelgrab als Zentrum der Liturgie und des Märtyrerkultes," *MDAI(R)* 112 (2005/2006): 248.

54. Giorgio Filippi, "Die Ergebnisse der neuen Ausgrabungen am Grab des Apostels Paulus: Reliquienkult und Eucharistie im Presbyterium der Paulsbasilika," *MDAI(R)* 112 (2005/2006): 385–86; R. A. Lanciani, "Delle scoperte fatte nel 1838 e 1850 presso il sepolcro di Paolo Apostolo," *NBArC* 23 (1917): 7–27.

55. Filippi, "Ergebnisse," 282–84.

56. Wanda Wolski and Ion Berciu, "Contribution au problème des tombes romaines à dispositif pour les libations funéraires," *Latomus* 32.2 (1973): 370–79.

57. On the broader Christian adaptation of Greco-Roman burial customs, see Lucrezia Spera, "Riti funerari e culto dei morti nella tarda antichità," *Aug* 45 (2005): 5–34; Paul-Albert Février, "Le culte des morts dans les communautés chrétiennes durant le IIIe siècle," in *Atti del IX Congresso internazionale di archeologia cristiana, Roma, 21–27 settembre 1975* (2 vols.; SAC 32; Vatican City: Pontificio Istituto di Archeologia Cristiana, 1978), 1:211–74.

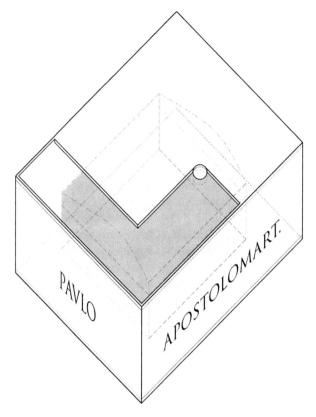

Fig. 1.9. Reconstruction of the original placement of *Paulo* slabs.
After Filippi; drawing by John Capen Brough.

balsams, and wet their faces with their tears" (Prudentius, *Perist.* 11.193–194, Thomson, emphasis added). The archaeological evidence suggests that such libations also took place at the tomb of Paul. A funnel-shaped hole in the sarcophagus lid led to its interior. The cover stone for the shrine surrounding the sarcophagus would have featured a round hole that lined up with the opening in the coffin's lid. Therefore, visitors could have brought wine or perfumes to pour into the casket and over the bones of the apostle. In some cases, the pouring of balsams or oil at Christian tombs was believed to alter the liquids into holy objects that had come into contact with the relics and were taken away in flasks placed beneath a hole in the bottom of the tomb.[58] When (or

---

58. This process of creating holy oil is described by Paulinus of Nola (*Carm.* 21.586–600), and archaeologists excavating at Apamea (Syria) found small reliquaries with funnel-shaped openings in the top and taps at the bottom for collecting the oil that had been

if) the entire sarcophagus of Paul is revealed, we will have more evidence concerning the possible collection of holy oil here.

This tomb structure's other function was to accommodate the celebration of the Eucharist by the bishop. As early as 406, Jerome confirmed this practice over the bones and graves of the apostles: "Does the bishop of Rome act wrongly, therefore, when he offers sacrifices to the Lord over the bones of the dead men Peter and Paul, which we consider to be venerable…, and judges their tombs worthy to be Christ's altars?" (Jerome, *Vigil.* 8). The practice in this basilica probably dates even earlier, to the late fourth century.

This grave-altar combination amplified the significance of Paul and the holiness of his traditional burial site, for it linked the death of the martyr with the death of Christ liturgically, spatially, and experientially. Those gathered saw the bishop or priest breaking the bread for the Eucharist above a table that featured the name of "Paul the apostle and martyr." Christ's body had been broken as the foundational event for the Christian faith, and Paul's body had been broken as a foundational event for the Roman church. The bodies of these two figures were present: one in the bread and wine, the other in his relics. This liturgical event would have augmented the belief that Paul's presence and sacred power could be accessed here in a special way. The resulting desire to access this presence and power led to other practices as well, including the placement of burials in the vicinity of Paul's remains.

1.3.2. Privileged Burials and Architectural Changes around the Tomb

The desire among Christians to be buried "near the saints" (*ad sanctos*) is widely attested in the ancient period. The mortal remains of holy people were believed to sanctify and heal anything with which they came into contact, including the ground around them.[59] It was advantageous, therefore, to be as close as possible.[60] As Christians lay in their tombs, they would receive a constant flow of blessing. The merit of the nearby martyrs would improve their

---

poured through. See Jean Lassus, *Sanctuaires chrétiens de Syrie* (BAH 42; Paris: Geuthner, 1947), 163–64. John Chrysostom (*Mart.* [PG 50:664–65]), Theodoret of Cyrus (*Hist. eccl.* 21), and Gregory of Tours (*Vit. Mart.* 1.2) are among those who witness to the miraculous power of holy oil in flasks.

59. In *Acta Thom.* 170, King Misdaeus goes to Thomas's tomb seeking one of the apostle's bones to heal his demoniac son. The body had been moved, but even the dust from that place is sufficient to effect the miracle.

60. E.g., an inscription for a woman buried in Velitrae (south of Rome) states that "for so many good deeds [she] gained a burial in the precincts of the saints" and "received what many desire to get" (*ICUR* 1:3127, cited in MacMullen, *Second Church*, 82).

own spiritual standing, culminating in the resurrection at the end of time. Those lying "near the saints" would benefit again at that point on account of their proximity to God's most favored souls.[61] As Maximus of Turin once preached, "This provision was made for us by our ancestors, that we should join our bodies to the bones of the saints, for since the underworld feared them, punishment may not touch us.... Sleeping with the holy martyrs, we have escaped the shadows of hell—if not by our own merits at least as sharers in holiness" (*Serm.* 12).[62] At the basilica of Paul, provision for such burials had a direct impact on the architectural development of the building.

1.3.2.1. Sarcophagi at the Theodosian Level

Interment in the immediate vicinity of Paul's grave was an honor reserved for influential members of the Christian community, and archaeologists have discovered several sarcophagi from the Theodosian building phase.[63] One of these lay just to the north of the apostolic tomb. An inscription identifies it as the burial of the presbyter Gaudentius and his wife Severa in 389 C.E.[64] This indicates that the builders put this sarcophagus in place during the construction of the Theodosian basilica, which was dedicated about a year later. Gaudentius's position as a leader in the Roman church (and perhaps as a patron of the basilica?) would explain how he secured a burial location so close to the tomb of Paul.

Another late fourth-century sarcophagus from the same level is of even greater interest, for it features an iconographical representation of the mar-

---

61. A comparable practice developed within Judaism at around the same time, as seen at the necropolis of Bet She'arim in the Galilee, where wealthy Jews from all over the Near East brought their dead to be buried near the remains of revered rabbis such as Judah ha-Nasi. See Zeev Weiss, "Social Aspects of Burial in Beth She'arim: Archeological Finds and Talmudic Sources," in *The Galilee in Late Antiquity* (ed. Lee I. Levine; New York: Jewish Theological Seminary of America, 1992), 357–71; Lee I. Levine, "Bet Še'arim in Its Patriarchal Context," in *"The Words of a Wise Man's Mouth Are Gracious" (Qoh 10,12): Festschrift for Günter Stemberger on the Occasion of His 65th Birthday* (ed. Mauro Perani; Berlin: de Gruyter, 2005), 197–225.

62. See also Grabar, *Martyrium*, esp. 1:487–532; Duval, *Auprès des saints corps et âme.* Augustine disputed this view in *Cur.* 6. He claimed that there was no direct benefit from being buried close to saints. The only indirect benefit was that people who came to a shrine sometimes also prayed for those buried in that vicinity. Duval has shown that Augustine reflected by far the minority view among Christians of his day.

63. On the issue of social class and its influence on burial locations in Rome, see Mac-Mullen, *Second Church*, 69–80.

64. *ICUR* 2:4823; *ILCV* 1130; Krautheimer, *Corpus basilicarum*, 5:115–16, figs. 94, 97. Unfortunately, we know nothing more about these individuals.

tyrdom of Paul (fig. 1.10).[65] In the panel to the viewer's right of center, Paul stands with his arms bound behind his back. He is bald and bearded and wears a long tunic. He faces a Roman soldier, who is clearly identifiable by

Fig. 1.10. Sarcophagus image of the martyrdom of Paul. In the Museo Pio Cristiano, Vatican Museums. Photograph by Robin Margaret Jensen.

---

65. Friedrich Wilhelm Deichmann, ed., *Repertorium der christlich-antiken Sarkophage* (Wiesbaden: Steiner, 1967), 1.1, no. 61. According to Jaś Elsner, "The allusion via images of the Roman saints to sites of cult and (implicitly) to times of festivals—effectively a visual refiguring of Rome through its martyrs—became prolific in the second half of the [fourth] century." See "Inventing Christian Rome: The Role of Early Christian Art," in *Rome the Cosmopolis* (ed. Catharine Edwards and Greg Woolf; Cambridge: Cambridge University Press, 2003), 90.

his style of dress.[66] The soldier advances toward Paul, carrying the sword with which he will behead the apostle. The viewer is transported into the moment just before the sword fell. This image brought the literary tradition of Paul's beheading into three dimensions, and it was then placed next to Paul's tomb. The scene both honored the memory of the apostle and linked the person buried in the sarcophagus with the legacy of Paul.

This coffin has another level of importance for the history of the cult. It is the earliest example of a group of sarcophagi that, like the poetry of Pruden-tius, explicitly locate Paul's martyrdom next to the Tiber River. The important visual clues lie in the background. Just behind Paul's head is the stern of a ship. The image of the boat indicates that the apostle died near a body of water large enough to allow for transport. The Romans used vessels known as "tree-trunk ships" (*naves caudicariae*) to transport goods from the port at Ostia to Rome, because large merchant ships could not sail up the river. These boats would have passed by the Ostian Road site regularly (Seneca, *Brev. vit.* 13.4; Martial, *Epigr.* 4.64.20–23). Also behind the apostle stands a tall reed, which places the scene along the swampy banks of the Tiber. Prudentius had declared that the "marshland of the Tiber" (*Tiberina palus*) witnessed the victorious deaths of both Paul and Peter (Prudentius, *Perist.* 12.7–10, Thomson), and here was iconographical validation. These two visual locators—the reed and the ship—evoked associations with the Tiber and confirmed the traditional martyrdom site adjacent to it. Both details appeared on other sar-cophagi featuring scenes of Paul's death.[67] Examples survive in the crypt of St. Victor in Marseille (ancient Massilia), the crypt of St. Maximinus in Saint-Maximin-la-Sainte-Baume (Villalata), and the cemetery of St. Sebastian in Rome. The sarcophagus of Junius Bassus in Rome does not have a ship but shows three tall reeds standing between Paul and his executioner. Another example from the cemetery of St. Sebastian also features a reed.[68] All these, including those now found in Gaul, were probably produced in Rome and based on the original buried in the Ostian Road basilica.

---

66. On the image of Paul in iconography, see Fabrizio Bisconti, "La sapienza, la con-cordia, il martirio: La figura di Paolo nell'immaginario iconografico della tarda antichità," in *San Paolo in Vaticano: La figura e la parola dell'Apostolo delle Genti nelle raccolte pontifi-cie* (ed. Umberto Utro; Todi: Tau Editrice, 2009), 163–76.

67. Umberto Utro, "I sarcofagi paleocristiani dal complesso di S. Paolo fuori le mura," in Utro, *San Paolo in Vaticano*, 57–63.

68. St. Victor: *DACL* 10:2282–83, fig. 7775. St. Maximinus: Elizabeth Struthers Malbon, *The Iconography of the Sarcophagus of Junius Bassus* (Princeton: Princeton University Press, 1990), 19, fig. 6. St. Sebastian: Deichmann, *Repertorium der christlich-antiken Sarkophage*, 1.1, no. 212. Junius Bassus: Malbon, *Sarcophagus of Junius Bassus*, 54–59. St. Sebastian: Deichmann, *Repertorium der christlich-antiken Sarkophage*, 1.1, no. 215.

The two sarcophagi that I have highlighted from the Theodosian level provide important information for our understanding of the Pauline cult. The tomb of Gaudentius and Severa confirms that privileged burials were part of the basilica from the outset, while the image of Paul's martyrdom on the second sarcophagus specifies this location along the Tiber as the site of Paul's demise. Caius's "trophy" and Constantine's basilica had identified the Ostian Road as Paul's burial site. Now, the iconography of this coffin agreed with Prudentius's poetry in placing the apostle's death here, as well.

1.3.2.2. Renovations and Burials in the Time of Leo I

In the middle of the fifth century, Bishop Leo I (440–461) altered the area around Paul's tomb.[69] In the Theodosian basilica, the floor level of the transept was 54 centimeters higher than that of the nave. Paul's sarcophagus had rested on the floor of the transept encased by the marble dedicatory slabs that I discussed earlier. Leo I raised a presbytery (an area reserved for the clergy) 64 centimeters high in the area immediately around the grave. He did not raise the sarcophagus, however, so only part of it remained visible.[70]

Leo did not want the *Paulo* inscription slabs to be obscured by the higher floor, so he removed them from their vertical position surrounding the sarcophagus and placed them in a horizontal position on the top of a new altar table over the sepulcher. The inscription now covered the funnel-shaped shaft through which the faithful poured their libation offerings. Therefore, Leo cut a round hole in the *Paulo* stone, in order to allow the continuation of this practice (fig. 1.11). This explains the awkward placement of the hole, which was cut well after the inscription of the stone and had to line up with the funnel-shaped opening already in place. The three small indentations next to the hole held a hinge for a metal plate that covered the libation hole when it was not in use (see fig. 1.8).

---

69. Leo's work on the basilica was not limited to the tomb area. He also made repairs to the building after it was partially destroyed by a lightning strike ("divine fire") in 443 (*Lib. pontif.* 47) and is credited with restoring a fountain of the atrium (*ICUR* 2:80). Some time before 537 c.e., a covered portico was built from the city wall to the basilica (Procopius, *Goth.* 2.4.9), and this could also go back to the time of Leo. On the possible fifth-century date for the portico, see Louis Reekmans, "L'implantation monumentale chrétienne dans le paysage urbain de Rome de 300 à 850," in *Actes du XIe congrès international d'archéologie chrétienne: Lyon, Vienne, Grenoble, Genève et Aoste (21–28 septembre 1986)* (CEFR 123; Rome: École française de Rome: 1989), 910.

70. Filippi, "La tomba di San Paolo: I dati archeologici," 350–52.

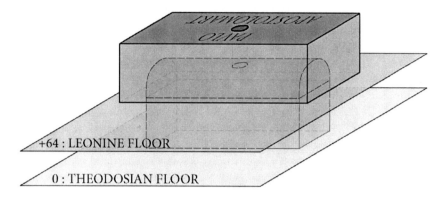

Fig. 1.11. Leonine renovations of the tomb area.
After Filippi; drawing by John Capen Brough.

By raising the floor, Leo created additional space for privileged burials near Paul's tomb.[71] Archaeologists discovered the so-called Dogmatic Sarcophagus in the northeast section of the Leonine presbytery. This Christian work features two friezes of scenes from the Hebrew Bible, the New Testament, and the Christian apocryphal writings.[72] The coffin probably was carved originally in the Constantinian period for a person of considerable means, based upon the expense of producing it. It was likely reused and placed here during Leo's renovations. The current lid is very rough compared to the detailed carving of the friezes, so it is possible that the original, fourth-century lid was broken prior to (or perhaps during?) its relocation to the altar area in the basilica.[73] Only a prominent member of the Christian community could have acquired such an expensive sarcophagus and the right to be buried in it so near the apostolic tomb.[74]

In 1959, while digging to run electrical lines between the organ and the altar, workers came across evidence for two additional burials from the Leonine phase. On the north side of Leo's presbytery, they discovered a pavement

71. Filippi, "Ergebnisse," 284–86.

72. Deichmann, *Repertorium der christlich-antiken Sarkophage*, 1.1, no. 43.

73. Jutta Dresken-Weiland, *Sarkophagbestattungen des 4.–6. Jahrhunderts im Westen des römischen Reiches* (RQ.S 55; Rome: Herder, 2003), 145, who credits Filippi for the suggestion. On the placement of the sarcophagus, see Francesco Tolotti, "Le confessioni succedutesi sul sepolcro di S. Paolo," *RivAC* 59.1–2 (1983): 127, fig. 15. Sarcophagi F, G, H, and M were found at the same elevation and may also have been inserted during the Leonine phase.

74. On the role of status in access to privileged burials, see Yasin, *Saints and Church Spaces*, 91–97.

slab and sepulcher of a certain Theodotus. According to the inscription, Theodotos was interred in 459 at the age of twenty-five. We know nothing else
about him, except that he came from the "land of the Gugutei," possibly in
the East.[75] Theodotos may have been a member of the clergy or a pilgrim—
or perhaps both—who had brought a sizable gift to the basilica before his
untimely death. This would explain how someone so young and with no obvious status in the Roman hierarchy could have been granted this privileged
burial position.

Workers also discovered the epitaph for a woman named Petronia, who
was buried on October 5, 472. Her husband was a deacon and later became
bishop of Rome under the name Felix III (483–492).[76] Felix's considerable
ecclesiastical influence explains his wife's illustrious burial site, yet she was
not the only member of the family buried in the basilica. On a nearby marble
paving stone are epitaphs for the children of Felix and Petronia, daughter Paula
(†484) and son Gordian (†485). There is also a reference to another member
of Felix's family, a consecrated virgin named Aemiliana (†489).[77] Immediately
adjacent to these inscriptions was an additional epitaph for a priest named
Felix, who died in 471. This may have been Felix III's father, whom Leo I
had charged with repairs to the church following a lightning strike in 443.[78]
According to the *Book of Pontiffs*, Felix III himself was eventually buried in
the basilica, making him the first bishop of Rome known to be interred here
(*Lib. pontif.* 50).[79]

The ties between this sacred place and Felix III's family were strong and
dated back perhaps to the time of Leo. The list of burials included the bishop
himself, his wife, their children, another relative, and perhaps his father. These
were all considered to be beneficiaries of Paul's radiating holy presence on

75. Filippi, "La basilica," 60–61; idem, *Indice della raccolta epigrafica di San Paolo Fuori
le Mura* (ISS 3; Vatican City: Monumenti Musei e Gallerie Pontificie, 1998), fig. 121; Filippi
and Sible de Blaauw, "San Paolo fuori le mura: La disposizione liturgica fino a Gregorio
Magno," *MNHIR* 59 (2002): 12, where they identify Theodotus's place of origin as Armenia.

76. Filippi, "La basilica," 60–61; idem, *Indice della raccolta epigrafica*, fig. 214; Filippi
and de Blaauw, "San Paolo fuori le mura," 16–17. The members of this family all died after
Leo, but their epitaphs were placed in the floor of the Leonine presbytery.

77. *ICUR* 2:4964; Louis Duchesne *Le Liber pontificalis: Texte, introduction et commen-
taire* (ed. Cyrille Vogel; 2nd ed.; BEFAR; Paris: de Boccard, 1955), 1:253 n. 2; Antonio
Ferrua, "Nuove iscrizioni della via Ostiense," *Epig* 21 (1959): 102–5. I am thankful to Nicola
Camerlenghi for making me aware of these family burials.

78. *ICUR* 1:371–73; Duchesne, *Liber pontificalis* 1:240 n. 7.

79. R. A. Lanciani, *Wanderings through Ancient Roman Churches* (Boston: Houghton
Mifflin, 1924), 154. Inscriptions attest to the later tombs of Paul I (757–767), John XIII
(965–972), and John XVIII (1004–1009).

account of their proximity to the apostolic tomb. This family's connection with Paul and this space rose to the surface again later, when another of Felix III's descendants, bishop Gregory I, undertook further embellishment of the basilica.[80]

1.3.2.3. Modifications and the Power of Paul's Presence in the Time of Gregory I

At the end of the sixth century, Bishop Gregory I (590–604) made extensive modifications to the sepulcher area. According to the *Book of Pontiffs*, "For St. Peter's he [Gregory] built a canopy over the altar with four columns of fine silver, provided a purple-dyed cloth to go above the apostle's body, and decorated it with the finest gold, weighing 100 lb; he brought it about that mass could be celebrated above St. Peter's body. At St. Paul's he made the same arrangements" (*Lib. pontif.* 66, Davis). As we have seen, the practice of celebrating the Eucharist over the apostolic tombs was in fact not new, yet the architectural renovations by Gregory were nonetheless significant and designed to bring Paul's basilica up to the standard of Peter's. Besides the magnificent canopy described in the *Book of Pontiffs*, Gregory built another, even higher presbytery around the sarcophagus. By raising the floor an additional 1.16 meters, he created a new level that was 1.8 meters above the Theodosian floor and even with the top of the Leonine altar table (fig. 1.12). The inscription plates were now at floor level, and Gregory built yet another altar table above this.[81]

Beneath the raised Gregorian floor level, excavators discovered more privileged burials. Inside one coffin archaeologists found a corpse that had been treated with a preserving agent and wrapped in bandages.[82] Mummification of the body, which was practiced in Rome at the time,[83] indicates a wealthy burial, probably for a member of the clergy or the Roman aristocracy. This is consistent with the status of those buried near Paul's tomb in the earlier

---

80. Ferrua, "Nuove iscrizioni della via Ostiense," 103, has argued for this family connection. Cf. Jos Janssens, "Le tombe e gli edifici funerari dei papi dell'antichità," in Guidobaldi and Guidobaldi, *Ecclesiae urbis*, 1:249–50. Janssens claims that the proximity of the apostle's grave played no role in the choice of the family's burial location, but I find this theory unconvincing.

81. Filippi, "La tomba di San Paolo: I dati archeologici," 350–52.

82. Dresken-Weiland, *Sarkophagbestattungen*, 146. A similar burial from the fourth century was found near the Basilica of St. Sebastian south of Rome (ibid., Kat. E.48, 383, fig. 28).

83. Laura Chioffi, *Mummificazione e imbalsamazione a Roma ed in altri luoghi del mondo romano* (Rome: Quasar, 1998).

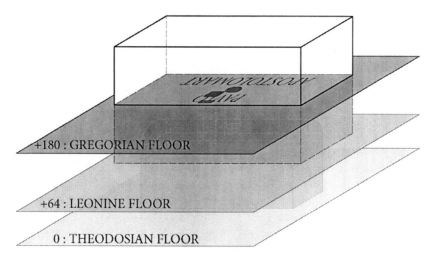

Fig. 1.12. Gregorian renovations of the tomb area.
After Filippi; drawing by John Capen Brough.

phases of the basilica.[84] Beyond this, unfortunately, we have no information about the identities of the individuals buried at the Gregorian level.

These burials in Gregory's time, like those in earlier periods, were motivated by the belief that Paul's relics radiated holiness into any other remains near the tomb. In a letter from 594, Gregory illustrated through two anecdotes how seriously Christians took this transfer of sanctity. The empress Constantina had asked for Paul's head or some other part of his body to place in a new chapel in the imperial palace at Constantinople. Gregory explained that he could not fulfill her request, because desecrating the graves of the dead violated Roman law and custom.[85] Not only that, but disturbing the bones of the martyrs could bring the penalty of death by supernatural forces. At

---

84. Heike Niquet has demonstrated that there was a large number of senatorial grave inscriptions in the burial ground around the basilica of Paul. See *Monumenta virtutum titulique: Senatorische Selbstdarstellung im spätantiken Rom im Spiegel der epigraphischen Denkmäler* (Stuttgart: Steiner, 2000), 38–40.

85. *Cod. Theod.* 9.17.7: "No one may transfer a human body to another place; no one may disturb a martyr; no one may sell [the remains]." Several bishops of Rome appealed to this statute in refusing relic transfers. In 519, Justinian asked for relics of Paul, Peter, and Lawrence, "according to the custom of the Greeks," to place in a new chapel. The papal legates explained to the emperor that this was "against the typical practice of the apostolic see." They suggested to Bishop Hormisdas that he send only *sanctuaria* (contact relics) "according to [Roman] custom" (Hormisdas, *Ep.* 77). In another instance, Gregory himself responded to a request for relics of Paul by sending *sanctuaria* to Constantius, the bishop

the basilica of Paul, one unfortunate laborer had died even for moving the remains of someone buried near the martyr:

> Yet I too wanted similarly to improve something near the most sacred body of Saint Paul the apostle and, as it was necessary that digging deeper should be done outside the tomb of the same saint, the man in charge of the place itself found some bones, not in fact connected with the same sepulcher. But since he presumed to lift them and bury them in another place, some sinister signs appeared, and he died a sudden death. (Gregory I, *Ep.* 4.30, Martyn)

The worker probably disturbed one of the privileged Christian burials from a previous building phase. He unwittingly stumbled upon some bones that had been so completely sanctified by lying near the saint that their removal carried the death penalty.

Another passage from this same letter describes an illicit attempt in 592 to transfer bones from otherwise nondescript burials near the basilica:

> For some Greek monks came here two years ago, and in the silence of the night, near the church of Saint Paul they dug up the bodies of the dead lying in the open field. Then they hid their bones, preserving them for themselves until they returned home. And when they had been held and had been carefully examined as to why they were doing this, they confessed that they were about to carry those bones to Greece, as if the relics of saints. (Gregory I, *Ep.* 4.30, Martyn)

These Eastern monks expressed no concern with the identities of those buried. The mere fact that the bodies had rested in the vicinity of the tomb—even in a field outside the church—was ample grounds for treating them as sacred relics. The monks planned to return to Greece[86] with the remains of these unknown people, "as if the relics of saints," on the grounds that they had been made holy by Paul's presence.[87]

---

of Milan (*Ep.* 9.184). However, the frequent reuse of coffins and relocation of bodies in the West reveal that this law was often violated.

86. The monks may have been surprised at the Roman resistance, given the relative ease with which relics circulated in the East, e.g. *Acta Thom.* 170, where Thomas's body is "stolen away ... to Mesopotamia" from India; Philostorgius, *Hist. eccl.* 3.2a, where Constantius brings relics of Andrew, Luke, and Timothy to Constantinople.

87. This notion of transferable holiness has survived well beyond late antiquity. In 1840 the monks of the Monastery of St. Paul reburied some bones that had been unearthed in 1838 near the altar of the basilica. The dedicatory inscription identified these as the "relics of unknown saints [*Reliquiae S.S. ignotorum*], which were discovered under this altar and were laid back here on May 12, 1840." In the time of Gregory, as in the nineteenth

Paul's tomb was the focal point for privileged burials during the Theodosian, Leonine, and Gregorian building phases. Many Christians believed in the power of proximity and its benefits in the world to come. Those still alive also desired Paul's blessing and traveled to the basilica in order to seek it.

1.3.3. The Basilica as a Pilgrimage Destination

While privileged burial was limited to a relatively small population, large numbers of the faithful came to Paul's tomb as pilgrims. Christian pilgrimage was a practice adapted from Greco-Roman religions and the Jewish tradition[88] and played an important role in the cult of the martyrs. Christians traveled to locations associated with particular saints in order to honor them[89] and receive spiritual and physical benefits, which resulted from close contact with the heightened aura of holiness that was believed to surround these sites. Some early Christian pilgrims traversed the entire Mediterranean, while others visited shrines in their own regions.[90]

century, burial location was considered sufficient to ensure that one would achieve sanctity. See Filippi, "Tomba di San Paolo e le fasi," 192; fig. 9, 198.

88. On pilgrimage in Greco-Roman religions, see Jaś Elsner and Ian Rutherford, *Pilgrimage in Graeco-Roman and Early Christian Antiquity: Seeing the Gods* (Oxford: Oxford University Press, 2005); Matthew Dillon, *Pilgrims and Pilgrimage in Ancient Greece* (New York: Routledge, 1997); Ian Rutherford, "Tourism and the Sacred: Pausanius and the Traditions of Greek Pilgrimage," in *Pausanias: Travel and Imagination in Roman Greece* (ed. Susan E. Alcock et al.; Oxford: Oxford University Press, 2001), 40–52; idem, " 'To the Land of Zeus': Patterns of Pilgrimage in Aelius Aristides," *AevumAnt* 12 (1999): 133–48; André Motte, "Pèlerinages de la Grèce antique," in *Histoire des pèlerinages non chrétiens: Entre magique et sacré, le chemin des dieux* (ed. Jean Chélini and Henry Branthomme; Paris: Hachette, 1982), 94–135; Ernst Künzl and Gerhard Koeppel, *Souvenirs und Devotionalien: Zeugnisse des geschäftlichen, religiösen und kulturellen Tourismus im antiken Römerreich* (Mainz am Rhein: von Zabern, 2002); Nicole Belayche, "Les pèlerinages dans le monde romain antique," in Chélini and Branthomme, *Histoire des pèlerinages non chrétiens*, 136–54. On Jewish pilgrimage, Allen Kerkeslager, "Jewish Pilgrimage and Jewish Identity in Hellenistic and Early Roman Egypt," in *Pilgrimage and Holy Space in Late Antique Egypt* (ed. David Frankfurter; Leiden: Brill, 1998), 99–225; Mark Friedman, "Jewish Pilgrimage after the Destruction of the Second Temple," in *City of the Great King: Jerusalem from David to the Present* (ed. Nitza Rosovsky; Cambridge: Harvard University Press, 1996), 136–46; Yoram Tsafrir, "Jewish Pilgrimage in the Roman and Byzantine Periods," in *Akten des XII. Internationalen Kongresses für christliche Archäologie, Bonn 22.–28. September, 1991* (ed. Ernst Dassmann and Josef Engemann; 2 vols.; Münster: Aschendorffsche Verlagsbuchhandlung, 1995), 1:369–76.

89. It is worth noting that the Greek equivalent to *peregrinatio*, the Latin word from which *pilgrimage* is derived, is προσκύνεσις, meaning adoration, homage, or veneration.

90. The anonymous Bordeaux Pilgrim traveled from Gaul to Jerusalem in 333 c.e., and the female pilgrim Egeria made her way from Spain as far as Egypt in the early 380s c.e.

The evidence from Rome points to lively pilgrimage activity by the fourth century. The church father Jerome studied in Rome around 365 and later reflected with great enthusiasm on the fervor of Christians in the city: "Where else do people rush to the churches and to the tombs of the martyrs with such zeal and frequency? Where does the 'Amen' resound like thunder, while the temples of idols are so empty?" (*Comm. Gal.* 2). Elsewhere Jerome recalled that he and some colleagues had the custom of making their own pilgrimages to various tombs of apostles and martyrs on Sundays. Some of these were underground and required descending into the subterranean darkness to visit the shrines: "Many times we entered the crypts, which were dug into the bowels of the earth.... Rarely some light entered from above and tempered our dread of the shadows.... We advanced one step at a time, surrounded by the gloomy night" (*Comm. Ezech.* 40.5). Prudentius wrote that many traveled to Rome on pilgrimage from other parts of Italy. In his poem on the martyr Hippolytus, he described the scene at the annual feast:

> Can you imagine what multitudes gather with God? The majestic city disgorges her Romans in a stream.[91] ... From Alba's gates the white-robed troops deploy and pass on in long lines. Loud sounds of rejoicing rise from diverse roads leading from different places; natives of Picenum and the people of Etruria come; the fierce Samnite and the Campanian dweller in lofty Capua meet together, and men of Nola too are there, everyone in happy mood with wife and dear children and eager to get quickly on the way. Scarcely can the broad plains hold the joyous multitudes. (Prudentius, *Perist.* 11.197–211, Thomson)

Prudentius has no doubt employed some poetic embellishment, yet his account confirms that Rome's wealth of martyrs made it a desirable destination for pilgrims.[92]

According to the *Life and Miracles of Saint Thecla*, the residents of Tarsus and Seleucia engaged in mutual pilgrimage between a shrine of Paul in Tarsus and one of Thecla in nearby Seleucia (Basil of Seleucia, *Mirac. Theclae* 4); Davis, *Cult of Saint Thecla*, 78–79. Studies on early Christian pilgrimage are numerous, but among the most important are Pierre Maraval, *Lieux saints et pèlerinages d'Orient: Histoire et géographie des origines à la conquête arabe* (2nd ed.; Paris: Cerf, 2004); Ousterhout, *Blessings of Pilgrimage*; E. D. Hunt, *Holy Land Pilgrimage in the Later Roman Empire, AD 312–460* (Oxford: Clarendon, 1982); Béatrice Caseau, Jean-Claude Cheynet, and Vincent Déroche, eds., *Pèlerinages et lieux saints dans l'antiquité et le moyen âge: Mélanges offerts à Pierre Maraval* (Paris: Association des amis du Centre d'histoire et civilisation de Byzance, 2006).

91. The shrine of Hippolytus was outside the city walls.

92. For other examples of pilgrimage to Rome, see Gustave Bardy, "Pèlerinages à Rome vers la fin du IVe siècle," *AnBoll* 67 (1949): 224–35; Victor Saxer, "Pilgerwesen in

We also have evidence for pilgrimage to the shrine of Paul on the Ostian Road. As mentioned earlier, the letter to Sallustius from the three emperors cited the "size of the assembly" as one factor in the decision to construct a larger basilica. At the end of the fourth century, Bishop Ambrose of Milan painted a similar picture. While in Rome, he had observed the crowd of pilgrims during the annual feast of Peter and Paul: "Around the circuit of so great a city a streaming throng makes its way. Celebrated on three roads is the feast of the sacred martyrs. One would think that the whole world is coming forth" (Ambrose, *Hymn.* 13.25–29). The Ostian Road was one of these "three roads."[93] A few years later, in describing the same festival, Prudentius observed, "All over Rome [people] are running about and rejoicing." The exhausted bishop, like the multitude of pilgrims, had to hurry across the city from the Vatican hill to the Ostian Road, in order to celebrate at both memorials on the same day (Prudentius, *Perist.* 12.2, 57–63, Thomson).

One regular member of these teeming crowds was Bishop Paulinus of Nola, a city just east of Naples. In a letter from 398/399, Paulinus describes his activities during a recent ten-day visit to Rome at the time of the festival. While endless meetings had occupied the afternoons and evenings, "I spent the mornings in votive prayer at the sacred memorials of the apostles and martyrs, whom I venerated with care" (Paulinus of Nola, *Ep.* 17.2). The basilica of Paul, recently dedicated, would have been an important destination among these morning vigils. From approximately 394 to 406, Paulinus made a pilgrimage to Rome each year for the "very popular apostolic birthday celebration" (*Ep.* 18.1). He referred to this annual voyage as his "solemn custom" and his "votive offering" (*Ep.* 20.2; 43.1). He even considered it a requirement, saying, "I went to Rome for that venerable day of the apostolic feast … which is indeed obligatory but nonetheless festive" (*Ep.* 17.1). He took this obligation upon himself, seeing the veneration of Paul and Peter at their shrines as his pious duty.

Christians across the Mediterranean knew the reputation of the Pauline basilica, from Prudentius in Spain to John Chrysostom in Syria. In 387 the priest of Antioch stated in a sermon, "In the imperial city of Rome, emperors, consuls and generals, putting aside everything else, rush to the tombs of a fisherman [Peter (Mark 1:16)] and a tentmaker [Paul (Acts 18:3)]" (John Chrysostom, *Jud. gent.* 9). Chrysostom himself desired to join this illustrious group of pilgrims, "If only now it were permitted to me to embrace the body

---

Italien und Rom im späten Altertum und Frühmittelalter," in Dassmann and Engemann, *Akten des XII. Internationalen Kongresses,* 1:36–46.

93. These three sites were on the Aurelian Road (the Vatican), the Ostian Road (Basilica of Paul), and the Appian Road (the Catacombs). The Appian Road site will be the focus of chapter 2.

of Paul, to be riveted to his tomb, and to see the dust of that body that filled up what was lacking from Christ (Col 1:24), that bore the marks, that sowed the proclamation everywhere, the dust of that body in which he ran about everywhere, the dust of that body through which Christ spoke clearly" (*Hom. Rom.* 32.3). The idea of visiting this sacred tomb appealed to Chrysostom because of the spiritual benefits that such a voyage would bring. He desired to complete just once the pilgrimage that Paulinus undertook every year, but, as far as we know, he never made it.

As we saw earlier, the architectural developments in the church from the fourth through the sixth century made Paul's sarcophagus increasingly less accessible to visitors. By Gregory's time the tomb lay entirely beneath the floor of the presbytery. The bishop understood that hiding the basilica's main attraction would lead to disappointment from pilgrims. Thus, he constructed a crypt beneath the presbytery that allowed visitors to get close to the apostolic tomb. A narrow staircase in the floor of the transept gave access to this crypt. There pilgrims could look (probably through an iron grate) into the chamber where the apostle's coffin lay (fig. 1.13).[94]

Gregory's construction of this crypt restored access to the apostolic tomb and allowed pilgrims to approach the sarcophagus along the ancient, sacred way (fig. 1.14).[95] After the bishop raised a higher presbytery, the easiest access to the tomb would have been from the nave (western side). Gregory could have cut a hole in the steps to expose the coffin, but instead he chose to excavate from the apse (eastern) side. I think that he did so in order to re-create an element of earlier Christian experience. According to tradition, Paul had been led from Rome down the Ostian Road and then to this spot. The early pilgrims to Caius's trophy had followed Paul's path from the road, and visitors

---

94. A large block to the lower left side of the grate bears the inscription "the salvation of the people" (*Salus populi*). Although this inscription has often been cited, its date and relationship to the construction layers of the basilica still require further study. See, e.g., Giulio Belvederi, *Le tombe apostoliche nell'età paleocristiana* (CACat 12; Vatican City: Pontificio Istituto di Archeologia Cristiana, 1948); Lanciani, "Delle scoperte," 13–14, 17–18; Tolotti, "Confessioni," 118–20; Apollonj-Ghetti, "Basiliche cimiteriali," 25, fig. 14; Filippi, "Ergebnisse," 291. Lanciani in particular bemoaned the fact that this inscription has not received more attention from archaeologists or epigraphists.

95. Cf. Beat Brenk, "Der Kultort, seine Zugänglichkeit und seine Besucher," in Dassmann and Engemann, *Akten des XII. Internationalen Kongresses*, 1:76. Brink has argued that all access to holy graves was limited to the "privileged." However, this interpretation is based on a misreading of Jerome (*Vigil.* 6), where Jerome states that the apostles and martyrs are well cared for in the world beyond, as if they were of senatorial rank. Brenk mistakenly applies this description to the visitors to the shrines of the saints. This misreading is restated in MacMullen, *Second Church*, 82.

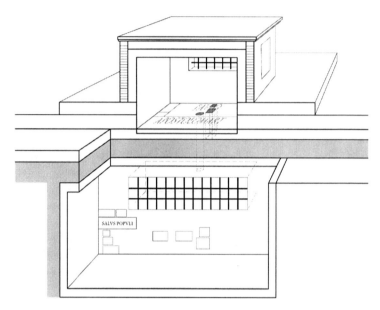

Fig. 1.13. The Gregorian crypt. After Tolotti; drawing by John Capen Brough.

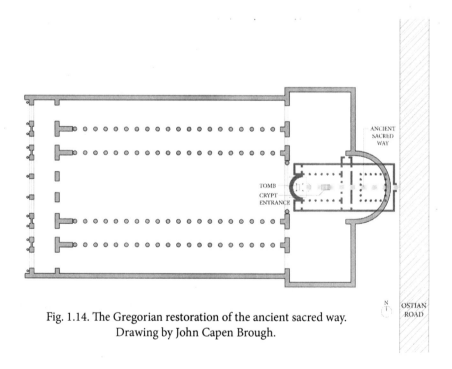

Fig. 1.14. The Gregorian restoration of the ancient sacred way.
Drawing by John Capen Brough.

to the Constantinian church had taken the same route through the basilica to see the tomb. All had approached from the east. The Theodosian builders had changed the orientation of the basilica and closed the access from the Ostian Road. By opening a crypt from the eastern side, Gregory allowed pilgrims to retrace the final few steps that Paul had traditionally taken. The pilgrimage trail to the Ostian Road once again ended where it had in ancient times, so pilgrims in Gregory's day could approach the tomb in the footsteps of the apostle and their spiritual forebears. At the end of their journey, Paul's sarcophagus and the relics within awaited them.

1.3.4. THE VENERATION OF PAUL'S RELICS

The relics of Paul provided a focal point for the veneration of the apostle. Even amid substantial architectural changes at the site, the coffin that contained his bones was held to be a source of radiating holiness. Paul's physical remains were not the only relic of the apostle in the basilica, however. Pilgrims also came to see a shroud and some chains that were believed to have come into contact with Paul just before his martyrdom. In Gregory's time, Paul's holiness was also mobile. Through the creation and distribution of secondary relics, the bishop encouraged the spiritual power of the apostle to travel far and wide. Even those who could not go to Rome in person could have contact with Paul through sacred objects brought back from the martyr's basilica.

Paul's remains were the most desirable of these relics. As we saw earlier, the dedicatory inscription above the main arch stated that Paul's body sanctified the entire basilica. Potential pilgrims such as John Chrysostom wanted "to embrace the body of Paul" and "to see the dust of that body." Others sought to possess pieces of Paul for themselves. Gregory's letter to Constantina was written in response to such a request. Gregory states that the empress had "asked from me that I should send over to you in answer to your commands the head of Saint Paul the apostle or something else from the saint's body." These relics were believed to be a conduit of divine power and had been the source of amazing deeds, "For the bodies of the apostles, saints Peter and Paul, gleam with such great miracles and terrors in their own churches that one cannot even enter there for prayer without great fear" (Gregory I, *Ep.* 4.30, Martyn). One of these terrors was certainly the death of the unfortunate worker who moved some bones near Paul's tomb.

The bones were not the only relics of the martyr that carried with them miraculous power. Gregory confirmed the presence in the basilica of two additional holy objects, a shroud (*sudarium*) and some chains that had once bound the apostle. Constantina had asked Gregory to send this shroud to Constantinople, but the bishop had responded that this was impossible, for it was buried with the body and could not be disturbed (Gregory I, *Ep.* 4.30, Martyn). This may have been the same shroud that appears in several literary accounts of Paul's death. In a fourth-century Latin text known as the *Passion of Saint Paul the Apostle*, Paul asks a woman named Plautilla for her scarf[96] on the way to his execution. He ties it over his eyes just before he dies and miraculously returns it to her later, stained with his blood (*Pass. Paul.* 14, 17).[97] A later version of Paul's death, the sixth-century Greek *Acts of the Holy Apostles Peter and Paul*, repeats this story but changes the woman's name to Perpetua and adds a healing account.[98] In this Greek rendition the pious Perpetua is blind in one eye. After receiving back her scarf soaked with Paul's blood, she places it over her eye and immediately receives her sight (*Acta Pet. Paul.* 80).

For those in Gregory's time familiar with the Perpetua story, the shroud would have held a double attraction. On the one hand, it was believed to contain the apostle's actual blood from his martyrdom. Because it preserved a physical remnant of Paul, it was a relic as powerful and coveted as the head, a finger, or even the whole body. As Gregory of Nazianzus once commented concerning saints such as Peter and Paul, "Even drops of their blood and small tokens of their passion [i.e., relics] are as powerful as their bodies" (*Or. 4* [*C. Jul.*] 69). On the other hand, the shroud offered the hope of miraculous healing. Just as the power of the shroud had healed the eye of Perpetua, so could it heal any affliction from which a pilgrim may have been suffering.[99] No one

---

96. *Sudarium* is one of the terms used in this story. This text is falsely ascribed to Linus, the traditional successor of Peter as bishop of Rome (Irenaeus, *Haer.* 3.3.3).

97. This story bears obvious parallels to another legend of a woman and an article of clothing, namely, that of Veronica's veil (also known as the Sudarium). According to this medieval account, a follower of Jesus named Veronica was standing alongside the road as Jesus was being led to his crucifixion. She used her veil to wipe the blood from his face. Miraculously, an impression of his likeness was left on the veil, which became a sacred relic. Paul, like Jesus, is being led outside the city to meet his death. Both Plautilla and Veronica are met along the way and singled out by the condemned. Both then offer a cloth to catch the sacred blood and have their item restored to them by the holy man. Veronica's veil was reportedly kept in St. Peter's in Rome for several centuries in the Middle Ages before disappearing. On this veil, see Neil MacGregor, *Seeing Salvation: Images of Christ in Art* (New Haven: Yale University Press, 2000), 90–94.

98. The author uses two different words to describe the item: ὡράριον and φακιόλιον.

99. John Chrysostom apparently knew about this object or about some very much like it: "Truly wonderous are the towels [σουδάρια] and aprons from [Paul's] flesh that are made marvelous" (*Hom. Eph.* 8). This is reminiscent of the story in Acts 19:12, where pieces of cloth that Paul had touched were used to cure the sick. This story was also referred to by Cyril of Jerusalem, "Handkerchiefs and aprons … that have touched the bodies of the infirmed have raised up the sick" (*Catech.* 18.16).

could physically touch the shroud as Perpetua had done. However, its holy power, like that of Paul's body, permeated the tomb area and could potentially heal those who came close enough. The presence of such a relic underscored Gregory's presentation of the basilica as a place for "great miracles."

Chains that had allegedly bound the apostle were also housed in the church.[100] In a sermon from the late fourth century, John Chrysostom spoke at length on the glory that Paul had earned by bearing his chains:

> I would wish now to be in those places—for it is said that the bonds still remain—and to see and marvel at those men because of their desire for Christ. I would wish to see the chains, which demons fear and which cause them to shudder, and which angels adore.... If I were free from the cares of the church and if my body were strong, I would not hesitate to make that trip abroad only to see the chains and to see the prison there. (*Hom. Eph.* 56–57)[101]

Paul's chains, like his physical remains, were sacred objects that Chrysostom longed to see in person. A reference to Paul's chains next appeared in 519 in a letter from Bishop Hormisdas of Rome to Justinian (see p. 50 n. 85). Justinian (not yet emperor) had asked Hormisdas for pieces from the chains of Peter and Paul, because he wanted to place them in a chapel built in honor of the apostles in Constantinople. Hormisdas declined the request and instead sent *sanctuaria* that had touched the chains (Hormisdas, *Ep.* 77–78, 81).

---

100. The current church still claims to have Paul's chains, although there is no evidence that these are the same as those kept in the ancient basilica. In the past, they were brought out only on feast days, but they are now displayed in a glass case above the sarcophagus.

101. Cf. Margaret M. Mitchell (*The Heavenly Trumpet: John Chrysostom and the Art of Pauline Interpretation* [Tübingen: Mohr Siebeck, 2000], 180–81), who has argued that Chrysostom was speaking of a pilgrimage site in Philippi, not in Rome. Charalambos Bakirtzis has similarly suggested that Philippi was a late antique pilgrimage site that may have claimed to have Pauline relics. See "Paul and Philippi: The Archaeological Evidence," in *Philippi at the Time of Paul and after His Death* (ed. Charalambos Bakirtzis and Helmut Koester; Harrisburg, Pa.: Trinity Press International, 1998), 47–48. An ancient location for Paul's chains or prison in Philippi has not been suggested by Mitchell or Bakirtzis, and the structure now labeled "Paul's prison" is known to have been a cistern in antiquity. The commemoration of Paul was established there only in the early medieval period, as demonstrated by Paul Lemerle, *Philippes et la Macédoine orientale à l'époque chrétienne et byzantine: Recherches d'histoire et d'archéologie* (BEFAR 158; Paris: de Boccard, 1945), 296–97; Elli Pelekanidou, "Ἡ κατὰ τὴν παράδοση φυλακὴ τοῦ Ἀποστόλου Παύλου στοὺς Φιλίππους [Concerning the Traditional Prison of the Apostle Paul at Philippi]," in Ἡ Καβάλα καὶ ἡ περιοχὴ τῆς [Kavala and Its Surroundings] (Thessaloniki: Institute for Balkan Studies, 1980), 427–35.

Although Gregory refused to send Paul's body parts or shroud to Constantina, he (unlike Hormisdas) was willing to send fragments of the chains,
which had healing properties. As Gregory explained,

> I shall hasten to send across to you a portion from the chains which the holy
> apostle Paul himself bore on his neck and hands, from which many miracles
> are shown in public. That is, if I shall succeed in removing it with a file. For
> many often come and seek a blessing from the same chains, so a priest stands
> by with a file to receive a small portion from the filings. For some of those
> seeking them, something is cut from the very chains so rapidly that there is
> no delay. But for others seeking them, the file is drawn over those chains for a
> long time, and yet there is no chance of anything coming off them. (Gregory
> I, *Ep.* 4.30, Martyn)[102]

The chains attracted so many pilgrims that a priest had to be stationed nearby
specifically to attend to the request for filings. Just as the body of Paul could
bring about either miracles or terrors, so could the chains be fickle in distributing their spiritual power. Some visitors received a blessing easily, while
others departed empty-handed. Those who received chain fragments carried
them away as pilgrim tokens, holy mementos of their visit to Paul's shrine.
These were not only symbols of the place and the saint; they were pieces of the
very chains that had bound the apostle. Some fortunate visitors departed with
these precious relics, which they believed could continue to perform miracles
and grant blessing wherever they were carried.

Paul's body, shroud, and chains were the primary relics in the basilica,
but Gregory also made provision for the production of secondary relics, or
brandea. These were usually pieces of cloth that had come into contact with
primary relics (a martyr's body) and carried with them the full measure of that
saint's spiritual power. Gregory described the creation process in his letter to
Constantina: "A silk cloth is simply put in a small box, which is placed near the
very holy bodies of the saints. When lifted out, the box is deposited with due
reverence in the church which is to be dedicated,[103] and through it miracles

---

102. Gregory records that he sent some filings from Paul's chains to Bishop Eulogius
of Alexandria in 603 (*Ep.* 13.43). The practice of taking filings also occurred at the Church
of St. Peter in Chains in Rome, and August 1 eventually became the feast day to celebrate
Peter's chains. See Louis Duchesne, *Origines du culte chrétien: Étude sur la liturgie latine
avant Charlemagne* (5th ed.; Paris: Fontemoing, 1909), 297. Gregory frequently sent pieces
of these chains, in reliquaries shaped as keys or crosses, to other dignitaries in the ecclesiastical or political hierarchies (*Ep.* 1.25, 1.29, 1.30, 7.23, 7.25, 8.33, 9.229, 11.43, 13.43).

103. Gregory refers here to the tradition of dedicating a church with relics, which
appears to have begun early but became a requirement only after the Second Council of

occur, as if the saints' bodies were specially brought there" (Gregory I, *Ep.* 4.30, Martyn).[104]

Gregory mentions the practice here in general terms, but I believe that he based his description on a particular practice that took place in the Ostian Road basilica. The entire letter concerned the relics of Paul and events that happened in and around the basilica, so it is reasonable to conclude that the method of creating *brandea* also had a connection to the Pauline basilica. Gregory's description also explains the two additional square holes in the *Paulo* inscription slabs (see fig. 1.8), which the bishop would have had cut for the production of secondary relics. They were appropriately sized to accommodate the insertion of small boxes containing pieces of cloth. These came into contact with Paul's tomb, just as Gregory had described to Constantina.[105] Spiritual power flowed into the cloths, resulting in the creation of *brandea* that could be taken away. The size and placement of all three holes in the *Paulo* slabs are therefore explained. The round hole was cut for the pouring of libations, while the square holes were added subsequently to permit the production of secondary relics.

The construction of privileged burials, the practice of pilgrimage, and the veneration of relics all contributed to the popular Pauline cult on the Ostian Road. The apostle's tomb was the focal point of these practices, for it was the most sacred space of the cult. The portability of relics, however, allowed Paul's sanctifying presence to travel to multiple locations, as if his body were specially brought there (to paraphrase Gregory). Pilgrims could carry home chain fragments and silk cloths from the basilica. These secondary relics were powerful enough to sanctify church altars and perform additional miracles abroad. The result was an expansion of the cult and a proliferation of the number of spaces "sanctified by the body of Paul."

Nicea in 787. See Bernhard Kötting, *Der frühchristliche Reliquienkult und die Bestattung im Kirchengebäude* (Cologne: Westdeutscher, 1965); Noël Duval, "L'espace liturgique dans les églises paléochrétiennes," *MD* 193.1 (1993): 7–29; Jean Gagé, "Membra Christi et la deposition des reliques sous l'autel," *RAr* 5/29 (1929): 137–53.

104. Cf. Gregory of Tours (*Glor. mart.* 27), who describes a similar process at St. Peter's in Rome. Elsewhere in the same letter, Gregory (of Rome) recounts that in the time of Leo I, some Greeks had doubted the veracity of *brandea*. Therefore, Leo cut one of the *brandea* with scissors, and blood flowed. Gregory does not specify if the *brandea* in question had come from the basilica of Paul, but this is a possibility.

105. Tolotti ("Confessioni," 137–43) discusses these holes as part of the *brandea* production process but fails to make the connection with Gregory's letter.

1.4. COMPETITION: A RIVAL HOLY PLACE

The tradition about Paul's death on the Ostian Road was largely fixed by the fourth century. Both the poetry of Prudentius and the iconography on sarcophagi identified the banks of the Tiber as the location of Paul's martyrdom. Nonetheless, by the sixth century a dissenting voice arose in Rome about the location of the apostle's demise. This divergence in the tradition can be seen by a comparison of two sixth-century texts: the Latin *Passion of the Holy Apostles Peter and Paul* and the Greek *Acts of the Holy Apostles Peter and Paul* (referred to previously).[106]

A few words are in order at the outset about the relationship between these two texts. Overall, they show great affinity with each other. Both include the same account of the adventures of Peter and Paul in Rome and an eventual conflict with Nero. Apart from some additional material at the beginning of the Greek *Acts* (on Paul's journey from Malta to Rome),[107] the Latin and Greek narratives are nearly identical throughout most of the story. There is certainly a close literary relationship between them. The sources diverge, however, at the point of Paul's death:

Latin *Passion*	Greek *Acts*
Paul was decapitated on the Ostian Road. (*Pass. Pet. Paul.* 59)	They led Paul three miles outside the city in order to decapitate him, and he was bound in irons. The three soldiers guarding him were of a large race. After they left the gate and had traveled about the distance of a bow shot, a pious woman came to meet them. When she saw Paul being dragged along and bound in chains, she felt great pity for him and wept bitterly. The name of the woman was Perpetua, and she had only one eye. Seeing her crying, Paul said to her, "Give me your scarf, and

---

106. From this point on I will refer to these texts as the Latin *Passion* and the Greek *Acts*.

107. This extra material may have been added to the Greek text as late as the ninth century. See J. K. Elliott, *The Apocryphal New Testament: A Collection of Apocryphal Christian Literature in an English Translation* (Oxford: Oxford University Press, 1993), 428.

as I am returning I will give it back to you." She took the scarf and gave it to him willingly. But the soldiers approached the woman and said to her, "Why do you want to lose your scarf, woman? Do you not know that he is going to be beheaded?" But Perpetua said to them, "I beg you, on behalf of the salvation of Caesar, to place this scarf on his eyes when you cut off his head." And it happened in that way. They decapitated him [Paul] at the estate called Aquae Salvias, near the pine tree. (*Acta Pet. Paul.* 80)[108]

The brief, almost passing, reference to the martyrdom in the Latin *Passion* coincides with the established tradition about the location of Paul's death on the Ostian Road. The Greek version, on the other hand, presents an alternative rendition. Paul died not on the Ostian Road but on an estate called Aquae Salvias. From other sources we know the location of this estate. It was south of Rome on the Laurentinian Road, not on the Ostian Road (fig. 1.1).[109] When the Ostian Road turned southwest to follow the Tiber toward the sea, the Laurentinian Road split off and headed straight south. The estate lay several kilometers south of the Ostian Road basilica, so this was clearly a distinct location.

When faced with these accounts, scholars have typically responded in one of two ways. Most have tended to conflate these stories in order to protect both traditions. Either they ignore the fact that the Aquae Salvias location is not on the Ostian Road, or they conclude that Paul must have died at Aquae

---

108. J. P. Kirsch has proposed that this reference to a pine tree, unique in the tradition, must have made sense only to the editors of the Greek *Acts* and to their contemporaries, because a later compiler would not have invented such a detail. See "Der Ort des Martyriums des Hl. Paulus," *RQ* 2 (1888): 237. V. Capocci has suggested that the topography of the Aquae Salvias site, which today is largely covered by pine trees, may explain this detail ("Sulla tradizione del martirio di S. Paolo alle Acque Salvie," in *Atti dello VIII congresso internazionale di studi bizantini, Palermo 3–10 aprile 1951* [Rome: Associazione nazionale per gli studi bizantini, 1953], 15–16).

109. Lucrezia Spera, "Aquae Salvias, Massa," in *Lexicon topographicum urbis Romae: Suburbium* (ed. Adriano La Regina; 5 vols.; Rome: Quasar, 2001), 1:147–48.

Salvias and been buried at the site of the Ostian Road basilica.[110] However, several centuries of tradition clearly placed the martyrdom on the Ostian Road. Prudentius was quite explicit on this point, as were the artists of the Roman coffins. The sarcophagus imagery suggests that Paul died next to a significant body of water. Ships traveled there, and reeds lined its banks. This description fits the Tiber but not the topography of the Aquae Salvias site, which lies nearly one-and-a-half kilometers from the nearest point of the Tiber.[111] In addition, I can find no visual reference on any sarcophagus to Paul's dying next to a pine tree, as the Greek *Acts* records.[112] In fact, no ancient work of art known to me reflects any awareness of the Aquae Salvias story. Scholars have been mistaken, therefore, to ignore the differences or to conflate the accounts. The story concerning the Aquae Salvias site simply does not coincide with the Ostian Road tradition.

A second approach has been to recognize the disparity but to discredit the Aquae Salvias version by arguing that the Greek *Acts* is the creation of monks from Cilicia, Paul's home region in eastern Asia Minor.[113] According to this theory, these monks came to Rome in the sixth century and established a monastery at the site known as Aquae Salvias. In order to add prestige to their new monastery, they fabricated the story that Paul had been beheaded at their location, not on the Ostian Road. They then sought recognition of

---

110. For example, the editors of the *DACL* recognized the particular iconographic elements of the St. Victor sarcophagus, which point to the Ostian Road, yet still concluded that it shows Paul's death "at a place called Aquae Salvias" (*DACL* 13.2:2695). R. A. Lanciani also failed to acknowledge this tension and even sought to add credibility to the pine-tree detail. He recounted that in 1875, while digging behind the chapel at the site, some monks found a mass of coins of Nero and some fossilized pine cones (*Pagan and Christian Rome* [Boston: Houghton & Mifflin, 1899], 156–57). Most recently, Giorgio Filippi ("Decennio," 29) has stated without any qualification, "The literary sources attest to Paul's coming to Rome, his decapitation at *Aquae Salvias* three miles from the city, and his burial on the Ostian Road two miles from the place of martyrdom" (my translation of the Italian).

111. The continuity in the road system shows that the path of the river in this area has not changed significantly since antiquity. Thus, it cannot be claimed that the Tiber passed next to Aquae Salvias in that period (Capocci, "Sulla tradizione del martirio," 15).

112. One sarcophagus places a palm tree behind Paul, but the soldier in this case is beating Paul with his fist, not carrying a sword (Deichmann, *Repertorium der christlich-antiken Sarkophage*, 1.1:57).

113. Tajra, *Martyrdom of St. Paul*, 151–54. Others who have simply dismissed the Aquae Salvias account on "historical" grounds include Jean-Marie Sansterre, *Les moines grecs et orientaux à Rome aux époques byzantine et carolingienne* (2 vols.; Brussels: Académie Royale de Belgique, 1982), 1:152; Louis-Sébastien Le Nain de Tillemont, *Mémoires pour servir à l'histoire ecclésiastique des six premiers siècles* (2nd ed.; 2 vols.; Paris: Robustel, 1701), 1:583–84.

their monastery as a center of veneration for the apostle. In order to establish this tale, the monks influenced the text of the Greek *Acts*, replacing the earlier Latin tradition with one of their own imagination.

This second approach also falls short, because it fails to recognize that the distinctive elements in the Greek text all come from Latin, even Roman sources. This can be seen by examining three elements in the Greek *Acts*: the Perpetua story, the name Aquae Salvias, and the description of the place as an estate (*massa*). Previously in this chapter (see above, pp. 58–59) I have discussed the story of Perpetua in relation to the "shroud" of Paul that was buried with his body. I showed that the Greek text depends directly on the story of Plautilla in the *Passion of Saint Paul the Apostle*, a fourth-century Latin work of Roman origin. The editor of the Greek *Acts* has changed the woman's name and expanded the story to include a healing account, yet the basic narrative is the same. Paul borrowed a scarf from a pious woman on the way to his execution and miraculously returned it to her after his death. This section of material, which is present in the Greek *Acts* but missing from the Latin *Passion*, was taken and modified from a Roman source and reflects a Roman tradition. This is an important piece of evidence for placing the origins of this unique piece of the Greek *Acts* account in a Roman setting.

Another significant indicator of the Roman origin of the Greek *Acts* is the fact that the Aquae Salvias reference itself reveals a Latin source. The name of the site in Greek Ἄκουαι Σαλβίας (*Akouai Salvias*) is a direct transliteration of the Latin *Aquae Salvias*. The editors of the Greek text must have learned the name of the site from a Roman source, and they took this directly into Greek. This key element of the story also has its roots in the Roman context.

Finally, the text says that Paul was taken "to the estate called Aquae Salvias" (εἰς μάσσαν καλουμένην Ἄκουαι Σαλβίας). The critical term for our purposes is "estate," μάσσα (*massa*). This is a transliteration of the Latin *massa*, a term that in later antiquity referred to an estate or a plot of land.[114] *Massa* was not a Greek word; it was a word only in Latin. If Greek-speaking, Cilician monks had invented this story about Paul's death, then surely they would have used a Greek term for an "estate." It is very unlikely that they would have inserted a foreign word into a story that they had concocted. The fact that the editors of the Greek text employed this Latin term, without even translating it, indicates that they received their information from a Latin source and simply transliterated the Latin term *massa* into Greek.

---

114. This Latin term was originally taken from the Greek μᾶζα (*maza*), referring to a lump of dough. It retained this original meaning in Latin but later took on the secondary meaning of estate. There is no evidence, however, that μᾶζα ever took on the additional meaning of "estate."

There are, then, three compelling pieces of evidence against the theory that the expanded Greek *Acts* account was the invention of Cilician monks: local, Latin sources lay behind the story of Perpetua, the name of the site (Ἄκουαι Σαλβίας), and the description of the place (μάσσα). The Greek *Acts* does indeed reflect an alternative tradition regarding Paul's martyrdom, but this tradition was already part of the Roman, Latin-speaking context in the sixth century and has survived in this text.

A letter from Gregory I supports my argument for a Roman source behind the description of Paul's death in the Greek *Acts*. In 604, Gregory wrote to Felix, a subdeacon who was overseeing some of the Roman church's holdings south of the city. The bishop explained that the basilica of Paul did not have enough lamps, so he was redirecting the income from certain church properties in order to pay for more. The primary source of revenue was to be "that estate called Aquae Salvias [*eamdem massam quae Aquas Salvias nuncupatur*], with all its farms." Gregory chose to transfer this specific patrimony because "it seemed to be highly incongruous and most unfortunate that that possession in particular should not be at his service, at the place where he assumed the palm-wreath of martyrdom and was beheaded so that he might live" (Gregory I, *Ep.* 14.14, Martyn).[115] It was right and proper, according to Gregory, that the revenue from the place of Paul's death (Aquae Salvias) should provide for the needs of the basilica that housed his body. Gregory's crucial phrase, "that estate called Aquae Salvias," is an exact equivalent of the expression from the Greek *Acts*, including the use of the term *massa*. Is it possible that Eastern monks had fabricated the Aquae Salvias story in Greek and that soon after the bishop of Rome himself (whose Greek was limited at best[116]) had been duped into accepting it as the authentic narrative of the martyrdom? This strikes me as very doubtful. It is far more likely that Gregory and the Greek *Acts* both knew a Latin tradition about Aquae Salvias that had originated in Rome and had gained some level of acceptance by the end of the sixth century.[117]

The Latin *Passion* and Greek *Acts*, therefore, bear witness in the sixth century to competing accounts within Rome concerning the location of the holy

---

115. This letter was later inscribed onto marble and placed in the basilica of Paul. It now rests in the monastery (*ICUR* NS 2:4790).

116. Joan Petersen, "Did Gregory Know Greek?" in *The Orthodox Churches and the West* (ed. Derek Baker; Oxford: Blackwell, 1976), 121–34; idem, *The "Dialogues" of Gregory the Great in Their Late Antique Cultural Background* (Toronto: Pontifical Institute of Mediaeval Studies, 1984), esp. 1–14, 151–91; Carole Straw, *Gregory the Great: Perfection in Imperfection* (Berkeley: University of California Press, 1988), 13.

117. In the seventh and eighth centuries, other literary sources perpetuated the story of Aquae Salvias as the location of Paul's martyrdom, e.g., *Loc. sanct.* 109; *Mirac. Anast.* 3; Bede, *Temp. rat.* 66.

place where Paul had been martyred. The Latin *Passion* stood in line with the older tradition that Paul died next to the Tiber on the Ostian Road and was buried at the same location. The Greek *Acts* reflected an alternative version of the story. Paul had died on the Laurentinian Road at Aquae Salvias, several kilometers from the river and the tomb. The date and identity of the Roman source for this latter account is unknown, but by the turn of the seventh century even the city's bishop was giving it credence.

These competing traditions have never been reconciled. Prior to the fire of 1823, a small altar sat just inside the main entrance of the Ostian Road basilica. It was said to mark the spot where Paul's head was discovered after his

Fig. 1.15. Central altar in the Basilica of St. Paul at the Three Fountains.
Photograph by Wilmar Santin.

Fig. 1.16. Traditional "prison of Paul" in the Church of Santa Maria in Scala Coeli.

execution.[118] The Aquae Salvias location also has a memorial for Paul's fallen head. According to the twelfth-century *Marvels of the City of Rome*, when the soldier cut off the apostle's head, it bounced three times on the ground as Paul cried out "Jesus, Jesus, Jesus." At each place that his head bounced, a spring miraculously appeared (*Mirabil.* 1.5). This story has given the location its present name, the Three Fountains. The current sixteenth-century church on the site has three altars that mark these spots (fig. 1.15). It also contains a partial column that is celebrated as the milestone to which Paul was bound for his execution, while a chamber in the crypt of the adjacent Church of Santa Maria in Scala Coeli is identified as the prison in which Paul was held before execution (fig. 1.16). For centuries, then, two separate basilicas in Rome had altars for Paul's head.

Today, as in previous centuries, the Ostian Road tradition has remained dominant in Rome. While tour buses stream to the Basilica of St. Paul Outside

---

118. An inscription at the spot read, "Here was found the head of saint Paul the apostle" (*Hic inventum fuit caput s. Pauli apostoli*). Nicola Camerlenghi has made me aware of this altar and the accompanying dedication. It is my hope that he will soon publish his research on the fascinating history of this altar.

the Walls, the Aquae Salvias site and the Basilica of St. Paul at the Three Fountains receive relatively few pilgrims. Nevertheless, the Three Fountains church
stands as a witness to an alternative tradition about Paul's death that has been
largely ignored or simply forgotten.

CONCLUSION

In this chapter I have sought to describe the central elements in the creation
of the Pauline cult on the Ostian Road. The literary and archaeological records
reveal the development of this localized cult based on a story that Paul had
died and been buried there. As a result, Christians designated the site a holy
place, a center of Pauline veneration. Through the sixth century, they fostered
the expansion of the cult at Paul's tomb through practices such as the placement of privileged burials "near the saint," pilgrimage, and the veneration
and proliferation of relics. Both Leo I and Gregory I undertook substantial
renovations to the tomb area, yet they allowed for and even encouraged the
continuity of these practices. In the sixth century a rival martyrdom site at
Aquae Salvias achieved some acceptance, yet the Ostian Road remained the
focal point and dominant site for the Pauline cult in Rome in late antiquity.

2

THE CULT OF PAUL ON THE APPIAN ROAD

The Ostian Road was the center of the Pauline cult in Rome in late antiquity, but it was not the only site in the city at which Christians venerated the apostle. Beginning in the third century, another location was established along the Appian Road, the main thoroughfare leading south from Rome into southern Italy (see fig. 1.1). Today the site is called the Church of St. Sebastian at the Catacombs. In the ancient period, it was known simply as "the Catacombs." Because Roman law prohibited burying the dead inside the city walls, it was common for tombs to be constructed along the roads outside the city. In the first century C.E., local inhabitants built several monumental tombs into caves in an abandoned quarry that lay at the third milestone on the Appian Road. This location came be to known as "the Catacombs," which comes from two Greek words (κατὰ κύμβας) meaning "near the caves." Since the medieval period, the term *catacombs* has been used to refer in general to any underground burial complex, but when ancient authors spoke of "the Catacombs," they meant this specific location. (I will observe the ancient custom here.) These first-constructed tombs remained in use for several centuries, and evidence suggests that they contained both pagan and Christian mausolea.[1]

By the middle of the third century, cultic practices honoring Paul and Peter were taking place here. The first part of this chapter will focus on three primary practices: commemorative meals, appeals to Paul as intercessor and patron, and architectural development. By drawing on archaeological, literary, and liturgical materials, I will reconstruct each of these practices and show how they functioned within the context of this space. The last section of the

---

1. Bisconti and Mazzoleni, *Christian Catacombs of Rome*, 14; John Bodel, "From Columbaria to Catacombs: Collective Burial in Pagan and Christian Rome," in *Commemorating the Dead: Texts and Artifacts in Context: Studies of Roman, Jewish, and Christian Burials* (ed. Laurie Brink and Deborah A. Green; Berlin: de Gruyter, 2008), 177–243. On the expanded use of the term *catacombs*, see Leonard Victor Rutgers, *Subterranean Rome: In Search of the Roots of Christianity in the Catacombs of the Eternal City* (Leuven: Peeters, 2000), 43.

chapter will take up the question of apostolic relics and their relevance to the site. Many have attempted to trace the foundation of this location to an early belief in the presence of the apostles' bodies. I will demonstrate, however, that such a belief was not attested until the sixth century and cannot be said to lie behind the establishment and development of the cult at the Catacombs.

2.1. PAUL AS DINING COMPANION: CULTIC MEALS IN THE CATACOMBS

By the latter half of the third century, Christians were holding special banquets at the Catacombs in honor of the apostles Paul and Peter. These took place in a complex constructed near the middle of the third century over the top of the older tombs in the caves, which had been filled in and taken out of use. Within the complex was a structure 23 meters long by 18 meters wide that included a paved courtyard and a dining room with benches along three walls. Paul Styger, the lead archaeologist at the site, labeled this room the *triclia* (fig. 2.1), a term derived from Latin and Greek words for a dining hall with three couches.[2] Within the *triclia* the excavators discovered a wall covered with numerous inscriptions crudely scratched into the stucco (fig. 2.2). They were written in Latin, Greek, or a mixture of the two. This use of both languages is not surprising. Both Latin and Greek were widely spoken in Rome in this period, and Greek was the official language of the Roman liturgy until the late fourth century.[3] Some of these inscriptions can be dated earlier than 260 C.E., based on the presence of an inscription that mentions the date August 9, 260. A certain Celerinus scratched it into the plaster over top of another inscription that invokes the name of Paul. It follows, then, that this Paul inscription

---

2. Paul Styger, "Il monumento apostolico della via Appia," *APARA.D* 2.13 (1918): 48–98; Fabrizio Mancinelli, *The Catacombs of Rome and the Origins of Christianity* (trans. Carol Wasserman; Florence: Scala, 1981), 17–18; Fabrizio Bisconti, "La Memoria Apostolorum," in *Pietro e Paolo: La storia, il culto, la memoria nei primi secoli* (ed. Angela Donati; Milan: Electa, 2000), 63–64; Jørgen Kjaergaard, "From 'Memoria Apostolorum' to Basilica Apostolorum: On the Early Christian Cult-Centre on the Via Appia," *ARID* 13 (1984): 59–68. The term *triclia* is clearly derived from Greek τρίκλινον and Latin *triclinium* but is not otherwise attested in either language. It was coined by Styger and has remained the technical term for this particular banquet hall at the Catacombs. On the use of benches of this type at cultic sites, see Février, "Culte des morts," 211–74; Sarah Braune, *Convivium funebre: Gestaltung und Funktion römischer Grabtriklinien als Räume für sepulkrale Bankettfeiern* (Hildesheim: Olms, 2008).

3. J. Spencer Northcote, *Epitaphs of the Catacombs: Or Christian Inscriptions in Rome during the First Four Centuries* (London: Longmans, Green, 1878), 18–21; Maura K. Lafferty, "Translating Faith from Greek to Latin: *Romanitas* and *Christianitas* in Late Fourth-Century Rome and Milan," *JECS* 11.1 (2003): 21–62; Bisconti and Mazzoleni, *Christian Catacombs of Rome*, 168.

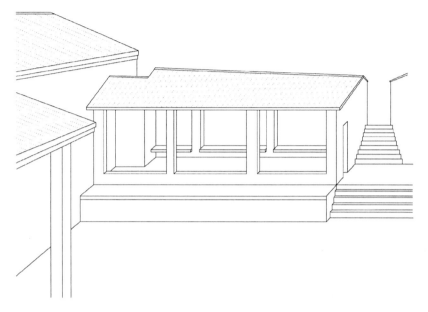

Fig. 2.1. Reconstruction of the *triclia*.
After Styger; drawing by John Capen Brough.

Fig. 2.2. *Triclia* graffiti to Paul and Peter. Scala/Art Resource, NY.

must be earlier than August 260. Studies done on the shapes of the letters have confirmed this as a possible date, for the forms are consistent with the style used from approximately 225 to 300 c.e.[4] Not all the inscriptions in the *triclia* date prior to 260, but it appears that at least some do, making them the earliest archaeological evidence for the apostolic cult.

Among these inscriptions are several that attest to the observance of commemorative meals in honor of the apostles:

> To Paul and Peter, [I/we] have held a banquet.[5]
> On March 19, I, Parthenius, have held a banquet in God—and we all (have held a banquet) in God.[6]
> To Peter and Paul, I, Tomius Coelius, have held a banquet.[7]

Parthenius, Tomius Coelius, and the others were participating in meals (*refrigeria*) that are earlier attested in the Greek and Roman traditions.[8] The participants gathered at tombs or shrines in order to honor and remember deities or deceased loved ones. The meals referred to here, as two of the inscriptions specify, were held for Paul and Peter, Rome's two greatest martyrs.

---

4. Robert Marichal, "La date des graffiti de la basilique de Saint-Sébastien à Rome," *NC* 5 (1953): 119–20; idem, "Les dates des graffiti de Saint-Sébastien," *CRAI* 97 (1953): 60–68; idem, "La date des graffiti de la Triclia de Saint-Sébastien et leur place dans l'histoire de l'écriture latine," *RevScRel* 36 (1962): 111–54; Hans G. Thümmel, *Die Memorien für Petrus und Paulus in Rom* (Berlin: de Gruyter, 1999), 78–79.

5. At Paulu(m) et Pet(rum) refri(gerav...). The inscription breaks off, so it is impossible to know if the verb is singular or plural (Styger, "Il monumento apostolico della via Appia," 61). The inscriptions relevant to Peter and Paul are also reproduced in Graydon F. Snyder, *Ante Pacem: Archaeological Evidence of Church Life before Constantine* (rev. ed.; Macon, Ga.: Mercer University Press, 2003), 251–58.

6. XIIII Kal Apriles refrigeravi Parthenius in Deo et nos in Deo omnes (Paul Styger, "Scavi a San Sebastiano," *RQ* 29.2 [1915]: 84–85; idem, "Gli Apostoli Pietro e Paolo ad Catacumbas sulla via Appia," *RQ* 29.3 [1915]: 163–64; idem, "Il monumento apostolico della via Appia," 61). In some cases Styger updated his transcriptions between the 1915 and 1918 publications. I will favor the later forms.

7. Petro et Paulo Tomius Coelius refrigerium feci (Styger, "Scavi a San Sebastiano," 85; idem, "Gli Apostoli Pietro e Paolo," 163–64; idem, "Il monumento apostolico della via Appia," 59).

8. Elisabeth Jastrzebowska, *Untersuchungen zum christlichen Totenmahl aufgrund der Monumente des 3. und 4. Jahrhunderts unter der Basilika des Hl. Sebastian in Rom* (EHS.A 2; Frankfurt am Main: Lang, 1981); Delight Tolles, "The Banquet-Libations of the Greeks" (PhD diss., Bryn Mawr College, 1943); Maureen Carroll, *Spirits of the Dead: Roman Funerary Commemoration in Western Europe* (Oxford: Oxford University Press, 2006), 30–58; Ulrich Volp, *Tod und Ritual in den christlichen Gemeinden der Antike* (VCSup 65; Leiden: Brill, 2002), 60–63, 77–86.

But what went on at these events? What did they look like, and what expectations did those in attendance bring? To address these questions, I will draw upon two texts from Italy and North Africa that describe similar commemorative meals. The records of these comparative practices allow us to identify some probable elements of the meals on the Appian Road and to understand the significance of these banquets for creating and celebrating the Catacombs as sacred space for the Pauline cult.

The first example comes from the Italian city of Lanuvium (about 30 kilometers south of Rome), where an organization of worshipers of the goddess Diana and the hero Antinous[9] wrote commemorative meals into its constitution. This document from 136 c.e. states that every year on the birthday of Diana (August 13) and the birthday of Antinous (November 27), four members of the group would be responsible for organizing and making provision for communal banquets: "Four men will provide an amphora of good wine each, loaves of bread worth two pounds each for every member of the association, four sardines [per member], the furnishings for the dining room, and hot water with service."[10] These banquets served as annual reminders of a shared community identity centered around two elevated figures. The group met in the temple of Antinous at Lanuvium. By holding their meals in that place, the members of the association marked off the space as sacred to the hero and goddess and to themselves.

The second example reflects a different context for honorific banquets from third-century North Africa. This dedication inscribed on stone comes from the burial site of a woman named Aelia Secundula:

> It seemed pleasing to us to place a stone table on which we commemorate the number of great things that she did. When the food and the cups and the covers are brought, so that the cruel wound that remains in our heart may be healed, at night we freely recount stories and the praises of our virtuous mother. The old woman sleeps.[11]

In this case the members of a family constructed and met at a designated spot at the tomb of a deceased relative. The diners were primarily Aelia Secundula's children, who came to remember their mother. The relationship was more

---

9. Antinous was Hadrian's young lover who died in the Nile River in 130 c.e. Hadrian promoted his cult as a hero and founded Antinoöpolis in Egypt in his honor.

10. *CIL* 14:2112.

11. Lapideam placuit nobis atponere mensam in qua magna eius memorantes plurima facta dum cibi ponuntur calicesq(ue) e copertae vulnus ut sanetur nos rod(ens) pectore saeuum libenter fabul(as) dum sera redimus hora castae matri bonae laudesq(ue) uetula dormit (*ILCV* 1570).

intimate than the example from Lanuvium, for those gathered here had an emotional attachment to the deceased ("the cruel wound … in our heart").

These examples provide important details about commemorative meals in the second and third centuries C.E. The Lanuvium text lists the components of the meal and focuses on the physical elements of the gathering. The Aelia Secundula inscription also describes the elements of the banquet but highlights the relational aspects of the meal. Together, these sources allow us to reconstruct the banquets at the Catacombs in regard to the temporal contexts for these meals, the physical elements of the meals, the commemoration practices that accompanied the meals, and the expectations that participants brought to the meals about communing with the dead.

First of all, we learn that the meals were held at special times. According to the Lanuvium inscription, the meals for Diana (August 13) and Antinous (November 27) were held annually on their "birthdays." August 13 marked the beginning of the Festival of Torches, a three-day celebration for the goddess Diana. The main event on this day was a procession of torches and candles around Lake Nemi, also known as "Diana's Mirror." As Ovid describes it, "In the valley of Aricia, there is a lake surrounded by a deep forest and made sacred by an ancient cult.… Along the hedgerows, like veils, hang many threads; and many plaques are placed out of gratitude to the goddess. Often a woman who is granted her prayer places a wreath on her brow and carries out from Rome burning torches" (*Fast.* 3.263–264, 267–270). Lanuvium lies only a few kilometers from Lake Nemi, so the August festival was a significant event on the civic calendar. No doubt the city saw its fair share of pilgrims at this time of year. As for November 27, it was to be celebrated across the empire as the birthday of Antinous as part of the cult promoted by the emperor Hadrian.[12] These dates in August and November, then, were recognized festival days and appropriate times for the organization to hold communal meals in honor of Diana and Antinous.

Christians adapted this practice of setting aside particular feast days for revered figures, and banquets for the apostles took place at the Catacombs on their annual festival day. In the previous chapter I discussed the *Burying of the Martyrs*, a fourth-century list of feast days in Rome for various saints. According to this text, on June 29, 258, Christians observed the "(feast of) Peter in the Catacombs, of Paul on the Ostian Road" (*Dep. mart.*). This Cata-

12. M. Zahrnt, "Antinoopolis in Ägypten: Die hadrianische Gründung und ihre Privilegien in der neueren Forschung," *ANRW* 2.10.1:669–706; Hugo Meyer, *Antinoos: Die archäologischen Denkmäler unter Einbeziehung des numismatischen und epigraphischen Materials sowie der literarischen Nachrichten: Ein Beitrag zur Kunst- und Kulturgeschichte der hadrianisch-frühantoninischen Zeit* (Munich: Fink, 1991).

combs reference to events on the annual feast of Peter and Paul focuses on Peter, yet the *triclia* inscriptions reveal that Paul was also an important figure on the Appian Road in this period. Among all the Catacombs inscriptions for the apostles that can be deciphered, the formula "Paul and Peter" (34 occurrences) outnumbers "Peter and Paul" (28), and Paul's name appears alone in nine additional cases.[13] This distribution demonstrates that visitors to the site would have revered both apostles at the June 29 meals. Christians may well have come to the site at other times of year to venerate Paul and Peter, but the annual feast day for the apostles on June 29 would have provided the primary context for commemorative meals.

Second, the examples from Lanuvium and North Africa describe the physical elements of the meal: the location, the menu, and the objects used by the diners. For Aelia Secundula, the family installed a permanent table at the tomb. While a similar practice occurred at many Christian sites in the third century,[14] archaeologists have discovered no such table at the Catacombs. The arrangement there was probably more like that in the Temple of Antinous, which had a "dining room." In this case the *triclia* provided the venue for the meals,[15] and participants reclined on the benches along the walls. They enjoyed their banquets in honor of the apostles in full view of prayers and petitions that previous visitors had scratched into the wall. The room would have accommodated approximately twenty-five to thirty diners at a time.[16] This might strike us as a small number, but in the mid-third century—before the construction of the Constantinian basilicas—the other cultic sites in Rome for the apostles were their "trophies." These were probably simple shrines in cemeteries that also could have hosted groups of very limited size. Feasting in a dining room would have been a step up from a roadside picnic among the tombs. At the completion of their meal, those attending could add their names: "To Peter and Paul, I, Tomius Coelius, have held a banquet."

From the Lanuvium text we also learn about the organization's typical menu for the celebrations. Those responsible were to provide wine, loaves of bread, and fish for the other members of the group. Artistic evidence from burial sites around Rome suggests that pilgrims to the Catacombs would have followed a similar menu. An early third-century painting in the cemetery of

---

13. This count is based on the inventory in Styger, "Il monumento apostolico della via Appia," 58–82.

14. Février, "Culte des morts," 211–74.

15. See Bisconti, "Memoria Apostolorum," 64; Richard Krautheimer, *Early Christian and Byzantine Architecture* (4th ed.; New York: Penguin, 1986), 33, labels the *triclia* the "funeral-banquet hall."

16. MacMullen, *Second Church*, 79.

Callistus, for example, shows seven figures seated around a dining couch (fig. 2.3). Some hold wine goblets. In front of them rest two large platters, each of which contains a fish. In the foreground are eight large baskets containing small loaves of bread. Scenes with similar elements were carved onto sarcophagi and painted on the walls of many cemeteries in Rome, including at the Catacombs.[17] Participants in these other cases also surround a dining couch and eat a meal of fish, bread, and wine.

Some scholars have sought to identify all such scenes when they are in an apparently Christian context as specific representations of the Eucharist, not of more general funerary meals. Wine and bread, they argue, were the elements designated by Christ at the Last Supper, and the fish was one of the earliest symbols of Christianity.[18] Others, however, have correctly pointed out that all these elements were also present in pre-Christian and non-Christian meals for the dead.[19] Indeed, bread, wine, and fish were common to many

Fig. 2.3. Banquet scene in the cemetery of Callistus. Scala/Art Resource, NY.

17. Elisabeth Jastrzebowska, "Les scènes de banquet dans les peintures et sculptures chrétiennes des IIIe et IVe siècles," *RechAug* 14 (1979): 3–90. According to Augustine, his mother's typical menu in North Africa had included "meal-cakes and bread and wine" (*Conf.* 6.2).

18. G. B. de Rossi, *Roma sotterranea* (ed. and trans. J. Spencer Northcote and W. R. Brownlow; London: Longmans, Green, Reader & Dyer, 1869), 213–32; Joseph Wilpert, *Fractio Panis: Die älteste Darstellung des eucharistischen Opfers in der "Capella Graeca"* (Freiburg im Breisgau: Herder, 1895); Bisconti and Mazzoleni, *Christian Catacombs of Rome*, 109.

19. Adolf Hasenclever, *Der altchristliche Gräberschmuck: Ein Beitrag zur christlichen*

meals in the period, as the example from Lanuvium shows. My goal is not to settle this larger debate here. For our purposes, it suffices to point out that the inscriptions in the *triclia* make no reference to the Eucharist. This suggests that the meals for Paul and Peter were general honorary banquets of the Lanuvium type enjoyed in the *triclia* with a menu of wine, bread, and fish.

The Aelia Secundula inscription also specifies the objects used by the diners. Family members brought covers for the table at the tomb and cups for drinking their wine. The inscriptions from the Catacombs do not mention these items, but archaeologists have discovered the remains of glass cups that may have been used at banquets in honor of the saints.[20] In the ancient Christian burial grounds around Rome, including the Catacombs, excavators have found the decorated bottoms of over five hundred glass drinking vessels. Many of these preserve the images of martyrs, including Paul and Peter. The breakage pattern in these cups suggests that they were intentionally broken in a way that preserved the images.[21] One example in the British Museum shows Paul and Peter facing each other (fig. 2.4). Their names are written above their heads, and they both wear mantles that are fastened in the front with circular brooches. The figure of Christ holds wreaths over their heads, symbols of their victory as martyrs. An inscription around the outside reads, "Biculius, the pride of your friends, may you live piously, and may you drink." It has been dated on artistic grounds to the fourth century c.e., and the inscription suggests that it was made for use in a ritual context.[22] The Vatican possesses

Archäologie (Braunschwieg: Schwetschke & Sohn, 1886), 225–37; F. J. Dölger, *Ichthys: Das Fischsymbol in frühchristlicher Zeit* (5 vols.; Münster: Aschendorff, 1943), 5:329–638; Friedrich Gerke, *Die christlichen Sarkophage der vorkonstantinischen Zeit* (StSKG 11; Berlin: de Gruyter, 1940), 73–94; Laurence Kant, "The Interpretation of Religious Symbols in the Graeco-Roman World: A Case Study of Early Christian Fish Symbolism" (PhD diss., Yale University, 1993), 518–85; Dennis E. Smith, *From Symposium to Eucharist: The Banquet in the Early Christian World* (Minneapolis: Fortress, 2003), 1–46, 285–87; Robin M. Jensen, "Dining with the Dead: From the *Mensa* to the Altar in Christian Late Antiquity," in *Commemorating the Dead: Texts and Artifacts in Context: Studies of Roman, Jewish, and Christian Burials* (ed. Laurie Brink and Deborah A. Green; Berlin: de Gruyter, 2008), 107–44; MacMullen, *Second Church*, 74–76.

20. This possible connection was first raised by Friedrich Wilhelm Deichmann, *Archeologia cristiana* (SAEB 63; Rome: "L'Erma" di Bretschneider, 1993), 319.

21. K. Painter, "Frammenti di coppa," in *Vetri dei Cesari* (ed. Donald B. Harden; Exposition Catalog: Milan, 1988), 279–81; Bisconti and Mazzoleni, *Christian Catacombs of Rome*, 80–81.

22. Donald B. Harden, *Glass of the Caesars* (Milan: Olivetti, 1987), 285, no. 160; Hermann Vopel, *Die altchristlichen Goldgläser: Ein Beitrag zur altchristlichen Kunst- und Kulturgeschichte* (Freiburg: Mohr Siebeck, 1899), 107–9.

Fig. 2.4. Gold glass image of Peter and Paul. In the British Museum, London. © Trustees of the British Museum.

Fig. 2.5. The martyrs Peter and Paul being crowned by Christ. In the Vatican Museums. Courtesy of the Vatican Museums.

a sizable collection of such artifacts, including images of the apostles being crowned as martyrs by Christ (fig. 2.5).[23]

Pilgrims probably used glasses of this type for banquets in the *triclia*. Because these visitors came to honor Paul and Peter, they used vessels that featured the images of the apostles. The participants broke the glasses after the commemorative meals and preserved only the most important portion with the images of the saint(s). Some left these pieces on site (even embedding them in the wall) as a memorial and perhaps as a form of protection for those buried in the cemetery. Others took them home as tokens of their pilgrimage.[24] The glass pieces now preserved in museums throughout the world, then, could be direct artifacts of the cult of Paul at the Catacombs.

Third, we learn from the Aelia Secundula inscription about a particular commemoration practice that occurred at the meals, where diners took turns sharing their recollections of the woman's life: "At night we freely recount stories and the praises of our virtuous mother." The memory of their mother provided a common thread that linked together the members of the family. By telling stories from her life and praising her good deeds, they renewed and strengthened the bonds of kinship and relationship both with her and with each other. The meal served not only a commemorative but also a communal function.

The practice of recounting stories at shrines was also part of the Christian cult of the martyrs. The female pilgrim Egeria experienced this during her trip to the eastern Mediterranean in the fourth century.[25] In her *Itinerary*, Egeria

---

23. Guy Ferrari and Charles R. Morey, *The Gold-Glass Collection of the Vatican Library: With Additional Catalogues of Other Gold-Glass Collections* (CMSBAV; Vatican City: Biblioteca Apostolica Vaticana, 1959), nos. 37, 50–51, 53–54, 58, 60–68.

24. Bisconti and Mazzoleni, *Christian Catacombs of Rome*, 81: "These iconographic choices demonstrate how the glass vessels became true protective objects for the Christians, a type of support for the images of saints as intercessors, whom the faithful selected as companions in life on earth and as guides in the afterlife." Cf. Charles Pietri, *Roma christiana: Recherches sur l'Église de Rome, son organisation, sa politique, son idéologie de Miltiade à Sixte III (311–440)* (2 vols.; BEFAR 224; Rome: École française de Rome, 1976), 1:605. Pietri argues that the glasses had domestic and familial use, instead of cultic use. Pietri's sharp dichotomy between the familial and the cultic does not hold up, as the Aelia Secundula inscription demonstrates. These meals could be both at the same time. Elsewhere Pietri argues that Christians gave such glasses as gifts on public or private feast days ("Concordia Apostolorum," 307). This would only strengthen my case for their possible use in banquets at the Catacombs.

25. Egeria is only one of many sources of evidence for this practice. See Baudouin de Gaiffier, "La lecture des actes des martyrs," *AnBoll* 72 (1954): 134–66; idem, "La lecture des passions des martyrs à Rome," *AnBoll* 87 (1969): 63–78; Hans Urner, *Die ausserbiblische Lesung im christlichen Gottesdienst* (Berlin: Evangelische Verlagsanstalt, 1952); Hippolyte

states that her visit to the shrine of the apostle Thomas in Edessa (modern Urfa, Turkey) included special readings: "When we had come [to Edessa], we immediately proceeded to the church and the martyr shrine of saint Thomas. Then, according to custom, prayers were made and other things that were customary in the holy places were done. Also, we read there a number of things by Saint Thomas himself" (*Itiner.* 19.2). These readings may have included excerpts from the *Acts of Thomas*, an early third-century account of the apostle's trip to India and the miraculous deeds that he performed there. The second-century *Gospel according to Thomas* and the fourth-century *The Book of Thomas: The Contender Writing to the Perfect* are other possible sources for the readings. These texts all probably came from Edessa, which in late antiquity was a center for the production of texts about Thomas.[26] Identifying the precise text(s) is not critical. The important point is that Egeria and other pilgrims read from works of this kind at a shrine that was considered sacred to Thomas and in a city that claimed a special association with his legacy. It was the appropriate setting for reading stories as a way of honoring this apostle.

Later in her journey, Egeria came to Seleucia (south-central Turkey) and the shrine of Thecla, a traditional companion of Paul. She recounts that "prayer was offered at the martyr shrine, and the whole of the *Acts of Saint Thecla* was read" (*Itiner.* 23.5). Egeria is probably referring to a portion of the *Acts of Paul and Thecla*, a late second-century account of the travels of the virgin Thecla alongside the apostle Paul. (This is the first part of the larger *Acts of Paul.*) Seleucia was believed to be Thecla's burial site and was a center for her cult in this period.[27] This made it the appropriate place for proclaiming her deeds to visiting pilgrims. In both these examples from Egeria's *Itinerary*, we see that the reading of texts by or about the saints could be an important aspect of the veneration practices at their martyr shrines.

Likewise, the faithful at the Catacombs would have praised Paul by narrating his marvelous deeds. By the middle of the third century, pilgrims had a wide variety of texts and stories from which they could choose. The Acts of the Apostles and the various epistles attributed to Paul told stories of his life and missionary journeys. The *Acts of Paul* and the *Acts of Peter*, among other

---

Delehaye, *Sanctus: Essai sur le culte des saints dans l'antiquité* (SHG 17; Brussels: Société des Bollandistes, 1927), 191–93; Gregory Dix, *The Shape of the Liturgy* (London: Dacre, 1945), 470–72.

26. Bentley Layton, *The Gnostic Scriptures: A New Translation with Annotations and Introductions* (Garden City, N.Y.: Doubleday, 1987), 357–409; K. A. D. Smelik, "Aliquanta ipsius sancti Thomae," *VC* 28 (1974): 290–94. Smelik has argued that Egeria is referring to the *Gospel according to Thomas*.

27. Davis (*Cult of Saint Thecla*, 39–40), who argues that the *Acts of Thecla* was circulating independently by this time.

texts, reported additional adventures and his eventual martyrdom in Rome. These texts existed alongside stories that had been passed along by word of mouth.[28] At the banquets in Paul's honor, then, those present could draw from a number of sources in order to recount the exploits and praises of Paul. As they shared these stories with each other, they underscored a sense of shared identity as the heirs to the faith that Paul had preached.[29] Just as family members used their recollections to honor Aelia Secundula as an excellent mother, so did pilgrims at the Catacombs venerate Paul by telling stories about this apostle, one of the spiritual fathers of Rome.

Finally, we learn from the North African inscription that these meals were a venue for participants' communion not only with each other but also with the one being honored. The inscription states, "The elderly woman sleeps." Here sleep serves as a euphemism for death, but the flexibility of this wordplay left open the possibility that Aelia Secundula was somehow in the midst of her family members whenever they gathered.[30]

For Christians, the relationship between sleep and death was especially dynamic, for the boundary between the two was thin and even permeable. The faithful would one day be resurrected, so those who died were merely "sleeping" until that moment arrived. Paul himself had explained this idea to the Christian community in Thessaloniki: "We do not want you to be ignorant, brothers, concerning those who have fallen asleep, lest you grieve like others who have no hope. For since we believe that Jesus died and rose again, then through Jesus God will bring those who have fallen asleep with him.... And the dead in Christ will rise first" (1 Thess 4:13–14, 16). The play between sleep and death is reflected in many other early Christian texts. The story of the healing of Jairus's daughter (Mark 5:21–43) and the raising of Lazarus (John 11) both employ the language of sleep to indicate death. John Chrysostom, Jerome, and others went so far as to remove death as a category for Christians. As Chrysostom stated it, "We no longer call it death, but sleeping and dreaming" (*Hom. Gen.* 29.7). In his letter against Vigilantius, who considered the cult of the saints a shameful practice, Jerome refused to admit that Paul was actually dead, for "in fact the saints are not called dead, but sleeping"

---

28. Dennis R. MacDonald, *The Legend and the Apostle: The Battle for Paul in Story and Canon* (Philadelphia: Westminister, 1983), 17–77. McDonald argues that oral tradition played a key role in the development of the Pastoral Epistles and the *Acts of Paul*.

29. On the communal aspects of the Christian cult of saints, see Paul-Albert Février, "À propos du repas funéraire: Culte et sociabilité," *CAr* 26 (1977): 29–46; Yasin, "Funerary Monuments and Collective Identity," 433–57; idem, *Saints and Church Spaces*, 240–85.

30. Johannes Quasten, "'Vetus superstitio et nova religio': The Problem of *refrigerium* in the Ancient Church of North Africa," *HTR* 33 (1940): 257.

(*Vigil.* 6).[31] Given the permeability of the line between sleep and death for many Christians, those gathered at the *triclia* probably expected Paul to be among them, although he was "asleep." The martyr was invisible to the naked eye, yet his spiritual presence could be experienced by those taking part in the meal. The result was a sense of communion that included both the banquet participants and the apostle himself. For those present, the *triclia* became a holy space in which Paul joined their celebrations.[32]

The examples of commemorative meals from Lanuvium and North Africa have allowed us to reconstruct a picture of the banquets held at the Catacombs. The annual feast of the apostles on June 29 was the primary occasion for these meals. At least as early as 258, Christians set aside this date for banquets in honor of Paul and Peter on the Appian Road. Those in attendance shared a dinner of bread, wine, and fish in a special dining area and may have used glass drinking vessels that featured images of Paul or Paul with Peter. They told stories and read Pauline texts, recalling the greatness of the apostle and reinforcing their own bonds of spiritual kinship. The account of Paul's martyrdom must have held a central place, given the occasion for these meals. Participants also welcomed the spiritual presence of Paul into their gathering, thereby communing directly with the apostle whom they were venerating. By holding these meals at the Catacombs, Christians designated and celebrated the location as sacred space and structured their cultic practices around it. It was a place of commemoration but also a special place of meeting between those in the physical realm and the apostle, who interceded for them in the presence of God.

2.2. PAUL AS PATRON: ACCESSING THE POWER OF THE MARTYR

Many ancient Christians believed that the prayers of martyrs had extraordinary merit. On account of their suffering for the faith, these saints had attained an intimacy with God that no mortal could experience. They had special access to the "throne of grace" (Heb 4:16), so their appeals had particular effectiveness. The belief in the martyrs' power is reflected in many places, including the *Martyrdom of Potamiaena and Basilides* (ca. 202 C.E.). In this account a woman of Alexandria named Potamiaena is sentenced to death on the charge of being

---

31. See also Jerome, *Ep.* 75.1; *Apos. Con.* 6.30.4; Basil of Seleucia, *Mirac. Theclae* 46.

32. On the active participation of the holy dead at such meals, see Éric Rebillard "Les chrétiens et les repas pour les fêtes des morts (IVe-Ve siècles)," in *Bestattungsrituale und Totenkult in der römischen Kaiserzeit* (ed. Jörg Rüpke and John Scheid; Stuttgart: Steiner, 2010), 281–90; Ramsay MacMullen, "Christian Ancestor Worship in Rome," *JBL* 129 (2010): 602–8. On the continuing presence of the holy dead, see Peter R. L. Brown, *The Cult of the Saints: Its Rise and Function in Latin Christianity* (Chicago: University of Chicago Press, 1982), 69–85.

a Christian. Basilides, her executioner, protects her from the insults of a mob prior to her death. In gratitude, she tells him that "she would intercede for him with her Lord, and it would not be long before she would reward him for his kind deeds toward her." Soon after Potamiaena's death, Basilides declares himself a Christian and is thrown into prison. Some local Christians come to see him as he awaits his own death and ask what led to his sudden conversion. He credits a series of dreams in which Potamiaena visited him and made good on her promise: "Potamiaena, indeed for three days after her martyrdom, standing before him at night, placed a crown upon his head and said that she had entreated the Lord on his account, and she had obtained her prayer and that before long she would take him with her. On this, the brethren gave him the seal in the Lord." The visions come true, as Basilides is beheaded soon after and receives his crown of martyrdom. Because of Potamiaena's particular merit in the eyes of the Lord, she is able to appeal successfully for the conversion and salvation of Basilides (Eusebius, *Hist. eccl.* 6.5, Cruse).[33]

The inscriptions from the *triclia* show that visitors invoked Paul and Peter to intercede in a similar way on their behalf (see fig. 2.2):

Paul and Peter, pray for Victor.[34]
Paul, Peter, pray for Eratus.[35]
10th day of [ ], Paul, Peter, keep Sozomen in mind and …[36]
Peter and Paul, may you keep Antonius in mind …[37]

---

33. I am grateful to Candida R. Moss for drawing my attention to this understudied martyrdom account. The story of Potamiaena in some ways parallels that of the North African martyr Perpetua. See Henk Bekker, "Potamiaena: Some Observations about Martyrdom and Gender in Ancient Alexandria," in *The Wisdom of Egypt* (ed. A. Hilhorst and G. H. van Kooten; Leiden: Brill, 2005), 343–45. Appeals for intercession by saints also appear in Prudentius (*Perist.* 1.10–12, 2.579–584, 4.189, 5.545–548) and in many other places throughout antiquity. See Cyrille Vogel, "Prière ou intercession? Une ambiguïté dans le culte paléochrétien des martyrs," in *Communio sanctorum: Mélanges offerts à Jean-Jacques von Allmen* (ed. B. Bobrinskoy; Geneva: Labor et Fides, 1982), 284–89.

34. Paule ed Petre petite pro Victore (Styger, "Scavi a San Sebastiano," 81–83; idem, "Gli Apostoli Pietro e Paolo," 165; idem, "Il monumento apostolico della via Appia," 58).

35. Paule Petre [petite] pro Erate rogate (Styger, "Scavi a San Sebastiano," 82–83; idem, "Gli Apostoli Pietro e Paolo," 165; idem, "Il monumento apostolico della via Appia," 59). *Petite* is added to the side of the inscription, possibly by a later hand.

36. X Kal […] Paule Petre in mente habete Sozomenum et […] (Styger, "Scavi a San Sebastiano," 86–87; idem, "Gli Apostoli Pietro e Paolo," 166; idem, "Il monumento apostolico della via Appia," 62).

37. Petrus et Paulus in mente (h)abeatis Antonius… (Styger, "Scavi a San Sebastiano," 87; idem, "Gli Apostoli Pietro e Paolo," 166; idem, "Il monumento apostolico della via Appia," 62).

Paul, Peter, remember Timocrates and bless Kina and Esor.[38]

Victor, Eratus, and the others appealed here for spiritual assistance through the prayers and blessing of the apostles. They were part of a Roman tradition that remained vibrant into the time of Bishop Leo I. On June 29, 441, Leo reminded his congregation, "As we ourselves have experienced and *as our ancestors have learned*, we believe and trust that, in all the labor of this life, *we are to be aided always by the prayers of these special patrons* [Paul and Peter] to attain the mercy of God. As we are hindered by our own sins, so we are encouraged by the apostles' merits" (*Serm.* 82, emphasis added).[39] The roots of Leo's belief in apostolic intervention lay, at least in part, in the appeals of pilgrims at the Catacombs dating back to the third century.

Leo's reflections highlight an additional aspect of the ancient bond between pilgrims and the apostles on the Appian Road. From the earliest days, this relationship was based not only on veneration and intervention but also on the establishment of patron-client relationships with Paul. The patron-client model of patronage in the Roman world was based on an agreement between two parties of different social standing. The patron would offer assistance to the less-powerful client, who would offer some form of service in return.[40] We see an example of this model at work in the writings of Marcus Cornelius Fronto, a prominent Roman orator of the second century C.E. Fronto wrote to the emperor Lucius Verus, who had once been his pupil. He asked Verus to assist a certain Gavius Clarus in securing a financial legacy. Clarus was Fronto's client and had fallen on hard times, but Fronto was sure that the emperor's intervention would be of great benefit to Clarus: "If ever you have loved me, or ever will love me, I ask that you will befriend this man who is handed over by me to your trust and protection" (*Vero Aug.* 2.7). Fronto here sought both assistance and protection for his client from the emperor. These patron-client networks permeated Roman society at all levels, from the emperor to the day-laborer. They were the glue that provided cultural stability and cohesion in a very stratified society.

Many Christians claimed patronage relationships that traversed the barrier between the living and the dead by taking martyrs as their patrons and

---

38. Παύλε Παίτρε μνημόνευαι Τιμοκράτην καὶ εὐτύχειαν Κίνα καὶ Εσῶρα (Styger, "Scavi a San Sebastiano," 85; idem, "Gli Apostoli Pietro e Paolo," 166; idem, "Il monumento apostolico della via Appia," 61).

39. The prayer book ascribed to the time of Leo reinforced this perspective, referring to Paul and Peter as "our intercessors" (*Sacrum. Leon.* 49, line 360). However, the ascription to the time of Leo is dubious. This work may date to the sixth or even the seventh century.

40. For bibliography on patronage, see p. 10 nn. 20–22.

protectors.[41] At the Catacombs in particular, they applied the patron-client model to the cult of Paul. As one group of pilgrims wrote, "Peter and Paul, protect your servants. Protect the holy souls. With offerings for the dead [...]."[42] The clients identified themselves as the "servants" of the apostles. Their request included "protect your servants," an appeal for physical protection, and "protect the holy souls," an appeal for spiritual safeguard. On account of their exalted positions in the presence of God, the martyr-patrons were in a position to honor both petitions. In return, the pilgrim-clients would honor Paul and Peter with offerings (i.e., banquets) at their shrine.

Requests for spiritual intercession were numerous at the site. To the examples above we can add the appeal of a certain Primitivus: "Peter and Paul, come to the aid of the sinner Primitivus."[43] Primitivus considered himself in need of assistance and called upon the apostles to grant him the help that he needed, to use their higher standing in the sight of God to improve his lower standing. Bolder still was this request: "Peter and Paul, may you keep us in mind and may you save us and those who to you [...] Rufinus [...] and Peter and [...] our parents."[44] The prayer was eternal in scope. Rufinus and Peter beseeched the saints not just as those whose appeals to God had a special effectiveness, but also as powerful martyr-patrons who could even help their clients attain salvation. The supplicants believed that intercession was critical to their eternal destiny and asked the apostles to include their parents in the salvific blessing that they were seeking.[45] On the same wall we find

---

41. Charles Pietri, "L'évolution du culte des saints aux premiers siècles chrétiens: Du témoin à l'intercesseur," in *Les fonctions des saints dans le monde occidental (IIIe–XIIIe siècle)* (CEFR 149; Rome: École française de Rome, 1991), 15–36; Edina Bozóky, *La politique des reliques de Constantin à Saint Louis: Protection collective et légitimation du pouvoir* (Paris: Beauchesne, 2006), 33–38; Skedros, *Saint Demetrios of Thessaloniki*, 124–31; Davis, *Cult of Saint Thecla*, 78–80; Brown, *Cult of the Saints*, 54–62. Brown proposed that one of Christianity's "unconsidered strengths" was adapting the social structure of the Roman Empire to the spiritual level. Along similar lines, Kate Cooper has argued that Roman Christians developed their patronage networks so that "often ... they follow a traditional, dynastic pattern." See "The Martyr, the *Matrona* and the Bishop: The Matron Lucina and the Politics of Martyr Cult in Fifth- and Sixth-Century Rome," *EMEur* 8.3 (1999): 299.

42. (Πέτρ)ος καὶ (Παῦλο)ς συντηρήσατε τοὺς δούλους πνεύματα ἄγεια συντηρήσατ(ε) ... αναγίσμοις ετε... (Styger, "Il monumento apostolico della via Appia," 60). The inscription breaks off and does not preserve the names of the petitioners.

43. Petre et Paule subvenite Prim[itivo] peccatori (ibid., 64).

44. Petre et Paule in mente n(os habeat)is salvetis et qui vobis ... Rufin ... (e)t Petru et Pat ... pare(nt)es nostri.... (ibid.).

45. Parents also appealed on behalf of their children, as we see in this prayer to the Roman martyr Basilla: "Lady Basilla, we, Crescentius and Micina, commit to your care our daughter Crescentina, who lived ten months and [ ] days" (*ILCV* 2379a).

another eternal appeal: "Peter and Paul, pray for F[...] Quinta so that we may be able to come to you."[46] Quinta and at least one other asked Paul and Peter to intervene with their prayers. Their desired goal was to be with the apostles in heaven, so they sought the assistance of their martyr-patrons to aid them in their spiritual journey. Potamiaena had successfully interceded on behalf of the soul of Basilides, and now Peter and Paul could draw Quinta and company heavenward by their prayers.

In the fourth century, Christians expanded their expectations of Paul as patron. No longer just personal, as at the Catacombs, Paul was considered a patron for the city as a whole. In concert with Peter, he was believed to fulfill the role previously played by the Capitoline trio of Jupiter, Juno, and Minerva, the gods of Roman state religion.[47] In the *Passion of the Holy Apostles Peter and Paul*, some visitors from Jerusalem congratulate the Romans for this relationship with the apostles: "Rejoice and be glad, because you have merited to have these great patrons and friends of the Lord Jesus Christ" (*Pass. Pet. Paul.* 64).

Among their roles as martyr-patrons was the defense of the city. In a homily on Paul's Epistle to the Romans, John Chrysostom claimed that Paul was protecting Rome, because his body provided an unassailable defense: "This body fortifies that city. It is more impenetrable than any tower and than countless defensive walls" (*Hom. Rom.* 32.4). Later, in 406, the Roman general Stilicho defeated a confederation of Germanic tribes that had entered northern Italy and was threatening Rome. Paulinus of Nola asserted that the city had been saved by the presence of Paul and Peter, the princes of Rome, along with the other martyrs (*Carm.* 21.28). This belief in the apostles' defensive role was again expressed centuries later in a legend concerning the year 452, when Attila the Hun was approaching Rome with his army. According to the fifth-century chronicler Prosper of Aquitaine, Bishop Leo I met Attila outside the city and persuaded him to turn back from attacking the city (*Epit. chron.* 1367). In an expanded, medieval version of the story, an anonymous biographer of Leo added the miraculous detail that Attila had seen Peter and Paul standing on either side of Leo, holding swords over Attila's head and threatening to kill him if he did not obey the bishop. Attila withdrew across the Danube, while Leo returned to Rome, giving thanks to God and the apostles Peter and Paul (*Vit. Leon.* 2.6).[48]

---

46. (Pe)tre e(t Paule pe)tite pro F ... Quinta (u)t possimu(s a)d vos venire(e) (Styger, "Il monumento apostolico della via Appia," 69).

47. Livy describes the role of this trio in *Urb. cond.* 1.10–12. See also J. R. Fears, "The Cult of Jupiter and Roman Imperial Ideology," *ANRW* 2.17.1:3–141.

48. This legend is reflected in a famous painting by Raphael from 1514.

The apostles' general patronage role for this city was also highlighted in Prudentius's poem on the gruesome martyrdom of the Roman deacon Lawrence. The poet placed in Lawrence's mouth a rousing prayer that the martyr allegedly delivered with his final breaths. He declared that Christianity was triumphing in Rome and that Paul and Peter were driving out Jupiter, the previous patron:

> Already there reign here the two chiefs of the apostles, the one is he who called the Gentiles, while the other occupies the foremost chair and opens the gates of eternity which were committed to his keeping. Away, thou lecherous Jupiter, defiled with the violation of thy sister! Leave Rome at liberty, flee from her people, who are now Christ's. Paul banishes thee hence, the blood of Peter drives thee out. (*Perist.* 2.459–70, Thomson)

As we saw in the previous chapter, Prudentius elsewhere replaced Rome's founding deity and founding pair: the Christian God for Father Tiber, and Paul and Peter for Romulus and Remus. Here he pushed the refoundation of Rome as a Christian city even further, supplanting the former, pagan patron deity in favor of the apostles. Jupiter could no longer abide in the same city as these two martyr-patrons. In this purging process, according to Prudentius, Paul takes the primary position: he is the first of the "two chiefs" and the first to banish Jupiter.

Victor, Eratus, Sozomen, Quinta, and many others like them called upon Paul and Peter to employ their merit as martyrs on their behalf. In order to do so more effectively, they traveled to the Catacombs, a site that in their minds had a special connection to Rome's two greatest apostles. There they appealed to Paul and Peter as influential martyr-patrons, brokers of spiritual power. They scratched their entreaties into the wall of the *triclia* as a way of declaring their veneration to the apostles, while at the same time reminding the saints of the requests that had been made. In response, the martyr-patrons were expected to help their pilgrim-clients. The apostles' protective patronage eventually extended to encompass Christian Rome as a whole. As their reach and influence expanded, so did the space in which they were honored.

2.3. THE CONSTANTINIAN BASILICA OF THE APOSTLES: THE EXPANSION OF CULTIC SPACE

The legalization of Christianity in the fourth century opened the door for expansion at a number of sites around Rome. On the Ostian Road, the Constantinian basilica replaced Caius's "trophy" of the apostle Paul. Similar changes occurred on the Appian Road. The *triclia* and its surrounding complex were largely destroyed at some point, perhaps as a result of an edict issued during the persecution by Diocletian.[49] On that same site, Constantine constructed the Basilica of the Apostles (*Basilica Apostolorum*) as part of his extensive, Christian building campaign.[50] The basilica measured nearly 75 meters in length and was oriented east–west, with the apse at the western end (fig. 2.6). It was designed on a U-shaped plan with a long central nave and a continuous aisle all the way around. Arched windows provided plenty of light for the nave, while the aisle was lit only by narrow slit windows. The altar sat in the center of the nave almost directly above the *triclia*, thus maintaining continuity with the former cultic center of the site.[51] An atrium connected the building to the Appian Road. This church for the apostles quickly became a major landmark on the sacred topography of Rome. When the Egyptian monk Ammonius visited Rome with Athanasius around 340, he neglected the other sites of the city, wishing "to see only the martyr shrine [μαρτύριον] of Peter and Paul" (Socrates Scholasticus, *Hist. eccl.* 4.23). The Basilica of the Apostles was the only shared cult site in Rome at the time—and μαρτύριον can simply mean "church"—so the Appian Road must have been Ammonius's destination. Constantine's new basilica also impacted the city's sacred architecture, serving as the model for the Roman churches of Saints Agnes, Lawrence, and Marcellinus and Peter.[52]

The large basilica provided substantial space for privileged burials. The nave and side aisles initially had no pavement, and Christians immediately began to bury their dead here. Archaeologists excavated about 150 tightly packed graves that were dug into the basilica's original earthen floor (fig. 2.7). In some cases, bodies were stacked several high in order to maximize the

---

49. Kjaergaard, "Memoria Apostolorum," 67–68. The edict appears in Lactantius (*Mort.* 12.1) and has been dated to 303 by W. H. C. Frend, *Martyrdom and Persecution in the Early Church* (Oxford: Blackwell, 1965), 491.

50. Brandenburg, *Ancient Churches*, 69; R. Ross Holloway, *Constantine and Rome* (New Haven: Yale University Press, 2004), 105–9; Alastair Logan, "When and by Whom Was the Roman Basilica Apostolorum Built?" *JOUHS* 5 (2007): 1–14. On the broader Constantinian building program, see Charles M. Odahl, *Constantine and the Christian Empire* (London: Routledge, 2004), 146–61; Bernard Green, *Christianity in Ancient Rome: The First Three Centuries* (New York: T&T Clark, 2010), 228–36.

51. A staircase in the northern side of the nave may have allowed access to the *triclia* itself. See Francesco Tolotti, *Memorie degli apostoli in Catacumbas: Rilievo critico della Memoria e della Basilica Apostolorum al III miglio della Via Appia* (CACat 19; Vatican City: Società "Amici delle catacombe," 1953), tab. 1, 7; Antonio Ferrua, *La basilica e la catacomba di S. Sebastiano* (CatRI 3; Vatican City: Pontificia Commissione di Archeologia Sacra, 1990), 25 fig. 5.

52. Brandenburg, *Ancient Churches*, 63–69; fig. 6.6.

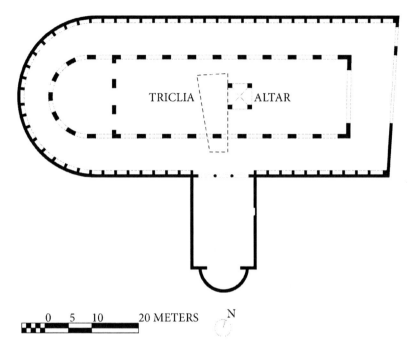

Fig. 2.6. Plan of the Constantinian Basilica of the Apostles.
After Tolotti; drawing by John Capen Brough.

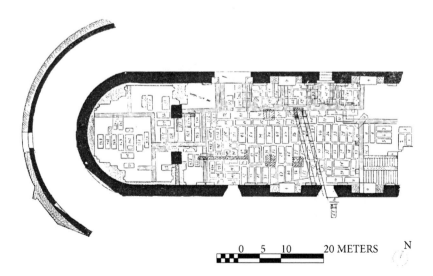

Fig. 2.7. Privileged burials in the floor of the Basilica of the Apostles. After Tolotti.

space.[53] A pavement was added soon after, and at this level excavators discovered epitaphs from the middle of the fourth century. One for a young child dates from 356/357: "Panegyrius, who lived one year and nine months, is buried in peace." Two others date from 350 and commemorate a child named Cassius and a man named Giminianus.[54]

Because the area within the church was filled so quickly, some wealthy Christians built mausolea against the outside walls of the basilica. This allowed them to increase the number of possible burials within the confines of this basilica built over the apostolic shrine. Due to the topography, these additional chambers were particularly numerous on the south side of the building and included a large, round structure near the southeast corner of the church. An epitaph commemorates a woman buried here in November 349. Her name does not survive, but she must have been a person of influence to be buried in such a large mausoleum in this location.[55]

Archaeologists have also discovered a number of sarcophagi from the area under and around the basilica. Some were of high quality and even included pillows for the deceased. The body of one anonymous person had been embalmed and mummified, an indication that the deceased was of high status.[56] The sheer quantity and density of these interments is evidence of the desire to be buried close to the *triclia*, a site considered holy to the apostles. As on the Ostian Road, the faithful here sought to honor the martyrs and to receive blessing from their proximity to this sacred space.[57]

Another outcome of the construction of the Basilica of the Apostles was the suppression of rival space. In the third century, the *triclia* had been used for Christian practices, yet the complex around housed sarcophagi with distinctly pagan imagery, such as the kidnap of Ganymede by the eagle of Zeus. No Christian symbols were present in these other areas. Prior to the building of the Basilica of the Apostles, then, the complex as a whole was shared and

---

53. Styger, "Il monumento apostolico della via Appia," 9–18; Lucrezia Spera, "Christianization of Space along the Via Appia: Changing Landscape in the Suburbs of Rome," *AJA* 107.1 (2003): 28–35.

54. *ICUR* 5:13300, 13298, 13297.

55. *ICUR* 5:13296, although the date is incorrectly given as 409. The addition of mausolea to basilicas was not uncommon. See MacMullen, *Second Church*, 44–45.

56. Dresken-Weiland, *Sarkophagbestattungen*, 381–88, Kat. E48. On Roman mummification, see Chioffi, *Mummificazione e imbalsamazione*, 24–26.

57. Richard Krautheimer, "Mensa-Coemeterium-Martyrium," *CAr* 11 (1960): 15–40; Bisconti, "Memoria Apostolorum," 64–65; Victor Saxer, "Il culto degli apostoli Pietro et Paolo dalle origini all'epoca carolingia," in *Pietro e Paolo: La storia, il culto, la memoria nei primi secoli* (ed. Angela Donati; Milan: Electa, 2000), 75–76.

perhaps disputed space between the different cultic traditions that used it.[58] By building this church, Christians sought to stamp their identity on the entirety of the space. The cult of the martyrs Paul and Peter was meant to displace rival practices. The site was now (ostensibly, at least) thoroughly Christian, a reflection of the social and cultic change in Rome brought about by an ascendant Christianity and an apostolic cult with imperial backing.

This process was not limited to Rome. In the northern Greek city of Philippi, we see a similar fourth-century takeover of space for the Pauline cult. In the Hellenistic period, a tomb shrine to a certain "Euphenes son of Exekestos" was built near the center of the city. The identity of Euphenes is unknown, but he may have been a local hero. Archaeologists found grave offerings of gold jewelry inside the tomb, which was surrounded by a large temenos (sacred precinct).[59] By the middle of the fourth century, Christians took control of the southern half of the temenos and constructed a single-aisle basilica. According to the dedicatory mosaic for the church, "Bishop Porphyrios made the mosaic of the basilica of Paul in Christ."[60] Porphyrios was a signer at the Council of Serdica in 343 (Hilary of Poitiers, *Fr. hist.* B.2.4), which provides an approximate date for the church. The temenos of Euphenes was nearly cut in half by this Christian structure, although the pagan cult site probably remained active.[61] In the early fifth century, Christians replaced the basilica of Paul with an octagonal church. This much larger structure measured 33 by 30 meters and subsumed the entire Hellenistic temenos. The architecture of the surrounding structures was also modified at that time, creating a complex of rooms and buildings dependent upon the church. The result was a complete dislocation of the pagan cult of Euphenes and a reidentification of the entire area as Christian cultic space with Pauline associations. Even the tomb may have become a cenotaph for the apostle.[62]

---

58. Brandenburg, *Ancient Churches*, 68; Snyder, *Ante Pacem*, 183–85. Some visitors may have taken part in both Christian and pagan rituals here. See Ramsay MacMullen, *Christianizing the Roman Empire (A.D. 100–400)* (New Haven: Yale University Press, 1984), esp. 74–85.

59. Chaido Koukouli-Chrysantaki, "Colonia Iulia Augusta Philippensis," in Bakirtzis and Koester, *Philippi at the Time of Paul*, 20. She suggests a possible association between Euphenes and the gods of Samothrake or Egypt.

60. Denis Feissel, *Recueil des inscriptions chrétiennes de Macédoine du IIIe au VIe siècle* (Athens: École française d'Athènes, 1983), 192 no. 226; Lemerle, *Philippes et la Macédoine orientale*, 270; Bakirtzis, "Paul and Philippi," 41–42.

61. Bakirtzis, "Paul and Philippi," 43–44. The rise of Christianity by no means signaled the immediate end of pagan practices in the region. See Timothy E. Gregory, "The Survival of Paganism in Christian Greece: A Critical Essay," *AJP* 107 (1986): 229–42.

62. Bakirtzis, "Paul and Philippi," 46; Stylianos Pelekanidis, "Kultprobleme im Apos-

The process at the Catacombs was very much like that at Philippi. Christians claimed part of a space and used it for their own practices. Eventually, they took over the entire space by constructing a large church, thereby evicting their pagan neighbors and suppressing a rival ideology by giving it no physical place for expression. At both Rome and Philippi, the cult of Paul lay at the heart of this aggressive expansion.

The construction of the Basilica of the Apostles allowed for the continuity and expansion of Christian sacred space. The architects designed the church so that altar sat above the *triclia*, reminding visitors of the prayers of their Christian predecessors. The sheer size of the basilica allowed for privileged burials at this holy site, both in the floor and in mausolea attached to the church's south side. The result was a Christian space no longer shared with those who worshiped other gods, but instead dedicated to the cults of Paul and Peter.

2.4 THE CONTROVERSY OVER RELICS

The *triclia* inscriptions and Basilica of the Apostles attest to the veneration of Paul and Peter on the Appian Road in late antiquity. This site stood alongside the Ostian Road for Paul and the Vatican hill for Peter as a center of an apostolic cult. It was the third of Ambrose's "three roads" (*Hymn.* 13.28–29). The question that naturally arises is why this apostolic association was attached to the Catacombs in the first place. It was not a traditional martyrdom site, as were the other two roads, so why did the apostolic cult develop here? Responses to this question have overwhelmingly focused on a search for relics. The assumption has been that a belief in the physical presence of the apostles must lie behind the veneration practices that we have examined. From this perspective, relics were a necessary condition for the creation of this site. The result has been a vast bibliography of scholarly studies and conjectures on when, how, or if the relics actually rested here.[63] I want to present a fresh approach to the question based on a systematic analysis of the data. Do the sources themselves link relics and the foundation of the site? If so, when? I

---

tel-Paulus Octogon von Philippi im Zusammenhang mit einem älteren Heroenkult," in *Atti del IX Congresso*, 2:393–97.

63. E.g., George La Piana, "The Tombs of Peter and Paul ad Catacumbas," *HTR* 14 (1921): 53–94; Hans Lietzmann, "The Tomb of the Apostles ad Catacumbas," *HTR* 16 (1923): 147–62; H. Stuart Jones, "The Memoria Apostolorum on the Via Appia," *JTS* OS 18 (1926): 30–39; Henry Chadwick, "St Peter and St Paul in Rome: The Problem of the Memoria Apostolorum ad Catacumbas," *JTS* NS 8 (1957): 31–52; Victor Saxer, "Früher Märtyrerkult in Rom," in *Märtyrer und Märtyrerakten* (ed. Walter Ameling; Stuttgart: Steiner, 2002), 35–58.

will present the relevant sources in two groups: those that date from the third through the fifth centuries, and those that date from the sixth century. My analysis will show that no source prior to the sixth century makes any explicit reference to relics at the site. Only in this later period, when the obsession with relics had grown significantly, did authors feel the need to explain the origin of the site through a foundation myth centered on relics. The Catacombs, rather, was the site of a cult without bodies, a phenomenon attested elsewhere in early Christianity, including in Rome itself.

2.4.1. THIRD- THROUGH FIFTH-CENTURY EVIDENCE

Apart from the *triclia* inscriptions, the earliest reference to the apostles in connection with the Catacombs appears in the *Burying of the Martyrs*, which I have discussed in the previous chapter. This calendar dates from around 336 C.E. and states that on June 29, 258, Christians were holding some kind of celebration in the Catacombs: "[Feast of] Peter in the Catacombs, of Paul on the Ostian Road, when Tuscus and Bassus were consuls" (*Dep. mart.*).[64] What, if anything, does this text tell us about the presence of relics?

Louis Duchesne, a prominent scholar in the early twentieth century, proposed a popular theory that 258 was the date of the translation (transfer) of the apostolic relics from their initial burial sites on the Ostian Road and at the Vatican to the Catacombs. According to this theory, Christians secretly moved the bodies during the persecution by the Roman emperor Valerian (253–260). In 258 Valerian issued a harsh edict against Christians that led to the execution of prominent figures such as the Roman bishop Sixtus II, the Roman deacon Lawrence, and Bishop Cyprian of Carthage. The Christians feared that Valerian's henchmen would desecrate the apostolic tombs, so they secretly moved the bodies temporarily to the Catacombs. When the danger had passed, they returned the bodies to their proper resting places. Such a momentous event would explain the establishment of the feast in that year. After the relics left, so goes the theory, the focus of the apostolic cults naturally shifted back to the original burial sites, but the association of the Catacombs with Paul and Peter lingered in popular memory and practice.[65]

---

64. III kal. Iul. Petri in Catacumbas et Pauli Ostense Tusco et Basso cons.

65. Duchesne, *Liber pontificalis*, 1:civ–cvii. The theory is still widely accepted. See, e.g., Antonio Ferrua, "Riliggendo i graffiti di S. Sebastiano," in idem, *Scritti vari di epigrafia e antichità cristiane* (Bari: Edipuglia, 1991), 313–14, who appeals to this translation as the motivation for the construction of the *triclia*. In formulating his theory, Duchesne encountered one major problem related to the cult of Peter: the *Burying of the Martyrs* does not mention the Vatican in connection with Peter. Perhaps feeling the need to defend the Vatican as the center of the Petrine cult, Duchesne simply altered the text by drawing

Nothing in the text itself, however, indicates a connection to relics. The title would be misleading if taken too literally, for the other entries show that this is a calendar of festivals, not a record of burial dates. The initial entry alerts us to this fact: "December 25: Birth of Christ in Bethlehem of Judea" (*Dep. mart.*).[66] The celebration of the nativity is a feast in honor of the birth of Jesus, not an interment. Similarly, February 22 is listed as the "Birth of the Seat of Peter" (*Dep. mart.*).[67] This is the festival commemorating Peter's first service as leader of the Roman church and the traditional establishment of the ecclesiastical hierarchy. These dates obviously reflect liturgical events, not burials.

Even among those festivals in the calendar honoring martyrs, the presence of relics was not a prerequisite, as the entry for Cyprian shows. Cyprian died and was buried in North Africa, yet the Romans also set aside a day and location in his honor. September 14 was the "Feast of Cyprian in Africa. At Rome it is celebrated in the cemetery of Callistus" (*Dep. mart.*). Cyprian's body lay in Africa, and he was honored there, yet Christians in Rome also held an annual celebration. The absence of his relics did not prevent the development of a center for the saint's cult in the cemetery of Callistus, which is on the Appian Road very close to the Catacombs. Likewise, the Roman Christians could have honored Paul and Peter at the Catacombs without their bodies. There is simply no reason to assume that relics were present in June 258. In fact, archaeologists have failed to discover any evidence for a structure that could have served as an apostolic grave.[68]

---

from a much later source, the sixth-century *Martyrology of Jerome*. This list of martyrs arranged by "birthday" drew on earlier martyr lists, including the *Burying of the Martyrs*, and the entry for June 29 includes a reference to the Vatican: "At Rome [the feast] of the birthday of the holy apostles—of Peter on the Aurelian Way at the Vatican, and of Paul on the Ostian Road, and of both, who were martyred under Nero, in the Catacombs, when Bassus and Tuscus were consuls" (*Mart. Hier.*: III kal. Iul. Romae via Aurelia natale sanctorum apostolorum Petri et Pauli Petri in Vaticano Pauli vero in via Ostensi utrumque in catacumbis passi sub Nerone Basso et Tusco consulibus). Duchesne labeled the omission of the Vatican in the *Burying of the Martyrs* an "accident" that needed correction (1:cv) using the later source. The methodological problems with Duchesne's approach are evident, but the results yielded what he was seeking: a text that both honored the traditional primacy of the Vatican and supported his theory of the transfer of the apostolic relics.

66. VIII kal. Ian. natus Christus in Betleem Iudeae.

67. VIII kal. Martias natale Petri de cathedra.

68. Brandenburg, *Ancient Churches*, 68; Kjaergaard, "Memoria Apostolorum," 69. On other "body-less" cults in late antiquity, see, e.g., Davis, *Cult of Saint Thecla*, 45–46; Skedros, *Saint Demetrios of Thessaloniki*, 85–104; Bernhard Kötting, *Peregrinatio Religiosa: Wallfahrten in der Antike und das Pilgerwesen in der alten Kirche* (2nd ed.; Münster: Antiquariat Th. Stenderhoff, 1980), 294–95.

The *Burying of the Martyrs* is certainly an important text for our study. It confirms active commemoration of the apostles at the Catacombs in the mid-third century, the period of the earliest *triclia* inscriptions. On the issue of relics, however, it is silent. There is no indication that the body of either Paul or Peter arrived at this date,[69] and we have seen that physical remains were not required for the establishment of a martyr's festival on the Appian Road in the third century. Christians did honor the apostles at the Catacombs, but Duchesne went well beyond the evidence to link these practices to an alleged translation of relics during the Valerian persecution.

The next relevant source from this period comes from the time of Bishop Damasus of Rome (366–384). During his episcopate Damasus undertook an extensive program of construction and expansion of Roman shrines dedicated to the martyrs. He also wrote poems in honor of the martyrs and placed them in a number of locations.[70] At the Catacombs he installed a marble plaque that stated,

> Here the saints abided previously. You ought to know this, whoever you are, you who seek equally the names of Peter and Paul. The East sent the disciples, which we acknowledge freely. On account of the merit of their blood and having followed Christ through the stars, they have traveled to the bosom of heaven and the kingdom of the righteous. Rome capably deserved to watch over its own citizens. Damasus records these things for your praise, O new stars. (*Epigr.* 20)[71]

---

69. Hippolyte Delehaye, "Tusco et Basso cons.," in *Mélanges Paul Thomas* (Bruges: Sainte Catherine, 1930), 201–7, argued against Duchesne that the 258 date reflected simply the establishment of an apostolic cult at the site and had nothing to do with the translation of relics. Delehaye's perspective has remained a minority opinion. Cf. Enrico Quentin, "Tusco et Basso consulibus," *APARA.R* 5 (1926): 145–47, who believes that the 258 date was originally a marginal note in the text of the *Burying of the Martyrs* noting the date of the martyrdom of Cyprian. Subsequently, it was incorrectly attached to the feast day of the apostles.

70. *Damaso e i martiri di Roma: Anno Damasi saeculari XVI* (ed. Carlo Carletti; trans. Antonio Ferrua; Vatican City: Pontificia Commissione di Archeologia Sacra, 1985); Mazzoleni, "Papa Damaso," 5–14.

71. Hic habitasse prius sanctos cognoscere debes / Nomina quisque Petri pariter Paulique requiris / Discipulos oriens misit quod sponte fatemur / Sanguinis ob meritum Christumque per astra secuti / Aetherios petiere sinus regnaque piorum / Roma suos potius meruit defendere cives / Haec Damasus vestras referat nova sidera laudes. The original does not survive, but a pilgrim copied it in the seventh century. Giovanni de Rossi produced an edition of the text in *ICUR* 2:152. There he argued that "abided" (*habitasse*) should be changed to "abide" (*habitare*), but this reading has had very little scholarly support.

Scholars have argued two main interpretations of this poem. Some have proposed that it commemorates temporary apostolic burials at this site, while others claim that it refers to a tradition that the apostles had lived at this location. After analyzing and showing the shortcomings of each, I will offer a new interpretation that better explains the hymn as a whole, which is not centered on relics.

Duchesne's 258 translation theory has driven the apostolic-burials interpretation of this text.[72] According to this line of thought, the bodies of the apostles must have "abided" in tombs on the Appian Road ("here") at some point. The fear that Roman authorities would descrecate the apostolic tombs prompted this relocation to the Catacombs, and the bodies had been returned well before the time of Damasus. In this poem the bishop is evoking this event as the basis of his praise for the Catacombs as a sacred site. For this reading, great weight is placed on the initial "here" (*hic*) as a specific indicator of a burial site at the Catacombs. Indeed, a survey of Damasus's other poems might at first glance seem to support this assumption.[73] In four other cases, Damasus opens a poem with an initial "here," as in "Here lies Festus" (*Epigr.* 12².1) and "Here lies a collected multitude of the pious" (*Epigr.* 16.1). In five other instances, "here" introduces a subsequent stanza within a poem, for example, "Here is placed a priest" (*Epigr.* 16.6) and "Here lie holy confessors" (*Epigr.* 16.7). In all these cases the "here" in question seems to refer to the very spot where Damasus placed the poem. These are all burials, which would seem to align with the translation story. As a result, the assumption has been that the "here" in the Catacombs poem must function in the same way as these others, namely, as a reference to a burial at a specific site.

Upon closer inspection, however, we see an important difference between these other cases and the hymn at the Catacombs. In all the other Damasene uses of "here," he attaches a verb that clearly refers to burials, most often a form of the Latin verb *iaceo*, "to lie" (e.g., "Here lies Festus," "Here lie holy confessors"). The Catacombs poem has no such verb. There is, in fact, nothing in the language of this hymn that can be shown to refer either to relics or burials; rather, "abided" is a verb more appropriate to the living than the dead.[74] This is a significant divergence from the pattern in the alleged parallels

---

72. Henry Chadwick, "St Peter and St Paul in Rome," 36–37; Victor Saxer, "Früher Märtyrerkult in Rom," 53–54. The translation theory is now standard fare in tourist guidebooks.

73. They are collected in Antonio Ferrua, *Epigrammata Damasiana* (SSAC 2; Vatican City: Pontificio Istituto di Archeologia Cristiana, 1942), 81–215.

74. Bruno Luiselli, "In margine al problema della traslazione delle ossa di Pietro e Paolo," *MEFRA* 98.2 (1986): 844–46. In one other place Damasus does use the verb "abide" in a metaphorical sense within a funerary context. However, there the verb is in the pres-

cited above, and it must be taken into account. It shows that the other Damasene uses of "here" are more problematic than they might initially appear and should not be determinative for the interpretation of the Catacombs poem. The divergence, rather, suggests that "here" may have a different meaning in this instance than it does in the other poems of Damasus, a point to which I will return momentarily. To the questionable nature of this interpretation of "here," we must add the significant weaknesses of the underlying 258 translation theory, which I have elucidated previously. We are left with a reading of this poem based on the dubious theory of Duchesne and supported by problematic epigraphical parallels—a reading that I would argue is not tenable.

The second traditional interpretation depends heavily on the word "abided" (*habitasse*). Because the overwhelming use of this verb relates to living persons, Paul and Peter must have "abided" at this location during their lifetimes. Damasus is reflecting the story that the apostles had a residence here during their Roman ministries.[75] Proponents of this theory present the following narrative: During the Valerianic persecution (note the importance again of the year 258), Christians may have been barred from the burial sites on the Ostian Road and at the Vatican. Thus, they went to the Catacombs to venerate the apostles. They could not honor the apostles where their bodies lay, so they did the next best thing and honored them at a site believed to be a former place of residence. As support for the theory, proponents point to the wall of one of the mausolea attached to the Basilica of the Apostles, where someone in the fourth century inscribed *domus Petri* ("house of Peter"). They view this as a reflection of a much older tradition that Peter had actually lived there.[76] Additionally, according to Acts 28, Paul arrived at Rome via the port at Puteoli, near Naples. He would have gone north and joined the Appian Road (at Sinuessa) to travel the rest of the way to Rome. Luke specifically mentions that Paul was met by Roman Christians at the Forum of Appius and the Three Taverns, two sites south of Rome along the Appian Road (Acts 28:13–15).[77] Thus, he could have stayed at the site of the Catacombs as he

---

ent tense, and the poem opens with the clear indication, "Here is the tomb of the martyr" (*Epigr.* 32.1–4). There is no mention of a tomb in the Catacombs poem, so this potential parallel also breaks down.

75. Luiselli, "In margine al problema della traslazione," 843–54; A. S. Barnes, *The Martyrdom of St. Peter and St. Paul* (London: Oxford University Press, 1933), 33–59; Cullmann, *Peter*, 133–35; J. M. C. Toynbee, "The Shrine of St. Peter and Its Setting," *JRS* 43 (1953): 13–14; Delehaye, *Origines du culte*, 265–68; La Piana, "The Tombs of Peter and Paul," 63–65.

76. Joseph Wilpert, "*Domus Petri*," *RQ* 26 (1912): 117–22; Anton de Waal, "Zu Wilperts *Domus Petri*," *RQ* 26 (1912): 123–32.

77. Pervo, *Acts*, 677 n. 73.

drew closer to the city. The second-century *Acts of Peter* (*Acta Pet.* 6) states that Peter took the same route from Puteoli to Rome, thus creating a potential connection between the Appian Road and both apostles.

This reading of Damasus's poem is equally problematic. A collection of possible references to the apostles' traveling along the Appian Road is not evidence for an apostolic stay there. As for *domus Petri*, it is hardly surprising to find a fourth-century inscription to one of the apostles on a site that had been a center for the apostolic cult for over a century and, by that time, featured a basilica in honor of Peter and Paul. It may tell us something about fourth-century piety, but it is going well beyond the evidence to use it as support for a hypothetical reconstruction of the historical circumstances of the first century. The final and most damaging challenge to this interpretation comes from the archaeological record, which indicates an absence of domestic buildings at the site in the time of the apostles.[78] There simply was no house here that the apostles could have inhabited in the middle of the first century C.E.

Ultimately, the relic-translation theory and the theory that the apostles had lived at this site share several weaknesses. Both start with the assumption that the physical presence of the apostles at the Catacombs, in one form or another, must necessarily lie behind the institution of cultic practices at this site. However, as we saw with the *Burying of the Martyrs*, body-less cults were no stranger to Rome and the Appian Road. Thus, there is no reason to assume from the outset that bodies or relics were a requirement for the apostolic cult here. Furthermore, both readings are highly speculative and based on hypotheses about what *might* have happened in the first century and during the Valerianic persecution in the third century. There is no external evidence, however, to support these speculations. Finally, the proponents of both focus on only the first two lines of the poem, ending with the reference to Peter and Paul. In doing so, they omit some important details from the later verses that are critical for a proper understanding of this hymn.

I propose an alternative reading, one that more adequately incorporates the entirety of text and fits with the historical context of Damasus's episcopate. Beginning with the initial "here," the bishop is trumpeting the importance of the city of Rome *as a whole*. The poem is not a recollection of a relic translation or an apostolic apartment at the Catacombs but a polemical work produced to

---

78. Brandenburg, *Ancient Churches of Rome*, 68. Brandenburg adds that the apostolic cult at the Catacombs "might be explained in the tradition of the apocryphal Acts, whose legendary narration, probably going back to the second century AD, relates that this is where the apostles lived." However, he does not cite a source for this claim, and I am unaware of any apocryphal stories that refer to a shared apostolic residence in Rome.

assert that the apostles now have a stronger association with Rome than they do with their homelands in the East. In composing this poem, Damasus identifies himself as the great patron of the apostolic cult in an effort to solidify his own position as bishop in a period when Rome was becoming increasingly marginalized in relation to the great Christian centers of the East.

If we look back at the poem as a whole, we notice that the initial "here" is only one of many spatial markers in these verses:

> *Here* the saints abided previously. You ought to know this, whoever you are, you who seek equally the names of Peter and Paul. *The East* sent the disciples, which we acknowledge freely. On account of the merit of their blood and having followed Christ *through the stars*, they have traveled *to the bosom of heaven* and *the kingdom of the righteous*. *Rome* capably deserved to watch over its own citizens. Damasus records these things for your praise, O new stars." (*Epigr.* 20, emphasis added)

The focus of the text is location and movement, and the opening "here" serves to orient the reader within a wider narrative about the history of the apostles. The East sent the apostles to Rome ("here"), where they "abided" for a time. Rome "deserved" the honor of welcoming them, but Paul and Peter then moved on from "here" after their deaths to the heavenly realms, where they now shine. "Here" was a stage along the apostles' journey. It was a critical sojourn for the church—particularly the Roman church—but it was still only one part of the story.

The initial "here" has not only spatial but also polemical force, for Damasus uses it to set up a contrast between "here" (Rome) and "there" (the East).[79] The bishop recognizes the geographical origins of Paul and Peter: "The East sent the disciples, which we acknowledge freely."[80] He concedes that they had come from "there," yet the most important parts of the story occurred "here." It was "here" that both apostles had "abided" as co-ministers of the gospel. "Here" was the meeting place of the temporal and spiritual realms, the point from which the apostles had departed on their heavenly voyages. Damasus then closes the poem with an explicit reference to Rome and its special relationship to Peter and Paul, thus making the city as a whole the clear point of emphasis. The reference to the East serves as a foil to the cen-

---

79. In the final stages of producing this book, I came upon an article by Noële Maurice-Denis Boulet, "À propos des fouilles de Saint-Pierre," *RSR* 34 (1947): 405–6. Boulet suggests that "here" could signify Rome but does not develop this point. The arguments that I present for this interpretation were developed independently of Boulet's work.

80. This expression parallels a line from another poem of Damasus from the Appian Road: "Here lie holy confessors, whom Greece sent" (*Epigr.* 16.7).

tral story that the bishop wants to tell, and this is a story about Rome, not just the Catacombs.

Reading "here" as Rome also makes sense in the context of Damasus's own ecclesiastical and political situation. Being bishop of "here" would have raised Damasus's standing vis-à-vis the bishops of the East at a time when the bishops of Rome had lost significant ground compared to their Eastern colleagues. There are many indications of this shift over the course of the fourth century. The year 324 brought the news that the emperor Constantine was moving the eastern capital of the empire from Nicomedia[81] to Byzantium, a city that he would rebuild, name after himself (Constantinople), and establish as the new, single capital of the empire. As Sozomen Scholasticus recounts the event, "He populated it with men of rank and their households, summoned from Old Rome and from other nations.... He named it Constantinople and New Rome ... and established another great council, which is called the Senate, and endowed it with the same honors and privileges as that of Old Rome" (*Hist. eccl.* 2.3.4–6). Constantine also constructed there the Church of the Holy Apostles, thus giving the city its own apostolic monument. *Old Rome* on the Tiber was being replaced by this *New Rome* on the Bosporus, and the Roman bishops felt the impact of this.

When Constantine called the first ecumenical council in 325, he held it not in the West (where he had begun his political career), but in Nicea, across the water from his new Eastern capital. Bishop Sylvester I of Rome was not present, and his two representatives, the priests Vitus and Vincentius, seem to have had no impact on the proceedings. In 341, ninety-seven bishops gathered in Antioch for the dedication of the great church there. On this occasion they wrote a letter to Bishop Julius of Rome (337–352). They confirmed their respect for Rome as a center of apostolic teaching, but they also pointed out to Julius that Peter and Paul had been in Antioch before they had gone to Rome (Sozomen Scholasticus, *Hist. eccl.* 3.8.2–5). The implication was clear. Because Paul and Peter preached in Antioch before going to Rome, the Syrian city enjoyed preeminence. This letter marked a direct challenge to any Roman claim to primacy over the Eastern cities based on an association with the apostles.[82]

---

81. Upon the establishment of the Tetrarchy in 293 c.e., Diocletian (Augustus of the East) took Nicomedia as his capital, while his Caesar (Galerius) took Sirmium. In the West, Maximian (Augustus of the West) established his capital at Milan, while his Caesar (Constantius Chlorus) took Trier. Rome never again regained its former position as a capital of the empire.

82. Chadwick, "St Peter and St Paul in Rome," 35–36.

The waning influence of Rome came to light again in 381 during the episcopate of Damasus himself, for the First Council of Constantinople took place
without the presence or influence of Damasus. The presiding bishops came
from the East: Meletius of Antioch, succeeded by Gregory of Nazianzus and
then Nectarius of Constantinople. Damasus's degree of alienation from the
proceedings is illustrated by the fact that he considered both Meletius and
Gregory illegitimate bishops of their respective cities, yet the Eastern bishops
at the council paid no heed to Damasus's protests on this point.[83] Canon 3 of
the council did grant Rome the preeminent position among Christian sees, but
this was merely on paper. The accompanying designation of Constantinople
as the "New Rome" was a truer indicator of the weakening Roman position.
Damasus tried to reassert himself by calling a council in Rome in 382, but
the Eastern bishops refused to attend and instead sent only three envoys with
a letter stating the decisions of the council the previous year (Theodoret of
Cyrus, *Hist. eccl.* 5.9). Damasus was facing the reality that the primary centers of Christian theology were in the Greek-speaking East, while Rome was
increasingly isolated in the West. In response to this situation—and in particular, in refutation of the letter of 341 from the bishops at Antioch—Damasus
produced this carefully crafted poem for the Catacombs. He recognizes the
importance of the East but reasserts Rome's primacy as the location of Paul
and Peter's true citizenship. The claims of any other city to the apostles were
categorically inferior to those of Rome. The poem, therefore, is at once both
explicitly pro-Roman and anti-Eastern.

Damasus's message here, that Rome's claim to the apostles supercedes any
prior claim by their region of origin, recalls the ancient Roman tradition of the
evocatio deorum ("calling-out of the gods"). The belief was that deities could
be coaxed to leave their temples in other cities and come to dwell in Rome.
The successful *evocatio* doomed these other cities to being conquered, because
they had lost their source of divine protection. In Roman lore this process was
seen as critical for the expansion of Roman power. Livy's *History of Rome*, for
example, tells the story of the conquest of Veii in 396 B.C.E. Roman forces had
besieged the city for some time and were on the verge of a final assault. Before
the attack the Roman commander, Camillus, called out to Juno, the patron

---

83. Norman P. Tanner, *Decrees of the Ecumenical Councils* (2 vols.; Washington, D.C.:
Georgetown University Press, 1990), 1:1–4, 21–30; R. P. C. Hanson, *The Search for the
Christian Doctrine of God* (Edinburgh: T&T Clark, 1988), 805–12. Damasus supported a
rival bishop in Antioch named Paulinus. In Constantinople he supported an Alexandrian
named Maximus on the basis of canon 15 of Nicea, which stated that a bishop could not
move from one city to another. Prior to being elected in Constantinople, Gregory had been
ordained bishop of Sasima, a backwater town in Cappadocia.

goddess of the city, "You, Queen Juno, who now dwell in Veii, I pray that you follow us the victors into our city, which will soon be yours as well, where a temple worthy of your greatness awaits you." After Veii fell, Juno's statue was brought without incident, as if with the aid of the goddess herself, to her new temple on the Aventine Hill in Rome (*Urb. cond.* 5.21–22). Like Veii, the conquests of Falerii, Isaura Vetus, Carthage, and many other cities were ascribed in the ancient sources to the removal of the deities.[84] Even the fall of Jerusalem in 70 C.E. may have been preceded by the *evocatio* of the God of Israel by the Roman general Titus.[85]

Damasus appeals to this *evocatio* tradition and claims that Peter and Paul had left another place, the East, and come to Rome to dwell. They were considered Roman citizens and, therefore, in some sense Roman property. Their powers of patronage and protection were now believed to reside primarily in Rome, as we saw earlier in this chapter. Damasus chooses to commemorate the city's claim to the apostles at the Catacombs, because it was *the* joint center of the apostolic cult in Rome; however, the status granted by possessing the transplanted apostles applied to the city as a whole. All of Rome's Christians, and especially its bishop, were in some regard superior to their counterparts in the East, because the apostles had left the East and established their citizenship in Rome.

Damasus's concerns were not limited to Eastern bishops. He also had to contend with ecclesiastical opponents within Rome itself, and this poem further served to solidify his position in the city. Conflict and controversy had surrounded the election of Damasus in 366. Many adherents of Liberius, the previous bishop, supported a deacon named Ursinus as Liberius's successor.

---

84. Gabriella Gustafsson, Evocatio deorum: *Historical and Mythical Interpretations of Ritualised Conquests in the Expansion of Ancient Rome* (AUU.HR 16; Stockholm: Elanders Gotab, 2000). After I completed this section on Damasus and the *evocatio* tradition, I discovered that Henry Chadwick had raised a similar idea in "Pope Damasus and the Peculiar Claim of Rome to St. Peter and St. Paul," in *Neotestamentica et Patristica: Eine Freundesgabe, Herrn Professor Dr. Oscar Cullmann zu seinem 60. Geburtstag überreicht* (NovTSup 6; Leiden: Brill, 1962), 314–16. My argument here is much more developed than Chadwick's and does not depend on his work.

85. John S. Kloppenborg, "*Evocatio Deorum* and the Date of Mark," *JBL* 124 (2005): 434–47. Jodi Magness ("The Arch of Titus and the Fate of the God of Israel," *JJS* 59 [2008]: 204–6) has argued that the spoils from Jerusalem shown on the Arch of Titus represent the Israelite God that had left Jerusalem (cf. Ezek 10:18–19) and been brought to Rome as a captive. The presence of these cultic objects made Rome a pilgrimage destination for some of the rabbis, according to David Noy, "Rabbi Aqiba Comes to Rome: A Jewish Pilgrimage in Reverse?" in *Pilgrimage in Graeco-Roman and Early Christian Antiquity: Seeing the Gods* (ed. Jaś Elsner and Ian Rutherford; Oxford: Oxford University Press, 2005), 373–85.

Although Damasus was elected, the supporters of Ursinus also consecrated their candidate as bishop. Violence erupted between the factions, and the emperor Valentinian I had to intervene to stop a riot that had lasted for several days and resulted in 137 deaths. At the end of the day, Damasus had more powerful political connections (and perhaps more political savvy), so the emperor recognized his election and banished Ursinus to Cologne. Nonetheless, the position of Damasus remained tenuous.[86]

Damasus endeavored to unify the faithful by spending large amounts of money on monuments and producing hymns honoring the heroes of Christianity[87] He presented himself as the great patron of the cult of the martyrs and sought to rally the Christians of Rome around this illustrious, shared heritage. (See, e.g., fig. 2.8, a gold glass fragment on which Damasus appears alongside Paul, Peter, and Pastor.[88]) This poem on the apostles contributed to his propaganda campaign. He reminded the Romans of the historical legacy of their "own citizens," which was superior to any claims made by "the East." "Here" Peter and Paul gave their lives and followed Christ to the "kingdom of the righteous." As the leader of the Roman church, he now stood as their successor and defended the faith for which they had died. The city's Christians should rally around him when they gathered to honor the memory of the

---

86. Variations of the story appear in Ammianus Marcellinus (*Res gestae* 27.3), Rufinus of Aquileia (*Hist. eccl.* 2.10), and *Lib. pontif.* 39. MacMullen (*Second Church*, 86) suggests that this riot may have taken place at the Catacombs, which would make it an appropriate location for a monument to reconciliation.

87. Trout, "Damasus," 517–36; Marianne Sághy, "*Scinditur in partes populus*: Pope Damasus and the Martyrs of Rome," *EMEur* 9.3 (2000): 273–87; Charles Pietri, "Damase évêque de Rome," in *Saecularia Damasiana: Atti del Convegno internazionale per il XVI centenario della morte di papa Damaso I (1984)* (Vatican City: Pontificio Istituto di Archeologia Cristiana, 1986), 29–58. Nicola Denzey has been harshly critical of Damasus as the patron of saints' cults, arguing that his efforts to unify the Roman church involved the suppression of powerful female patrons in the city. See *The Bone Gatherers: The Lost Worlds of Early Christian Women* (Boston: Beacon, 2007), 176–204.

88. Damasus also composed a separate hymn specifically in honor of Paul, which gives a brief history of the apostle's life and concludes, "In these verses briefly, I confess, I Damasus have attempted to show your triumphs, most blessed doctor and saint" (*Epigr.* 1.25–26). The identity of the figured identified as Pastor is not certain. There was a presbyter in Rome named Pastor who died ca. 160 c.e. (feast day July 26). He is credited with founding the Basilica of St. Pudentiana and, according to tradition, was a brother of Pius I. However, it must also be noted that the *Shepherd of Hermas* (*Hermae Pastor* in Latin) was a very popular text in Rome. An image from the cemetery of Callistus, for example, reflects a scene from this text (*DACL* 6:2286). It is possble, then, that this *Pastor* is being pictured here alongside the bishop and the apostolic martyrs.

Fig. 2.8. Gold glass fragment showing Damasus with Pastor, Peter, and Paul.
In the Vatican Museums. Courtesy of the Vatican Museums.

apostles in this sacred space.[89] Just as this poem was overtly pro-Roman, so
was it also pro-Damasene.

The poem of Damasus was not a reference to the temporary burial of apostolic relics on the Appian Road. Instead, it was a declaration of the apostles'
association with all of Christian Rome. Paul and Peter had left behind their
Eastern identities to become Romans. This claim was meant to elevate the
position of Rome and its bishop at a time when the center of Christian theol-

_____

89. Kate Cooper ("The Martyr, the *Matrona* and the Bishop," 312) has argued that
Damasus is particularly focused on bringing into the fold the Novatianist sect, which she
thinks may have controlled the Catacombs in the fourth century. Cooper was not the first
to associate the Novatianists with the site. For the theory that the Novatianists founded
the site, see Alfons Maria Schneider, "Die Memoria Apostolorum an der Via Appia,"
NAWG.PHK 3 (1951): 1–15; Leo Kunibert Mohlberg, "Historisch-kritische Bemerkungen
zum Ursprung der sogenannten 'Memoria Apostolorum' an der Appischen Strasse," in
Colligere Fragmenta: Festschrift Alban Dold zum 70. Geburtstag am 7.7.1952 (Beuron in
Hohenzollern: Beuroner Kunstverlag, 1952), 52–74; Jérôme Carcopino, *De Pythagores aux
Apôtres: Études sur la conversion du monde romain* (Paris: Flammarion, 1956), 342–59. Cf.
Kjaergaard, "Memoria Apostolorum," 69, who sees a Novatianist connection with the site
as unlikely.

ogy and ecclesiastical power had shifted to the East. Damasus was attempting to refute the claims of the bishops at Antioch and reclaim some of Rome's former influence by asserting his city's ancient and intimate ties to the two greatest apostles. His position as primary patron of their cult would raise his own status vis-à-vis both the bishops of the East and those within Rome who were opposing him. The Catacombs, the center of the shared apostolic cult in Rome, was the place he chose to monumentalize his statement.

Our final source in this group is the *Passion of St. Sebastian*, a fifth-century account of a martyrdom that supposedly occurred in 287/288. In the story Sebastian is a Roman soldier whose good conduct earns him favor in the eyes of Diocletian. The emperor promotes him to captain among the elite Pretorian Guard in Rome, but Sebastian harbors a secret. He is a Christian and does not shy away from aiding other Christians who face execution at the hands of the Roman government. Diocletian becomes aware of Sebastian's sentiments and activities, which he considers treasonous, and condemns him to death by being shot with arrows. Sebastian survives this ordeal and finally dies by being beaten to death with clubs. The executioners deny him the dignity of proper burial by throwing his body into a sewer. Soon after, the martyr appears in a dream to a pious matron named Lucina and asks her to bury him "in the Catacombs … next to the remains [*vestigia*] of the apostles" (*Pass. Sebast.* 88). It must first be said that the reference to Lucina signals that this is a later work of pious fiction. Lucina is a stock character in martyrdom accounts from late antiquity. Over the course of three centuries, she appears in numerous stories as the one who comes forward to care for the bodies of the dead.[90] The story of Lucina and her dramatic visitation by Sebastian, therefore, belongs to the realm of hagiography. It tells us nothing about the situation at the Catacombs in the third century but instead reflects only the imagination of the fifth-century author.

But what exactly were these "remains" that this later author places at the Catacombs? The term *vestigia* referred to footprints or some other trace that a person had left behind. The use of *vestigia* for a person's physical remains is virtually unknown.[91] For physical relics, authors of martyrdom and hagiographical accounts overwhelmingly preferred *reliquiae* (relics) or *pignora*

---

90. "If all were historical she [Lucina] must have lived a long life of about 300 years spent in devotion to the care of the departed" (Chadwick, "St Peter and St Paul in Rome," 40). The fictitious nature of the stories about Lucina (and her near double Lucilla) is also discussed by Cooper, "The Martyr, the *Matrona* and the Bishop," 308; Denzey, *Bone Gatherers*, xi–xviii. Denzey maintains that such stories still have value for social historians, because "fictive characters like Lucina might conceal real women … who inspired these narrative re-creations" (xvi).

91. Luiselli, "In margine," 848–52.

(pledges).[92] In the context of the *Passion of St. Sebastian, vestigia* could reflect the tradition that both Peter and Paul had entered Rome via the Appian Road,[93] or it could point to any other trace of the apostles, including secondary relics. The church of Santa Francesca Romana (formerly Santa Maria Nova) in Rome, for example, claims to have the very stones on which Peter and Paul knelt when they prayed to strike down Simon Magus during their showdown in Rome (*Pass. Pet. Paul.* 56). When the apostles dropped to their knees, they left impressions in the stones that would constitute *vestigia*. These stones are now displayed in the wall of the church (*Mirabil.* 1.7). By the time the *Passion of St. Sebastian* was written in the fifth century, it is very possible that secondary relics had been brought from the Vatican and the Ostian Road to the Catacombs. The presence of any object of this kind would constitute the "remains of the apostles," thus making the Catacombs a desirable location for Sebastian's burial.

The only relics in the story belong to Sebastian, and this fact brings us to another important point, namely, how we should interpret this text in light of its *function*. The *Passion of St. Sebastian* was produced as a foundation myth justifying the cult of Sebastian at the Catacombs. By the early fifth century, Christians had begun to associate Sebastian with this site, as an inscription from the time of Bishop Innocent I (401–417) testifies: "In the time of the holy bishop Innocent, Proclinus and Ursus, presbyters of the Byzantine title, offered this votive to the holy martyr Sebastian."[94] This votive must have been placed in or very near the Basilica of the Apostles. Soon after, bishop Sixtus III (432–440) "built a monastery at the Catacombs" (*Lib. pontif.* 46), the first such monastery in the outskirts of Rome. The original dedication is not recorded, but it may have been built in honor of Sebastian, for Bishop Nicholas I (858–867) later renovated and rededicated this monastery "at the Catacombs in the cemetery of Sebastian, the holy martyr of Christ" (*Lib. pontif.* 107). A cult of this martyr, therefore, was developing at the Catacombs by the early fifth century, when the *Passion* was produced. The story of placing Sebastian's relics next to the "remains" of Paul and Peter served to create continuity between him and the apostles. They were co-martyrs, honored side by side at a location with strong apostolic associations going back to the third century, the

---

92. Thomas Head, "The Cult of the Saints and Their Relics," *On-line Reference Book for Medieval Studies*; online: http://www.the-orb.net/encyclop/religion/hagiography/cult. htm.

93. See above, p. 99. In the Latin version of the *Martyrdom of Ignatius*, for example, Ignatius considers landing at Puteoli, where Paul had landed on his way to Rome (Acts 28:13), as proceeding in the "footsteps [*vestigia*] of Paul the apostle" (*Mart. Ign.* 5.3).

94. Antonio Bosio, *Roma sotterranea* (Rome: Facciotti, 1632), 177.

same period in which (the author would have us believe) Sebastian was buried there. Linking this martyr with the apostles granted legitimacy to his emerging cult on the Appian Road. The *Passion of St. Sebastian*, therefore, is a story about the interment of Sebastian's relics in an apostolic cult space, not in an apostolic burial ground.

The *Burying of the Martyrs*, the poem of Damasus, and the *Passion of St. Sebastian* reflect popular associations between the apostles and the Catacombs. Commemoration of Paul and Peter took place here as early as the third century, making this a desirable site at which Damasus could honor them jointly as Rome's "own citizens." Even another martyr such as Sebastian is presented as desiring burial in this space set aside in their honor. On the issue of apostolic relics at the site, though, all three sources are ultimately silent. They provide no indication that the presence of the bodies of Peter and Paul (dead or alive) lay at the origin of the connection between this site and the apostles.

2.4.2. The Sixth-Century Witnesses

In the sixth century, stories at last appear that place apostolic relics at the Catacombs. We have three such texts, all claiming to recount events from earlier centuries. As we will see, there is significant variation among them on issues such as chronology, yet they all assert that apostolic relics were at the Catacombs at some point.

The *Book of Pontiffs* includes two references to the Catacombs and the bodies of the apostles. In the entry for Bishop Cornelius (251–253), the author recounts,

> In his time, at the request of a certain matron, he [Cornelius] took up the bodies of the apostles saints Peter and Paul from the Catacombs at night. In fact, first of all blessed Lucina took the body of St. Paul and put it on her estate on the Ostian Road close to the place where he was beheaded; the blessed bishop Cornelius took the body of St. Peter and put it close to the place where he was crucified ... on the Vatican. (*Lib. pontif.* 22, modified from Davis)

This passage refers explicitly to the translation of the bodies of the apostles. With the approval of the bishop, Lucina moved Paul's body from the Appian Road to her own property on the Ostian Road. The timing is clear: the apostles' bodies lay in the Catacombs in the early 250s, but Cornelius handed Paul over to Lucina and moved Peter himself between 251 and 253. This move *from* the Catacombs obviously conflicts with Duchesne's theory of a move *to* the Catacombs in 258, but Duchesne simply dismisses the account in the *Book of*

Pontiffs as an "obvious anachronism."[95] His disregard for the historical nature of this passage is probably warranted, for as with the *Passion of St. Sebastian*, the mention of Lucina here suggests that this story belongs in the category of hagiography.[96]

Later in the *Book of Pontiffs*, the author links the Damasus inscription with these pre-Cornelian burials: "At the Catacombs, the place where lay the bodies of the apostles St Peter and Paul, he [Damasus] adorned with verses the actual tablet at the place where the holy bodies lay. He searched for and discovered the bodies of many saints, and also proclaimed their [acts] in verses" (*Lib. pontif.* 39, Davis). The author claims that the poem of Damasus marks the place from which Cornelius had removed the bodies of Peter and Paul. In this case the myth of Cornelius and Lucina leads to the reinterpretation of the Damasus poem, a misinterpretation that continues to survive but that I have attempted above to correct. Contributors to much later additions to the *Book of Pontiffs* perpetuated this translation legend. The entries for bishops Leo III (795–816) and Nicholas I (858–867) also refer to the Catacombs as the site where the apostolic relics had once been kept (*Lib. pontif.* 98; 107). Behind all these later references lay the fictional Cornelius and Lucina story about an alleged translation at the time of the earliest *triclia* inscriptions. This reflects the perspective of the sixth century and later, when the foundation of this sacred space had to be anchored in and justified by the former presence of relics, even if they had subsequently been moved.

Both the Latin *Passion of the Holy Apostles Peter and Paul* and the Greek *Acts of the Holy Apostles Peter and Paul* (introduced in chapter 1) assert the existence of the apostles' relics on the Appian Road. According to these nearly identical accounts, following the death of Nero, Christians from the East[97] took the bodies of Paul and Peter with the intention of carrying them back to their home regions. As they departed, a violent earthquake occurred. The alarmed Romans rushed out of the city and caught up with those carrying the bodies "in a place that is called the Catacombs on the Appian Road at the third milestone from the city." They seized the relics and placed them there "until they built the places in which they would lay their bodies." It was as if Paul and Peter had intervened with a powerful sign to prevent their translation.[98]

---

95. Duchesne, *Liber pontificalis*, 1:cvii.

96. Cf. Holloway, *Constantine and Rome*, 153–54, who accepts this story about Cornelius as historically viable.

97. The Latin text calls them "Greeks." Latin authors often used this as a general designation for Greek-speaking residents of the Eastern empire.

98. In the medieval period, it was widely believed that saints could prevent the translation of their bodies by causing storms or earthquakes. See Patrick J. Geary, *Furta Sacra: Thefts of Relics in the Central Middle Ages* (rev. ed.; Princeton: Princeton University Press,

With great pomp the Romans then carried the relics to their permanent locations on the Ostian Road and at the Vatican. The Latin *Passion* specifies that the bodies remained for a year and seven months at the Catacombs, while the period was a year and six months according to the Greek *Acts* (*Pass. Pet. Paul.* 66 [quoted]; *Acta Pet. Paul.* 87).

These sources push the connection between the apostles and the Catacombs very early. Nero died in 68 C.E.—within a few years of the traditional dates of the deaths of the apostles—and the narratives both move directly from his death to the attempt to take the bodies to the East. The implication seems to be that in the first century the bodies of Paul and Peter were taken from Rome, intercepted, buried on the Appian Road, and then later moved to their permanent locations. This is the earliest source to link the apostles to the Catacombs in the first century, but this striking claim received support soon after from Bishop Gregory I.

In Gregory's correspondence with the empress Constantina from 594, as we saw in the previous chapter, the bishop denied her request for the head or some other body part of Paul. He responded with a story of the terrible fate of someone who had disturbed the area around Paul's tomb. He also expressed disbelief at the practice of the Greeks, who had no qualms about desecrating tombs and relocating bodies (as the Greek empress was asking him to do). It was, after all, Greek monks who had attempted to take bones indiscriminately from the field near Paul's sepulcher and carry them home as relics. This was not the first instance of such scandalous behavior, according to Gregory. The most egregious example concerned the remains of Paul and Peter themselves:

> But what shall I say about the bodies of the blessed apostles, when it is certain that at the time of their martyrdom, believers came from the East to recover their bodies, as if they were their own citizens? The bodies were taken as far as the second milestone[99] of Rome, and were deposited in a place that is called the Catacombs. But when their whole multitude came together and tried to remove them from there, the violence of the thunder and the lightning so terrified them and put them to flight through excessive

1990), 108–14; Heinrich Fichtenau, "Zum Reliquienwesen im früheren Mittelalter," *MIÖG* 60 (1952): 73.

99. The fact that Gregory places this event at the second instead of the third milestone is not significant. In different periods, there were various points of reference from which the Romans calculated distances on the roads leading out of the city. In the Republican period, the Servian Wall was the primary marker, but Augustus replaced it with his Miliarium Aureum. By the time of Gregory, the Aurelian Wall may or may not have been the starting point, so some variation is to be expected (Carlos F. Noreña, e-mail message to author, November 29, 2006).

fear, that they did not presume on any account to try such a thing again. But
then the Romans went out there and raised the bodies of those who deserved
it, by their piety towards the Lord, and put them in the places where they are
now buried. (*Ep.* 4.30, Martyn)

Gregory's account is comparable to the Latin *Passion* and the Greek *Acts* on
two significant points.

First, Gregory agrees that the bodies of the apostles lay at the Catacombs
at a very early date. In fact, he eliminates the chronological ambiguity present
in the Latin *Passion* and the Greek *Acts*. The Appian Road burials took place
not just some time after Nero's death but precisely "at the time of their martyrdom." This would place the bones of the apostles in the Catacombs before
the year 70 c.e. Gregory does not specify how much time passed between the
initial burial of the bodies and the attempt to move them to the East, nor does
he say how much later the Romans came and took the remains to "the places
where they are now buried." Did he think that all this happened right after the
martyrdoms of Paul and Peter? Or did he believe that decades, or even centuries, may have elapsed? The text seems to suggest the former, but Gregory is
not explicit on the timing of the subsequent events. He is clear, however, on
the fact that Christians from the East lay Peter and Paul to rest in the Catacombs in the immediate aftermath of the apostles' deaths.

Second, Gregory also includes a story about a miraculous sign that prevented Greeks from taking the relics from the Romans. His reference to the
disrespect for burials among those in the East, supported by the account of the
unscrupulous Greek monks, set the polemical context for this story about the
apostolic relics. These "believers came from the East to recover their bodies,
as if they were their own citizens" (emphasis added).[100] This qualifying clause
recalls the poem of Damasus, which identifies Paul and Peter as Rome's "own
citizens." Christians from the East, says Gregory, thought they could still
claim the apostles as their own, but they were mistaken. The terrible storm
that scared away the crowd is presented as an act of supernatural, apostolic
intervention. The citizenship of these martyrs now lay in Rome. They were no
longer Easterners, and their bodies belonged in the West.

Not every detail is identical between Gregory's letter and the accounts in
the Greek *Acts* and Latin *Passion*, yet these stories are quite similar. Both place
the apostolic remains on the Appian Road at a very early date, thus legitimiz-
ing the claims of this site as Christian sacred space. The Catacombs had not
been merely a temporary repository for the relics; it had been the original
apostolic burial site. These stories also explicitly settled the dispute between

100. Cf. Mark 6:29; Matt 14:12, where John's disciples recover his body for burial.

Rome and the East over Paul and Peter. The believers from the East were the first to take their bodies, which they believed to be theirs by right. However, a storm or earthquake stopped the transfer of the relics to the East. This allowed the rightful claimants, the Romans, to guard the bodies of their own from desecration by the Greeks. Rome, not the East, was most sacred to the apostles, and their remains sanctified their new home.[101]

For previous scholars, the question of relics has been the guiding issue in the establishment of the Catacombs as a sacred site. I have argued for an alternative approach. A belief in the one-time presence of the apostolic relics cannot be demonstrated until the sixth century, when the Christian obsession with relics was in full vigor. Given the prominence in that period of a relic-centered piety among many Christians, it is easy to understand why relics would lie at the heart of foundation myths produced at that time. Nonetheless, these stories tell us little about the Pauline and apostolic cults in earlier centuries. Relics were not a necessary condition for the establishment of martyr shrines in the third century. Some locations, like the Ostian Road, did claim to have relics attached to them from an early period. However, Rome and many other places also had "body-less" cult sites, like the location for the cult of Cyprian very near the Catacombs. In fact, merely invoking the name of a saint was sufficient for rendering a site holy to that saint.[102] The evidence—or, rather, the lack thereof—suggests that such was the case at the Catacombs. Only in the sixth century did authors feel compelled to imagine apostolic burials at the origin of the cult on the Appian Road. The one-time contact with the relics guaranteed the continuing sanctity of the space.

---

101. An addendum to the Syriac *Acts of Sharbil* provides yet another rendition of a similar story. In this version, however, the earthquake occurred at the precise moment that the assembly from the East began to remove the bones. They replaced the relics immediately, and the Romans invited them to stay in the city. See William Cureton, trans., *Ancient Syriac Documents Relative to the Earliest Establishment of Christianity in Edessa and the Neighbouring Countries* (London: Williams & Norgate, 1864), 61–62. I have confined this text to a note because the date is uncertain, the account does not mention the Catacombs, and the chronology within the text is very confused. It is interesting to note that in this Eastern version those who tried to take the bodies are nonetheless treated well by the Romans, and there is no hint of Roman supremacy based on the citizenship of the apostles.

102. Yasin, *Saints and Church Spaces*, 239. Moreover, she has shown that the function of a space as a Christian worship site was sometimes sufficient to render it sacred. Relics or even invocations of a saint were not always required to justify a site's sanctity (34–44).

CONCLUSION

The Catacombs was the second most important site for the cult of Paul in Rome. As early as the mid-third century, Christians gathered here to honor Paul along with Peter, the two greatest martyrs of the Roman church. Popular veneration in the *triclia* took the form of commemorative banquets and appeals to the apostles as martyr-patrons. As was the case on the Ostian Road, Constantine's construction of a basilica allowed the cult a more prominent spatial presence, which was further extended by the addition of mausolea for privileged burials. The impetus for the establishment of this sacred site remains somewhat obscure. Scholarly arguments for the physical presence of the apostles, while alive or dead, are not supported by any sources prior to the sixth century. Although these later authors use the relic stories to justify the foundation of the Catacombs site, they also incorporate a strong anti-Eastern polemic. The possession of the martyrs' burials is proof that Rome, not the East, is now the true home of the apostles. In this regard, authors such as Gregory I echo the sentiments expressed two centuries later by Damasus in his hymn at the Catacombs. Paul and Peter are presented as thoroughly Roman, the founding figures of the spiritual capital of the West. On account of their abiding presence and the observance of their cult in this sacred space at the Catacombs, the martyr-patrons continued to grant ecclesiastical legitimacy and preeminence to Rome.

PART 2
THE EXPANSION OF THE CULT OUTSIDE ROME

3
THE SPREAD OF THE PAULINE CULT IN LATIN EUROPE

The cults of Christian saints typically had particular geographical centers. These locations were linked to key events in the lives or deaths of the saints and became focal points for veneration practices. Cults, however, were not confined by geography. Through a variety of means, Christians could transfer the sanctifying influence of a particular figure to new locales. This process, known as *translocation*, extended the cult and granted status to a saint's new dwellings and locations. This phenomenon is widely attested in late antiquity, including in relation to the cult of Paul. The Romans declared their claim to Paul through their local shrines and practices, but other places in Latin-speaking Europe also associated themselves with the apostle. They did so by designating certain places as sacred to Paul, by securing relics or other cultic objects, by establishing local rituals that mirrored those in Rome, and by claiming spiritual patronage relationships with Paul. As a result, a growing number of holy sites appeared in the Latin West. The reception and appropriation of Paul in these settings was not uniform, however. It varied from region to region and even within regions. In some cases, Christians observed the cult of Paul as a means of promoting intimate ties with the Roman church. In other contexts, they distanced themselves from Rome by elevating their local saints as replacements for Paul. This chapter analyzes these developments in the Pauline cult in the city of Milan and the regions of Gaul and Spain.

3.1. AMBROSE OF MILAN AND THE PROMOTION OF THE PAULINE CULT IN THE "NEW ROME"

Milan was a relatively obscure settlement until the Roman imperial period. The city began to grow as a result of its strategic location on the main communication routes between Rome and the northern provinces of the empire. A major status change occurred in 293, when Diocletian reorganized the imperial administration into the Tetrarchy, with himself as Augustus (emperor) in the East and Maximian as Augustus in the West. Maximian made Milan his capital[1] and undertook a massive building program in the city. Milan, not Rome, was the Western political capital from 293 to 404, when the emperor Honorius moved the capital again, this time to Ravenna. In the ecclesiastical sphere, Milan also grew in prominence during the fourth century, particularly during the episcopate of Ambrose (374–397).[2] As I will demonstrate, Ambrose employed the cult of Paul and Peter as a means of increasing the fame of his city. Through liturgy and architecture, he sought to establish continuity between the Roman cult and the practices in Milan, thereby creating a city that was the legitimate heir to Rome not only politically but also spiritually.

A few words about Ambrose's career are essential for our analysis of his actions as bishop.[3] Ambrose did not start out with visions of a career in the church. His father had risen to become prefect of Gaul, one of the highest political positions in the imperial government. After his father's death, the young Ambrose moved with his family to Rome, where he received the elite education available to someone of his lofty social class. He studied law and gained the attention of certain government officials through his abilities in the courtroom. He was eventually appointed consular governor for the northern Italian region of Aemilia-Liguria and moved to its capital, Milan, in 370 to take up this new post. Ambrose became immensely popular with the people, but his career took a dramatic turn in 374.

Bishop Auxentius of Milan died in that year, and the stage was set for a vicious battle to fill the episcopal seat between the pro-Nicene and anti-Nicene factions in the city. The disagreement became so heated that Ambrose was summoned to the city's basilica to intervene in a riot. While he was attempting to restore order, someone shouted out, "Ambrose bishop!" The cry was repeated and gained force, and Ambrose found himself unexpectedly tapped to be the city's next bishop. He was not yet even baptized, so he was rushed through the remaining stages of his catechism, baptized, and consecrated bishop. He exercised his new role with great enthusiasm and became one of the most influential bishops of his day.

I want to highlight two key points from this story. First, Ambrose was groomed to be a politician, so he understood well the connection between

---

1. The Western Caesar (subemperor), Constantius Chlorus, was based in Trier. In the East, Diocletian established his capital at Nicomedia, while his Caesar, Galerius, chose Sirmium.

2. At that time Augustine of Hippo visited the city and was deeply influenced by Ambrose's preaching. It was in Milan that Augustine had his famous conversion experience.

3. My account of Ambrose's early career is based on John Moorhead, *Ambrose: Church and Society in the Late Roman World* (New York: Addison-Wesley Longman, 1999), 19–36.

creating the perception of legitimacy and being able to assert influence. Second, although he was born in Gaul, he spent many years living in Rome during a period when Christianity and the Pauline cult were on the rise. Thus, he was intimately familiar with the Roman traditions. Both these factors were to prove critical to his work as bishop in attempting to expand Milanese prestige and power by promoting the apostolic cult.

In 378, Ambrose preached a sermon in which he celebrated the June 29 feast of Peter and Paul in Milan. He highlighted the two apostles as bringers of daylight (i.e., the church) to those who had been in the dark (i.e., the synagogue). He declared, "Today on their very same birthday the Holy Spirit has cried out, saying, 'The day spews forth the word of the day.' That is to say, from the secret treasury of the heart they preach the faith of Christ. And doubly good is the day that has vomited forth the true light to us" (Ambrose, *Virginit.* 19.124).[4] Ambrose specified that the Holy Spirit's proclamation occurred "on their very same birthday," meaning on their traditional, shared anniversary of martyrdom. This day was "doubly good," and the Christians of Milan were commemorating the deaths of the two great heralds of daylight on their festival day, just as the Christians in Rome were doing.[5]

Tradition also ascribes to Ambrose the *Passion of the Apostles*, a hymn written for the feast of Peter and Paul. In the opening lines, the author states, "The passion of the apostles has consecrated this day of the year, displaying the noble triumph of Peter and the crown of Paul" (*Hymn.* 12.1–4). This initial declaration sets the work in a liturgical context. The bishop is addressing the Christian community in Milan, seeking to focus their attention on the cultic significance of the day. At the end of this hymn, Ambrose directs the audience's focus specifically toward Rome: "Around the circuit of so great a city a streaming throng makes its way. Celebrated on three roads is the feast of the sacred martyrs. One would think that the whole world is coming forth." The closing stanzas then hail Rome as the "elect, the head of the nations and the seat of the master of the nations" (12.25–32). Ambrose points his Milanese hearers back to Rome, the original site of the festival and the "head of the nations," while also exhorting them in their local veneration of the martyred

---

4. Ideoque hodie natali eorum spiritus sanctus increpuit dicens: Dies diei eructat verbum, hoc est, ex intimo thesauro cordis fidem praedicant Christi. Et bonus uterque dies, qui nobis verum lumen evomuit. This graphic imagery is jarring but not unique to the time. Augustine once preached, "Saint John belched forth this opening to his gospel [hoc enim principium evangelii sanctus Joannes ructuavit], because he had drunk it in from the Lord's own breast" (*Serm.* 119.1).

5. On Ambrose's dedication to the cult of Peter in particular, see Neil B. McLynn, *Ambrose of Milan: Church and Court in a Christian Capital* (TCH 22; Berkeley: University of California Press, 1994), 279.

Fig. 3.1. The apostles on the silver reliquary of San Nazaro. In the Museo Diocesano, Milan. Courtesy Archaeological Institute of America/ *American Journal of Archaeology* (Morey 1919, fig. 1).

apostles on this special day. The cult of the apostles had fully come to Milan, Rome's successor.

In addition to liturgical practice, architecture was another means by which Ambrose promoted the apostolic cult in Milan. In 382 Ambrose began construction of a church in honor of the apostles, thereby creating a space for their cult. The bishop built his Roman Basilica (which others called the Basilica of the Apostles) on Milan's Roman Road (*Via Romana*), the major route leading out of Milan toward Rome. Here he placed relics of Paul and Peter that were purportedly sent by Bishop Damasus of Rome. Ambrose made reference to this event in a letter concerning the dedication of another basilica in Milan: "For when I had dedicated the basilica, many as if with one voice began to cry out, saying, 'Dedicate it as you did the Roman Basilica.' I responded, 'I will, if I find relics of martyrs'" (Ambrose, *Ep.* 22.1). The holy relics that had been present at the opening of the Roman Basilica were lacking in this other case. Ambrose's biographer, Paulinus of Milan, confirmed the presence of relics in the Roman Basilica: "At that time he [Ambrose] transferred the body of the holy martyr Nazarius ... to the Basilica of the Apostles [i.e., the Roman Basilica], which is on the Roman Road.... There long ago the relics of the holy apostles had been deposited with the greatest devotion of all" (Paulinus of Milan, *Vit. Ambr.* 32–33).

Neither Ambrose nor Paulinus specified the nature of these relics, but a discovery in Milan in 1578 may provide an important clue. The city's arch-bishop at the time, Charles Borromeo, was constructing a new altar in the basilica and ordered excavations under the ancient altar. Workers uncovered there a small, decorated silver box measuring 19.9 centimeters square by 20.1 centimeters high (fig. 3.1). On the lid Christ is flanked by two figures, clearly identifiable as Paul and Peter by their iconographical types. Borromeo opened the box and found several pieces of fabric. These were not the bones that the archbishop had perhaps hoped to find, yet they were probably secondary relics (*brandea*) from the apostolic tombs in Rome. This silver reliquary disappeared and was rediscovered in 1894, thus allowing scholars to examine it closely. Significant debate arose concerning the date and authenticity of the item. Some claimed that it was a sixteenth-century forgery, while others argued that it was ancient. Graffiti written on the box was finally deciphered and identified conclusively as a late Roman hand. Since that time, scholars have overwhelmingly agreed that this reliquary dates from the fourth century. It is possible that this is the very box that held the relics of the apostles at the time that Ambrose dedicated his Roman Basilica.[6]

In constructing this basilica and promoting the apostolic cult, Ambrose was both pointing attention back to Rome and reflecting his desire to establish Milan as a new Rome. The location of the church was significant in this regard (fig. 3.2). The Roman Road linked the two cities and was the major thorough-fare (*decumanus*) leading into Milan from the south. For a distance of nearly 600 meters, from a four-sided triumphal arch to the city wall, a colonnaded portico covered the street. In Ambrose's time, this was the imperial triumphal way that led into Milan and had replaced the ancient triumphal way in Rome that passed through the Field of Mars. The Roman Basilica sat immediately adjacent to it at about the midway point. It dominated the north side of the

---

6. Gemma Sena Chiesa and Fabrizio Slavazzi, "La capsella argentea di San Nazaro: Primi risultati di una nuova indagine," *AnTard* 7 (1999): 187–204; P. L. Zovatto, "L'urnetta argentea di S. Ambrogio nell'ambito della rinascenza teodosiana," *CrArte* 13–14 (1956): 2–14; E. Villa, "Un autografo di Sant'Ambrogio," *Ambr* 30 (1954): 65–68; Charles R. Morey, "The Silver Casket of San Nazaro in Milan," *AJA* 23.2 (1919): 101–25.

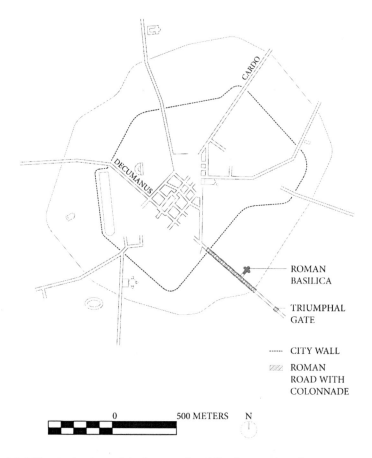

ROMAN
BASILICA

TRIUMPHAL
GATE

------ CITY WALL

▨▨▨ ROMAN
ROAD WITH
COLONNADE

0   500 METERS   N

Fig. 3.2. Milan in the time of Ambrose. After Villa; drawing by John Capen Brough.

road and, like Constantine's basilicas in Rome, served as a monument to the prominence of the Christian church. Victorious emperors entering Milan had to pass Ambrose's Roman Basilica along the Roman Road, a reminder of the importance of the Christian faith to the welfare of their empire. Milan was now the political capital of the West, and the bishop was attempting to establish it as a spiritual successor of Rome as well.

In addition to the name and location of the basilica, Ambrose also evoked associations with Rome by building a church that followed Roman examples. The site on which the basilica was built was a necropolis with some Christian tombs, a context that paralleled the major basilicas of Rome. Constantine had constructed churches for the apostles in burial grounds in the cases of the original basilica of Paul on the Ostian Road, the Basilica of the Apostles on the Appian Road, and the basilica of Peter at the Vatican.[7] In the 380s, the three emperors did likewise in building the new, larger Ostian Road basilica. Ambrose matched this effort in the 380s in Milan by building an enormous church in honor of the apostles in the midst of a cemetery. As in Rome, new, privileged burial sites were created for the wealthy and influential. There is evidence, for example, that four Milanese bishops of the early fifth century (Venerius, Marolus, Glicerius, and Lazarus) were buried in the Roman Basilica.[8]

By promoting the veneration of the apostles, Ambrose not only sought to fashion the city of Milan as another Rome; he also presented himself as an equivalent to the Roman bishop, as another Damasus.[9] Like his Roman contemporary, Ambrose was the one who adorned the shrine to Paul and Peter in his city, thus establishing himself as patron of their cult in Milan. Just as the apostolic cult saw expansion in Rome under Damasus, so did it grow in Milan under Ambrose during the same period. The Roman bishop had employed his patronage of the cult of the saints as a unifying factor in his city. It was a powerful propaganda tool in establishing his position against challengers and detractors. Ambrose had likewise entered a fiercely divided situation in the church in Milan. The city's two main factions were on opposite sides of the Nicene question, but they shared a high regard for Paul and Peter. A church in honor of the apostles was a sacred site that would appeal to both sides, and Ambrose, as patron of the cult, would gain status in the eyes of all in Milan.

His patronage of the Milanese cult served Ambrose in an additional way. He was bishop of a new political capital that lacked the apostolic pedigree of Rome. Milan's struggle for legitimacy within the Western church was real. While the city's secular authority was assured by the presence of the imperial residence, the city had no corresponding building of equal spiritual importance when Ambrose became bishop. By building the Roman Basilica on the Roman Road, Ambrose gave the "new Rome" a recognized cultic space dedicated to the martyr-patrons Paul and Peter and sanctified by their relics. This new basilica legitimized both the city and the bishop who had authority over it.

---

7. Suzanne Lewis ("Function and Symbolic Form in the Basilica Apostolorum at Milan," *JSAH* 28.2 [1969]: 92) has argued that Ambrose sought to imitate Constantine's sacred "crown" around Rome.

8. Fedele Savio, *La Lombardia* (vol. 1 of *Gli antichi vescovi d'Italia dalle origine al 1300*; Florence: Libreria Editrice Fiorentina, 1913), 21–47.

9. Lewis ("Function and Symbolic Form," 92) has suggested that Ambrose was "inspired" by the efforts of Damasus, but she has underestimated the ambitions of the bishop of Milan.

The veneration of Paul and Peter was vibrant in fourth-century Milan, thanks to the efforts of Ambrose.[10] He promoted the liturgical celebration of the annual feast of the apostles on the Roman model. He also constructed his Roman Basilica on the Roman Road and adorned it with relics, thereby creating an important new place for the cult of the apostles. This church represented a connection with Rome in more than name only, for it followed the model of the apostolic churches in the ancient capital. It rose from a necropolis and towered above the landscape, declaring the apostles' victory over death through their martyrdoms. Through both liturgy and architecture, Ambrose claimed a connection between Rome and his city and between bishop Damasus and himself. Milan and Ambrose were legitimate heirs to the spiritual legacy of Rome, for the re-creation of Roman sacred space had given Milan its own identity as a "new Rome," an apostolic city with an apostolic bishop.

3.2. The Cult of Paul in Gaul:
Venerating and Supplanting the Apostle

Ancient sources do not record the arrival of Christianity in Gaul, but two texts in the New Testament and a passage in the *Martyrdom of the Holy Apostle Paul* left room for speculation that associated Paul with this event. The first of these texts is 2 Tim 4:10, where Paul[11] says: "Demas abandoned me, because he

---

10. The Pauline cult also traveled from Rome to Milan through sarcophagus art. A coffin that probably dates from the sixth century features a scene of Paul's martyrdom; see Raffaele Garrucci, *Storia della arte cristiana nei primi otto secoli della chiesa* (Prato, Italy: Guasti, 1872), fig. 353, no. 4. The date is difficult to fix precisely, but Paul's posture and the gesture of the soldier mimic sarcophagi of the Junius Bassus type. The quality of workmanship was inferior to that of the Roman workshops of the fourth century, but the artists were clearly imitating Roman models.

11. For the sake of simplicity, I refer to the author here as Paul. Most modern critical scholars deny the Pauline authorship of the Pastoral Epistles (1 and 2 Timothy, Titus), while ancient interpreters accepted them as authentically Pauline. It is not my goal here to attempt to settle this debate. I am treating 2 Timothy as an important source for very early traditions about Paul's life and travels, whether or not it came from the pen of the apostle himself. For a summary of recent scholarship on the authorship of 2 Timothy, see I. Howard Marshall, *A Critical and Exegetical Commentary on the Pastoral Epistles* (ICC; Edinburgh: T&T Clark, 1999), 57–91. Marshall himself assigns the letters to the period soon after Paul's death. Cf. Jerome Murphy-O'Connor, *Paul: A Critical Life* (Oxford: Clarendon, 1996), 356–71. Murphy-O'Connor contends that the strongest arguments against Pauline authorship of the Pastoral Epistles are based on issues in 1 Timothy and Titus, not 2 Timothy. Therefore, 2 Timothy should be treated separately and, in his mind, as authentically Pauline. Others have agreed that the three letters should not be grouped

loved this present age, and went to Thessaloniki. Crescens went to Galatia [εἰς Γαλατίαν] and Titus to Dalmatia." Most interpreters have understood this as a reference to the region of Galatia in Asia Minor. According to the Acts of the Apostles, Paul visited Galatia and Phrygia (another region in Asia Minor) on at least two occasions, "strengthening all the disciples" there during his second visit (16:6; 18:23). It was logical that Crescens, a disciple of Paul, would be going to an area that the apostle had previously visited.[12] This is the tradition reflected in *Apos. Con.* 7.46, where Crescens is identified as the first bishop of the churches of Galatia. The seventh-century *Chronicon paschale* identifies Crescens as one of the seventy disciples of Jesus who became "bishop of Chalcedon in Galatia" (PG 92:1061),[13] where he preached, died, and was buried under Nero (PG 92:609). However, not all have shared this opinion. Since antiquity, some have understood εἰς Γαλατίαν as a reference to Gaul. From a literary perspective, this reading would be defensible. Numerous authors writing between the second century B.C.E. and the second century C.E. used "Galatia" to refer to Gaul. The list includes Polybius, Diodorus of Sicily, Josephus, Plutarch, Appian, and Cassius Dio. This usage, then, was contemporary with the writing of 2 Timothy.[14]

Early in the manuscript tradition of 2 Tim 4:10, some scribes sought to eliminate any ambiguity in the passage by replacing "to Galatia" (εἰς Γαλατίαν) with "to Gaul" (εἰς Γαλλίαν).[15] This reading appears in manuscripts of the Greek text as early as the fourth century, including Codex Sinaiticus (א), a very important early manuscript discovered in St. Catherine's Monastery on Mount Sinai. The fourth-century Greek fathers Eusebius of Caesarea, Epiphanius of Salamis, Theodore of Mopsuestia, and Theodoret of Cyrus also knew

---

together on the issue of authorship, e.g., Rüdiger Fuchs, *Unerwartete Unterschiede: Müssen wir unsere Ansichten über "die" Pastoralbriefe revidieren?* (Wuppertal: Brockhaus, 2003), 175–222; Jens Herzer, "Rearranging the 'House of God': A New Perspective on the Pastoral Epistles," in Empsychoi Logoi: *Religious Innovations in Antiquity: Studies in Honour of Pieter Willem van der Horst* (ed. A. Houtman et al.; Leiden: Brill, 2008), 547–55.

12. In both cases Luke clarifies the location of this Galatia by pairing it with Phrygia.

13. Here Chalcedon is incorrectly placed in Galatia, instead of Bithynia.

14. For a complete list of authors using "Galatia" for Gaul, see Ceslas Spicq, *Saint Paul: Les Épîtres pastorales* (2 vols.; EBib; Paris: Gabalda, 1969), 2:810–12. The confusion between Galatia and Gaul is further witnessed by the references to Crescens in the *Chronicon paschale*. In both cases the editor uses the term Γαλλία, which can mean Gaul, but the specific reference to Chalcedon makes it clear that the eastern region is meant.

15. Philip H. Towner, *The Letters to Timothy and Titus* (NICNT; Grand Rapids: Eerdmans, 2006), 623 n. 22.

this reading.[16] In addition, some manuscripts of the Latin Vulgate, Coptic (Egyptian), and Ethiopic translations of 2 Timothy include this variant.[17]

This distribution of witnesses is intriguing. It is not difficult to imagine a Western scribe inserting an explicit reference to Gaul, in order to increase the importance of his own region. If this were the case, then we would expect the preponderance of manuscripts and witnesses to be in Latin and from the West. The Eastern tradition would maintain the prominence of Galatia in Asia Minor. However, our evidence presents nearly the opposite picture. Not all versions of the Vulgate contain this reading, while Codex Sinaiticus (possibly of Egyptian origin), several Greek fathers from the regions of Syria and Palestine, and the Coptic tradition do. The Eastern textual evidence for a mission of Crescens to Gaul is actually stronger than the Western evidence. This distribution suggests that a tradition linking Gaul and a Pauline emissary was known in parts of the West and East at an early date.[18]

Romans 15:24–28 is another passage that leaves room for Pauline associations with Gaul. Here Paul states his desire to go to Spain. As we will see later in this chapter, many ancient Christian authors believed that he eventually made this voyage. If Paul did go to Spain by way of Rome, then he made at least one stop in Gaul along the way. Ancient sea routes followed the coastline as much as possible. The unpredictability of current and weather patterns in the Mediterranean could make crossings over open water dangerous. A ship sailing from Rome's port at Ostia to Spain would have followed a route to the

---

16. Rowan A. Greer, trans., *Theodore of Mopsuestia: The Commentaries on the Minor Epistles of Paul* (SBLWGRW 26; Atlanta: Society of Biblical Literature, 2010), 730–31. Robert C. Hill has suggested that the reference to the Gauls (τάς Γαλλίας οὕτως ἐκάλεσεν) in Theodoret's commentary on the Pauline Epistles is actually a reference to the Galatians of Asia Minor: "Theodoret, in fact, if we interpret him aright, seems to suggest *Gallias* would not be an improper reading as related more closely to the origin of the Galatians as 'Galli' from Gaul(s)." See Robert C. Hill, trans., *Theodoret of Cyrus: Commentary on the Letters of St. Paul* (2 vols.; Brookline, Mass.: Holy Cross Orthodox Press, 2001), 2:251. The text of Theodoret, however, is more ambiguous on the point than Hill suggests.

17. The most significant Greek manuscripts are the uncials ℵ and C and the miniscules 81 and 104. Bruce M. Metzger has described the witnesses for εἰς Γαλατίαν as "chiefly Alexandrian" in *A Textual Commentary on the Greek New Testament* (2nd ed.; Stuttgart: Deutsche Bibelgesellschaft, 1994), 581. He ascribes the change either to deliberate scribal alteration or to the accidental misreading of the second *alpha* in Γαλατίαν as a *lambda*, thus leading to the suppression of the *tau*.

18. Oddly, Crescens is not mentioned by any of the earliest Gallic sources. He is later identified as the founder of the church of Vienne and a martyr, but this may be attributed to the confusion of Paul's companion with a third-century Gallic bishop of the same name (*AASS* June 5.27). Crescens is elsewhere identified as the founder of the church in Mainz (*Menologion* May 30).

north of Corsica and on to Marseille (fig. 3.3). From Marseille it would have continued to Spain, possibly stopping at Narbonne (ancient Narbo in Gaul) before arriving most likely at Tarragona (ancient Tarraco).[19] The stops in Marseille and Narbonne would have permitted Paul to evangelize in the port cities of Gaul.[20]

Finally, an intriguing reference in the *Martyrdom of the Holy Apostle Paul* links the apostle to the region through Luke: "Luke, who had come from Gaul

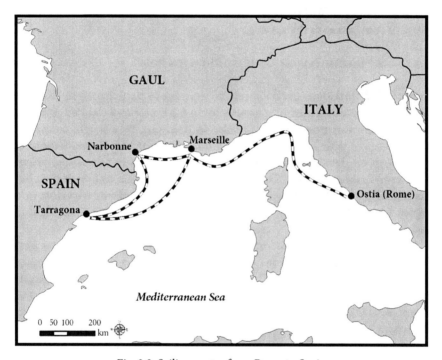

Fig. 3.3. Sailing routes from Rome to Spain.

---

19. The most direct route from Ostia to Tarragona, which passed through the narrow strait between Corsica and Sardinia, was notoriously perilous and almost never attempted when sailing from east to west. Pascal Arnaud, *Les routes de la navigation antique: Itinéraires en Méditerranée* (Paris: Errance, 2005), 164–65. On the dangers of navigation in general, see Chantal Reynier, *Saint Paul sur les routes du monde romain* (Paris: Cerf, 2009), 69–86.

20. J. B. Lightfoot, *S. Clement of Rome: The Two Epistles to the Corinthians* (London: Macmillan, 1869), 50 n. 1: "It is not improbable also that this western journey of S. Paul [to Spain] included a visit to Gaul." Prudentius mentions a "Paul" as the patron saint of Narbonne, but this is the Paul who was traditionally sent ca. 250 C.E. to reestablish the church at Narbonne, which had been nearly wiped out during the Decian persecution (Gregory of Tours, *Hist. franc.* 1.30).

[Λουκᾶς ἀπὸ Γαλλιῶν], and Titus, who had come from Dalmatia, were waiting for Paul in Rome" (*Mart. Paul.* 1). From an early date, Luke was associated with Paul through the personal connection suggested in Acts (e.g., Eusebius, *Hist. eccl.* 3.4.6), so finding a mention of Luke in the *Martyrdom* is not surprising. Luke's connection with Gaul, however, is otherwise unattested in the ancient period.[21] These three passages are, of course, not proof of any Pauline activity in Gaul, yet for those in Gaul who considered the apostle one of the church's greatest martyrs, the possibility that Paul had once sent a missionary to their region—or had even visited in person—would have invited a greater sense of connection to the apostle.

3.2.1. The Pauline Cult as Connection with Rome

Many Gallic Christians in late antiquity were active participants in the Pauline cult. They established numerous sites in his honor and claimed him as a source of spiritual power and authority. In doing so, they sought to associate themselves with the apostolic tradition originating in Rome. Others in Gaul, however, invoked Paul yet promoted local saints to a rank equivalent to or even greater than his. They still spoke of the apostle in lofty terms, but his importance served to highlight the status of his equals or superiors in a region in which some were struggling to establish an ecclesiastical identity apart from Rome.

Tours (ancient Caesarodonum/Civitas Turonorum) is by far the best documented city of late antique Gaul, so our study of the Pauline cult begins there (fig. 3.4). In the year 460/461, Perpetuus became bishop of the city. At that time a small church existed over the tomb of Martin, a former bishop of Tours (371/372–397) who had come to be venerated locally as a holy figure. Perpetuus claimed that constant miracles were taking place at Martin's tomb and decided that the diminutive sanctuary was "unworthy of such miracles." Being from an aristocratic family, he had the financial means to address this problem. Therefore, Perpetuus built a new, much larger structure in honor of Martin over the saint's tomb, yet he salvaged part of the former building for a basilica in honor of the apostles: "Since the arch of the preceding chapel had been constructed elegantly, the priest [Perpetuus] decided that it would be improper for such a work to disappear. Therefore, in honor of the blessed apostles Peter and Paul he constructed another basilica in which he placed that

---

21. Theodor Zahn has suggested that Luke may be substituted here for Crescens. See *Geschichte des neutestamentlichen Kanons* (2 vols.; Erlangen: Deichert, 1892), 2:888.

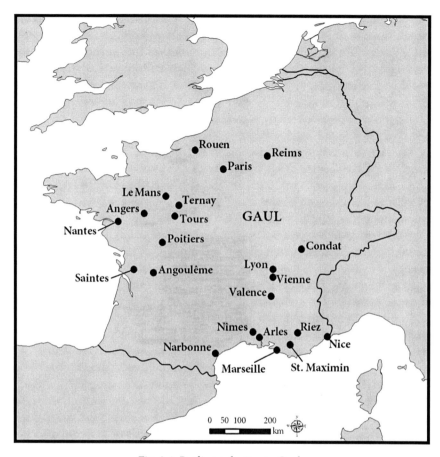

Fig. 3.4. Pauline cult sites in Gaul.

arch" (Gregory of Tours, *Hist. franc.* 2.14).[22] This apostolic basilica became the center of the apostolic cult in Tours, as we learn from a liturgical calendar that Perpetuus formalized for the city. Notable among the days to be observed annually was the feast of the apostles: "The birthday of the holy apostles Peter and Paul at their basilica" (*Hist. franc.* 10.31.6).

The architectural development of Perpetuus's Tours coincided with liturgical development, and on both fronts Perpetuus created a local adaptation of

---

22. Cf. Eugen Ewig, "Le culte de Saint Martin à son époque franque," *RHEF* 47 (1961): 3 n. 11. Ewig has argued that the earlier basilica was also in honor of the apostles, hence the designation of the new basilica as "another basilica" in their honor. This argument is not supported by the context, however.

the Roman martyr cult. The festival in Tours was an annual reminder of the dependence of the Gallic churches on the Roman traditions associated with the apostles. The festivities took place in a basilica that Perpetuus built for Paul and Peter. We do not know if he drew any architectural inspiration from the churches in Rome, but he built, seemingly at his own expense, a space for the apostolic cult in his city. The founders and martyr-patrons of the Roman church now had a place in this Gallic city, a basilica that honored them and reflected the influence and authority of Rome in fifth-century Tours.

In the sixth century, Bishop Gregory of Tours (573–593/594) reemphasized this Gallo-Roman relationship. He did so primarily through securing relics, as two separate events from 590 demonstrate. The first involved Gregory's dispatch of a deacon named Agiulf to Rome to procure relics. Through the intervention of a deacon also named Gregory—who soon after became Bishop Gregory I—Agiulf received relics from Bishop Pelagius of Rome. Thus, "Our deacon [Agiulf] returned from Rome and brought us the relics of holy men" (Gregory of Tours, *Vit. patrum* 8.6, James; *Hist. franc.* 10.1). During the trip back to Tours, the authenticity and power of these holy objects were put to the test. Agiulf left the port at Ostia on a ship bound for Marseille. Along the way, a strong wind arose and was driving the ship toward the rocks. As the sailors began to fear for their lives, Agiulf lifted his reliquary and called out for protection to the individual saints whose relics he possessed. Suddenly, "out of respect for the holy relics," another wind arose and blew the ship back into the safety of the open sea, saving the lives of all aboard. Gregory (of Tours) records in his chronicle, "By the grace of the Lord and the protection of the saints they arrived at the port they had hoped for. For these were relics of the saints whose sacred feet had been washed by the hands of the Lord, of Paul, Lawrence, Pancratius, Chrysanthus, the virgin Daria, and John and his brother, the other Paul. Rome, the capital of the world, piously celebrates their struggles and the prizes of their victories" (Gregory of Tours, *Glor. mart.* 82, Van Dam).

The act of sending Agiulf to Rome showed Gregory's deference to the status of the "capital of the world." He sought to transfer relics, focal points of spiritual power, to his own city. The passengers on the ship believed that the saints had acted through their relics to save the lives of all aboard, in order that their remains might arrive safely in their new home in Gaul. Foremost among these were Peter and Paul. The reference to foot washing recalls John 13:3–10, where Jesus washes the feet of his disciples. Peter is the only disciple mentioned by name in this Gospel account, and he is the only one of the Twelve with a traditional relationship to Rome, so there can be little doubt that he was among those "whose sacred feet had been washed by the hands of the Lord." Gregory then places Paul at the head of a list of other martyrs, all of whom had traditionally died in Rome. The sanctifying presence of these martyrs had come to Gaul by the intervention of the saints themselves. This was a sign that Tours, through the transfer of relics, was a recognized daughter of the Roman church.

The second event from 590 occurred during the rebuilding of the basilica of Martin. Prior to Gregory's time as bishop, fire had destroyed much of the church that Perpetuus had built in the fifth century. In the process of constructing a new, larger basilica to Martin, Gregory discovered in the treasury several forgotten reliquaries. He recounts that one of these contained "relics of the holy apostles along with other martyrs. I was amazed at this gift given by God and gave him thanks. Then, after observing vigils and saying a mass, I placed these things in the church" (*Hist. franc.* 10.31.19). In the same year that Agiulf went to Rome to bring back apostolic relics, Gregory allegedly discovered that Tours already possessed some. We cannot discount Gregory's story out of hand, but it must be read with caution. Unexpected, miraculous discoveries of relics were a great ally to uneasy bishops in late antiquity. As we have seen, Damasus entered a tumultuous and hotly contested setting in Rome. He was said to have "searched for and discovered the bodies of many saints" (*Lib. pontif.* 39, Davis) as part of his promotion of the cult of the saints. As the one who found these relics, he was recognized as the patron of their cults, which granted him considerable political as well as ecclesiastical influence. Similarly, Ambrose lived in Milan at a time of considerable unrest within the church and benefited from the discovery of important relics. He unearthed the body of the previously unknown martyr Nazarius and placed it in his Roman Basilica (Paulinus of Milan, *Vit. Ambr.* 32). Another of Ambrose's churches (commonly known as the Ambrosian Basilica) lacked relics, but a miraculous event occurred to solve this problem. Augustine tells the story in his *Confessions*: "It was at that time too that you [God] revealed to your bishop Ambrose in a vision the place where the bodies of the martyrs Protasius and Gervasius were hidden" (*Conf.* 9.7, Pine-Coffin). Ambrose placed them with great pomp in the basilica, thus staking his own claim to authority over it and thwarting the plans of the empress Justina, who had tried to secure control of the church for the anti-Nicene faction in the city. In the case of both Damasus and Ambrose, miraculously finding relics at the right moment and becoming a cult's patron were powerful tools of episcopal self-protection and self-promotion.

We may view Gregory of Tours' discovery of apostolic relics in a similar light. His tenure as bishop was also marked by significant conflict. At many points he faced opposition from secular authorities, including the Frankish kings and the counts of Tours. Even other clerics from Tours were involved in plots to remove him from office.[23] To strengthen his position, Gregory sought

---

23. Van Dam, *Saints and Their Miracles*, 68–81.

to control the city's primary cultic center, the shrine of Martin. Finding these forgotten reliquaries immediately increased the status of both Gregory and the basilica. Gregory saw himself as the patron of this sacred space, which became a source of even greater spiritual power now that it housed the relics of Paul and Peter alongside those of Martin.[24] Gregory enjoyed the sanction of the local saint, Martin, and of Rome's two greatest martyrs. He also controlled a considerable cache of relics, including those that Agiulf brought back from Rome. The security of Gregory's position in part depended on the relics of the Roman martyrs, for they granted legitimacy and prestige to the church at Tours under his leadership.

Gregory tells us that other cities in Gaul shared an interest in securing relics of the apostle. He was not the first Gallic bishop to send someone to Rome for this purpose: "A deacon from that province [Anjou] was sent to Rome to bring back relics of the blessed apostles and other saints that fortify that city." The deacon never reached Rome, for reasons that we will examine later, but instead declared, "I was looking for Peter. I was looking for Paul, Lawrence, and the others who bring fame to Rome by their own blood" (*Hist. franc.* 6.6). The sending bishop saw the benefits of linking Angers (ancient Iuliomagus/Andes) to Rome through relics and desired to bring some of that "fame" to his own region through the possession of remnants of "their blood." While Angers did not secure relics of Paul and Peter on this occasion, a site between Tours and Le Mans (ancient Suindinum) did have such items. A villa near Ternay (ancient Ternacum) featured an oratory in which "the relics ... are of the most blessed apostles, that is, of Peter and Paul." Gregory notes that Ternay was in the territory of Le Mans but in his time was "now controlled by the authority of this holy church [i.e., Tours]" (*Vit. Mart.* 4.12, Van Dam). In other words, Gregory had successfully secured jurisdiction over an apostolic cult site that was not traditionally part of his territory.

A letter from Paulinus of Nola to Bishop Victricius of Rouen (ancient Rotomagus) suggests that Rouen also had a shrine for apostolic relics. In the late 390s, Victricius obtained for his city some relics from several Italian bishops. Paulinus wrote that Victricius had transformed Rouen "into the entire appearance of Jerusalem, as it is famed in the East, even including the presence of the apostles.... And they have found with you a most suitable lodging for themselves. Clearly these friends of God, the leaders of the true people of Israel (that is, the people approaching to him), take delight in lingering in

---

24. Peter R. L. Brown, *Relics and Social Status in the Age of Gregory of Tours* (Reading: University of Reading, 1977). Yasin (*Saints and Church Spaces*, 259–84) has shown that appeals to saints as a means of reinforcing hierarchy, particularly the place of the bishop, were ubiquitous in late antiquity.

your city and aiding you in your work" (*Ep.* 18.5, Walsh). Paul and Peter are not explicitly named, but Paulinus points to the presence of "the apostles," who are also "the leaders," a likely reference to the apostle to the Gentiles and the apostle to the Israelites. Through the presence of their relics, they dwelt in Rouen as "a most suitable lodging." This linked Rouen with Jerusalem, where both apostles had stayed while alive, as well as with their current "lodging" in Rome. In Paulinus's eyes, this connection raised the ecclesiastical status of Victricius's city.

Venantius Fortunatus, a poet from northern Italy who traveled widely in Gaul in the late sixth century, attests to the presence of relics of Paul and Peter in the city of Nantes (ancient Namnis). When Felix, bishop of Nantes, dedicated a new basilica in the city, Fortunatus composed a poem "In Honor of Those Whose Remains Are Kept Here in Nantes—That Is, of Peter and Paul" (*Carm.* 3.7). He thus points to an apostolic cult in Nantes, probably centered on secondary relics, but also claims that the presence of these relics symbolizes the dependence of the Gallic Christians on Rome: "O Gaul, clap your hands joyfully. Rome sends salvation to you; the apostolic glory visits the Allobroges" (*Carm.* 3.7.17–18).[25] According to Fortunatus, the gospel had originally come to Gaul through the apostles, and now their remains were resting in Nantes. In a subsequent poem in honor of Nantes, Fortunatus even goes so far as to say, "Here a new Rome appears" (*Carm.* 3.8.9–20). He paints this Gallic city as a successor to the sacred city of the apostles.

Yet another story of relics comes from Condat Abbey in the Jura Mountains (eastern France). In the *Life of Eugendus* (†512/514),[26] this abbot of Condat has a dream of three men approaching him on the road from Geneva. Their dress and demeanor are strange, so he asks who they are. One responds, "I am Peter, and this is my brother Andrew, and that is our brother Paul." Eugendus asks how it is possible for them to be there, since their bodies rested in Rome and, in the case of Andrew, Patras. They respond that they have now come to dwell also in Condat, and then Eugendus awakes. At the very moment along the Geneva road, two monks return who had left Condat two years earlier. They announce that they have returned from Rome with the relics of Peter, Paul, and Andrew, a confirmation of the vision of Eugendus.

---

25. The Allobroges were an ancient Celtic tribe that resided in southern Gaul. Fortunatus invokes them here to symbolize the entirety of Gaul.

26. This source seems to have been produced within a decade of the death of Eugendus, but there has been debate over the possibility of much later interpolations. The most complete treatment of the arguments is found in François Martine, ed., *Vie des pères du Jura* (SC 142; Paris: Cerf, 1968), 1–44. Martine favors the antiquity of the text and the identity of the author as one who was a contemporary of Eugendus.

The abbot takes the reliquaries and with due reverence places them under the altar of the monastery's church (*Vit. patrum Iur. Eug.* 153–156 [3.15–16]).[27] Condat becomes a center for the apostolic cult by the announcement of the apostles themselves.

There were many other sites in Gaul that were dedicated to Paul and Peter. By the end of the sixth century, churches named for the apostles existed in Vienne (ancient Vienna), Le Mans (Subdinnum), Saintes (Mediolanum Santonum), Angoulême (Iculisma), Poitiers (Limonum), Arles (Arelate), and possibly Lyon (Lugdunum) and Reims (Durocortorum).[28] Clovis I (ruled 481–511), the first king of a united Frankish kingdom, built a basilica to the apostles in Paris (Lutetia) and was buried there (Gregory of Tours, *Hist. franc.* 2.43). In Riez (ancient Rhegium), Bishop Maximus (†460) constructed a similar church that also served as his sepulcher (Faustus of Riez, *De sancte Maxime*; Dinamius Patricius, *Vit. Maxim.* 15). Sacred buildings for the apostles dotted the landscape of Gaul, and some would have contained secondary relics like those found in Tours, Nantes, and Condat. These regional shrines served as outposts of an expanding apostolic cult with Rome at its center.

Sarcophagus art was another medium through which Christians in Gaul appropriated Roman expressions of the Pauline cult. Iconographical representations of Paul's death appear on several late antique coffins found in southern Gaul but believed to be of Roman origin. One example comes from Saint-Maximin-la-Sainte-Baume. The apostle stands with his hands bound behind his back. His head is (ironically) not preserved. Next to him a soldier draws his sword to carry out the execution. Behind Paul stands a tall reed, and a

27. The *Life of Eugendus* is the third and final part of the *Lives of the Fathers of Jura*. The critical edition assigns numbers to the *Lives* as a whole and to the *Life* individually, so I have given both designations here.

28. Vienne: Louis Duchesne, *Fastes épiscopaux de l'ancienne Gaule* (2 vols.; Paris: Fontemoing, 1900), 1:183. Le Mans: Margarete Weidemann, ed., *Geschichte des Bistums Le Mans von der Spätantike bis zur Karolingerzeit: Actus pontificum Cenomannis in urbe degentium und Gesta Aldrici* (3 vols.; Mainz: Römisch-Germanisches Zentralmuseum, 2002), 3:550. Saintes: Gregory I of Rome, *Ep.* 6.50 (to Palladius, who had built a church in honor of Peter and Paul and wanted relics for altars). Angoulême and Poitiers: Élie Griffe, *La Gaule chrétienne à l'époque romaine* (3 vols.; Paris: Picard, 1965), 3:36. Arles: *CIL* 12:936; *ILCV* 1808. Lyon: Gregory of Tours, *Glor. mart.* 48. Reims: Flodard of Reims, *Flod. hist. rem. eccl.* 1.6. Paris: Gregory of Tours, *Hist. franc.* 2.43. This list is by no means exhaustive. Additional churches to the apostles, either together or individually, are listed in Nancy Gauthier, Jean-Charles Picard, and Noël Duval, eds., *Topographie chrétienne des cités de la Gaule, des origines au milieu du VIIIe siècle* (14 vols.; Paris: de Boccard, 1986–2007). Unfortunately, many lack reliable dating.

column rises between the two men, topped by the prow of a ship (fig. 3.5).[29] The reed and the ship are references to the banks of the Tiber as Paul's martyrdom site. An image with similar elements is now housed in Marseille.[30] In this case a tall reed separates the apostle and his executioner, and the artist has sketched the prow of a ship just behind Paul's head. A third example comes from a fragmentary sarcophagus at Valence (ancient Valentia).[31] Paul faces his executioner, who has begun to draw his sword, while a reed and ship appear prominently in the background. A coffin from Nîmes (Nemausus) is simi-

Fig. 3.5. Scene of Paul's martyrdom on a sarcophagus from Gaul. In the crypt of the Basilique de la Madeleine, Saint-Maximin, France. From Le Blant, 1886.

---

29. E. Le Blant, *Les sarcophages chrétiens de la Gaule* (Paris: Imprimerie Nationale, 1886), 150–52, no. 212, fig. 54.1–3.

30. Ibid., 45–47, no. 58, fig 11.3.

31. Joseph Wilpert, *I sarcofagi cristiani antichi* (2 vols.; MAC; Rome: Pontificio Istituto di Archeologia Cristiana, 1929), 1:fig. 142.1; David R. Cartlidge and J. K. Elliott, *Art and the Christian Apocrypha* (London: Routledge, 2001), 144.

lar, except that a monumental capital rises between Paul and the soldier.[32] A final and slightly different image was discovered at Arles. Here two soldiers surround and arrest Paul, and the one on the viewer's right displays a sword at his side.[33] Residents of Gaul imported these Roman sarcophagi as physical manifestations of their veneration of Paul and the relationship between Gaul and Rome. By securing these objects for their own burials, Christians brought the Roman artistic tradition—and through it the Roman cult—to their own region. They laid claim to the story of Paul as their own story and to the Roman saint as their own saint. As a result, they established new sacred sites in the apostle's honor and hoped to receive spiritual benefits equal to those experienced in Rome.

All the above sarcophagi were transported to the southern part of Gaul, but Victricius of Rouen provides compelling evidence that the residents of northern Gaul also knew the iconographical tradition related to Paul's martyrdom. Earlier we looked at a letter from Paulinus to Victricius in which the bishop of Nola congratulates the church in Rouen for being a "suitable lodging" for the apostles. We now turn to Victricius's response to the arrival of these relics from Italy, a hymn entitled *On the Praise of the Saints*. In the opening lines, Victricius writes the following:

> We see no assassin. We do not know the sword drawn from its sheath, and we place altars of the divine powers. No one today is a cruel enemy, and we are enriched by the passion of the saints. No torturer now oppresses us, and we carry the trophies of the martyrs. No one's blood is poured out in our time, nor does a persecutor assail us, and we are filled up with the joy of the triumphant. (*Laud. sanct.* 4–9)

Victricius's description of the plight of Christians in former times—a plight that he did not share in his own time—displays a striking similarity to the sarcophagus scenes of Paul's death. He refers to the "assassin," the "cruel enemy," the "torturer," and the "persecutor," all represented by Roman soldiers on the sarcophagi. These soldiers, likewise, "oppressed" and "assailed" Paul by their rough handling. Paul above all was familiar with "the sword drawn from its sheath," for in the sarcophagus images a soldier draws a sword to behead him. The literary accounts of Paul's death probably also informed Victricius's description, because the apostle's blood was "poured out" at his execution and soaked up by shrouds. Iconographical representations of other martyrdoms were certainly known to Victricius, but the textual image of martyrdom

---

32. Le Blant, *Sarcophages*, 112–13, no. 135.
33. Ibid., 33, no. 48, fig. 12.1.

that he crafts in this poem matches up very closely with the scenes of Paul's death on Roman sarcophagi, some of which had been brought into Gaul. The language of Victricius seems too specific to be accidental. For anyone familiar with the images of Paul's beheading, the details in this hymn would have brought to mind that particular scene. The death of Paul, as represented on Roman sarcophagi, was a foundational event in Victricius's conception of what it meant to be a martyr. Paul's martyrdom was the model—a model not much followed in late fourth-century Gaul, but the model nonetheless. This connection between Roman image and Gallic text suggests the strong influence in Gaul of the Pauline cult imported from Rome.

The figure of Paul as martyr loomed large in late antique Gaul. His cult expanded across the region through relics, architecture, liturgy, images, and texts. Just as Roman sites were considered sacred space based on their association with the martyr, so, too, were places on the Gallic landscape believed to be transformed by the arrival of the apostle's cult, even to the point of creating a "new Rome." For many, this process of translocation highlighted the authority of the Roman church as the privileged source of access to the saint. Practices honoring Paul in Gaul, therefore, somehow pointed Christians back to the spiritual capital of the West. Not everyone in Gaul, however, received and appropriated the Pauline cult and its Roman overtones with as much enthusiasm.

3.2.2. GALLIC SAINTS AND THE SUPERSESSION OF PAUL

The traditional association between Paul and Rome prompted others to react to the cult in a very different way. Seeing Paul as a symbol of Roman authority and recognizing his influence in Gaul, they intentionally used his authority to subvert his cult in favor of the veneration of local figures. Paul himself was not attacked but rather became a standard by which they set up a hierarchy of Gallic saints and sought to establish an identity for Gaul that was independent of Rome and yet no less glorious. To do so, they presented these Gallic saints as the preferred patrons of the region, equal or even superior to Paul. Chief among the local saints honored in this way was Martin of Tours.

Martin was treated as a holy person even during his time as bishop. Some collected threads from his clothing or the straw on which he had slept and considered them relics.[34] He was a figure of considerable importance in the Gaul of his day. Martin himself demonstrated a strong desire to commemorate and honor the apostles: "In the monastery that is now called Marmoutier, he built a basilica in honor of the holy apostles Peter and Paul" (Gregory

---

34. Van Dam, *Saints and Their Miracles*, 13–14.

of Tours, *Hist. franc.* 10.31.3). The bishop established this monastery as his residence in an area outside Tours, preferring to live in a monastic house dedicated to the apostles rather than in the city itself.

According to one account, Martin's relationship to the apostles went well beyond veneration. Sulpicius Severus composed his *Dialogues on the Virtues of St. Martin* soon after Martin's death, sometime between 397 and 404. He includes numerous stories about the saint's life, some of which the author claims to have witnessed. On one occasion, Sulpicius and another man were standing guard outside Martin's cell. Suddenly, terror overcame them, "as if we were angels having received the mission of keeping guard before the tabernacle." Although Martin was alone inside, they could hear the murmur of voices and felt that something divine was inside the cell. When Martin emerged, they questioned him about this. On the condition that the men would not repeat it, Martin admitted that Saints Agnes, Thecla, and Mary had visited him, as they did frequently. Sulpicius continues, "He [Martin] did not deny that even Peter and the apostle Paul were seen by him quite often. As for demons, whenever one would come to him, he would rebuke it in their names" (*Dial.* 2.13.6). Martin enjoyed a type of patronage relationship with these intimate spiritual friends who visited him frequently. He appealed to them in times of distress, and they aided him in chasing away evil spirits. Their presence in his cell contributed to its transformation into a holy and fearful place comparable, in Sulpicius's mind, to the tabernacle, the dwelling place of the divine presence.

For Sulpicius, though, Martin did not have to rely on the power of the apostles, for he was their equal in every way. In another work, the *Life of Martin*, Sulpicius tells a story about the saint's miraculous intervention to spare a catechumen. The man had joined the monastic community of Hilary of Poitiers but fell violently ill with a fever and died almost immediately, before he had even been baptized. Martin arrived to find the man dead; being filled with the Holy Spirit, Martin ordered everyone out of the room. He prayed fervently for the mercy of the Lord, and a few hours later the man was revived. Later, the catechumen said that he had been standing before the judgment seat of God and was being condemned, when two angels interjected that Martin was praying on his behalf. The angels were then ordered to restore him to life, based on Martin's prayer. Sulpicius finishes the story by commenting, "From that time on the name of the blessed man [Martin] shone forth, such that the one who had already been considered holy now was also considered powerful and *truly like an apostle*" (Sulpicius, *Vit. sanct. Mart.* 7.7, emphasis added). Sulpicius created an image of Martin as one having influence with God and supernatural authority equal to that of figures such as Paul and Peter.

Martin may have performed miraculous deeds like an apostle, but Sulpicius faced one significant obstacle in equating him with these other figures.

Paul and Peter had earned their spiritual status by suffering and dying as martyrs at the hands of an evil Roman emperor. By contrast, Martin died peacefully along the banks of the Loire in a religious center that he had founded. Sulpicius was aware that his lofty portrayal of the former bishop had encountered some resistance on this very issue. He responded to Martin's detractors in a series of three letters that were appended to the *Life of Martin*. In one addressed to a priest named Eusebius, he asserts that Martin was indeed a match for the apostles in terms of his afflictions, for he had barely escaped a horrific fire: "Why do you say, whoever you are, that Martin is therefore not powerful and not holy? Because he was spared from the fire? O blessed man, equal to the apostles in everything, even in his sufferings!" Sulpicius goes on to explain that Martin's trials were in no way inferior to those of Paul. Yes, Paul had been shipwrecked and bitten by a deadly viper, but Martin's sufferings were every bit as real and severe (*Vit. sanct. Mart., Ep.* 1.5–8).

In another of these letters, addressed to the deacon Aurelius, Sulpicius turns his attention specifically to the apparent discrepancy between the apostles' violent martyrdoms and Martin's peaceful death. Here he adapts for Martin a passage from Hilary of Poitiers' *Against Constantius*. Hilary had claimed that he (Hilary) would endure torment for the gospel, if only he had the opportunity to face the dangers that saints of the past had faced, including Paul: "If only, omnipotent God … you had granted in my age and time that I might carry out the ministry of my confession in the times of men like Nero and Decius." Hilary says that he would not have feared the rack, the flames, or the cross. In fact, "I would not have trembled at the depths of the sea or the devouring swirls of the Black Sea, because through Jonah and Paul you taught that for the faithful there is life in the sea" (*C. Const.* 4).

Sulpicius borrows this motif from Hilary and ascribes the same commitment to Martin. Although Martin had not died as a martyr, he *would have* gladly done so, if he had had the opportunity:

> Therefore, he [Martin] is preserved with the apostles and prophets … and is inferior to no one among that flock of the righteous. Above all, as I hope, believe, and am convinced, he is added to the flock of those who have washed their robes in blood. Free from any stain, he follows the lamb, their leader. For the circumstances of the time did not make it possible for him to suffer martyrdom, but *he will not be deprived of a martyr's glory, since by his desire and virtue he was able and wanting to be a martyr.* But if it had been possible for him to take up arms in combat in the time of Nero or Decius, in the struggle that existed at that time, then—and I call upon the God of heaven and earth as my witness—he would have immediately mounted the rack.… And if, following the example of the teacher of the Gentiles [Paul], he had been designated for death by the sword, and had been led out among other

victims, as has often occurred, he would have been the first of all to seize the palm branch of blood by forcing the hand of the executioner. (*Vit. sanct. Mart., Ep.* 2.8–10, emphasis added)[35]

Here Sulpicius compares Martin's hypothetical martyrdom to Paul's actual martyrdom at two points. First, he states that Martin would have gone into spiritual combat "in the time of Nero or Decius." Christians remembered both of these emperors as persecutors of Christians, and the most famous martyrs of Nero's reign were Paul and Peter. If Martin had lived under Nero, then he would have behaved exactly as the apostles did, facing death unflinchingly and holding fast to the Christian faith. Second, if condemned to execution by the sword, as Paul was, Martin would have carried himself bravely to death, as had Paul. In fact, Martin would have provoked the executioner, so that he could be the first one to shed his blood. Sulpicius, therefore, presents Paul and Martin as parallel in life and death. Paul *did* stand firm in the face of persecution by Nero, and Martin *would have* done so. Paul *did* die by the sword at the hand of a brutal executioner, and Martin *would have* pushed forward to be the first in line to suffer the same fate. Sulpicius evokes Paul as the image of a model martyr, but Martin is his successor and equal in every way.

Sulpicius also compares Martin favorably to Paul in the *Dialogues*, where he places praise for Martin in the mouth of a Gallic monk named Postumianus: "And rightly does this Sulpicius compare him [Martin] to the apostles and prophets, because his strength of faith and works of power are seen to be equal to theirs" (*Dial.* 2.5.2; cf. 1 Cor 2:4). Later in the same work, Sulpicius claims in his own voice that those who had heard the preaching of Martin were just as fortunate as those who had heard Paul: "Blessed in fact is Greece, which merited hearing the apostle's [Paul's] preaching, but the Gauls were in no way ignored by Christ, for he granted to them to have Martin" (*Dial.* 3.17.6). A possible Pauline mission to Gaul, either in person on his way to Spain or through Crescens, was no longer of significance, for Martin was this region's evangelist sent by Christ himself. Gaul now had its own apostolic hierarchy with Martin at the apex.

The sixth-century poet Venantius Fortunatus of Poitiers incorporated this exalted view of Martin into his list of apostolic missions. While Peter was in Rome, Paul went to Illyricum (Balkans) and Scythia (Black Sea), Matthew to Ethiopia, Thomas to Persia, Bartholomew to India, Andrew to

---

35. Following Hilary, Sulpicius includes comparisons not only to the apostles but also to Isaiah, who went to the rack to be sawn in two (*Mart. Ascen. Isa.* 5), and to the "young Hebrews" (Shadrach, Meshach, and Abednego), who were thrown into the fiery furnace (Dan 3).

Achaia (Greece), and, "by the excellent faith of ancient Martin, Gaul took up the weapons of light" (*Carm.* 5.2.1–16). Fortunatus places Martin alongside Christ's other apostles, thus confirming his exalted status in the spiritual hierarchy. Christ had indeed sent Martin in the same way and with the same authority as Paul. By constructing his account of the apostolic missions in this way, Fortunatus reiterates Sulpicius's alternative foundation myth for Christianity in Gaul. Christianity had come to Gaul not through the preaching of Paul or Crescens. Instead, the faith had arrived through Martin. Fortunatus's version is striking in that it speaks of Martin as if he had been a contemporary of the other apostles. There had in fact been Christians in Gaul for at least two centuries prior to Martin's lifetime, yet for Sulpicius and Fortunatus, Martin stood alone as Gaul's patron saint, the founder of Christianity in their region.

Proponents of the cult of Martin were seeking to replace Paul's powerful presence with that of Martin. Two inscriptions from the basilica of Martin in Tours illustrate the extent to which some adopted this new ideology. Both were found in the area of Martin's tomb. The first declares Martin's position in the loftiest levels of Christianity's spiritual hierarchy: "Confessor by his merits, martyr by his cross, apostle by his action, Martin presides from heaven here at his tomb."[36] Martin occupies the faith's most exalted roles in ascending order. He is confessor, one who had suffered for professing the faith; martyr, one who had died for the faith; and apostle, one sent as an envoy by Christ himself. The rhetoric of Sulpicius had effectively created these identities for the former bishop. Martin was therefore considered worthy of veneration equal to Paul and Peter, for as the powerful martyr-patron of Tours, he "presides from heaven here at his tomb."

In the other inscription, the author applies the text of 2 Tim 4:7–8a to Martin. The original text states, "I have finished the race. I have kept the faith. From now on there is laid up for me the crown of righteousness, which the Lord, the righteous judge, will award to me on that day." This passage is considered one of the most overt references in the New Testament to Paul's impending martyrdom. The apostle's death is near, but he awaits it knowing that he has been faithful to the very end. In the inscription for Martin, the text reads, "He fought the good fight; he finished the race; he kept the faith. From now on a crown of justice has been set aside for him, which the Lord, the just judge, will give to him on that day."[37] At Martin's tomb someone altered the text from first person to third person, and the subject became Martin, not Paul. In Tours, Martin was the great warrior, the great runner, the great

---

36. Luce Pietri, *La ville de Tours du IVe au VIe siècle: Naissance d'une cité chrétienne* (CEFR 69; Rome: École française de Rome, 1983), 809–10, appendix 6, no. 15.

37. Ibid., 809, appendix 6, no. 14.

defender of the faith. He had earned a crown of martyrdom every bit as glorious as the one that Paul had received. Martin had followed in Paul's footsteps and had now actually supplanted the apostle to the Gentiles as the city's "new Paul."[38] The sacredness and power surrounding Martin's tomb were in no way inferior to those surrounding the tomb of Paul in Rome.

As a new martyr-patron of Gaul, Martin was expected to come to the aid of its residents. According to Gregory of Tours, he did so miraculously at Ternay, a site that (as mentioned earlier) possessed relics of Paul and Peter. An old, blind woman stayed day after day in the oratory where the relics were kept. Although the relics belonged to the apostles, she constantly appealed to Martin for help. Finally, "During the night before a Sunday her eyes began to sting with pain. Then she knelt before the holy altar, and when blood flowed [from her eyes], she recovered her sight. But the relics in that place are of the most blessed apostles, that is, of Peter and Paul; nevertheless this woman insisted that she had been healed by the power of the holy bishop [Martin]" (Gregory of Tours, *Vit. Mart.* 4.12, Van Dam). Even in the presence of relics of Paul and Peter, this woman clung to Martin as her helper and healer. In her mind it was the power of Martin, not the apostles, that dominated this place and brought about this miraculous healing.

Local saints also replaced Paul (and Peter) at other locations. A deacon from Angers, whom I mentioned above (see p. 132), was sent to Rome to retrieve relics. He never arrived at his destination, however, on account of an experience that he had along the way. Before he left Angers, the parents of a local man who was both deaf and mute heard about the voyage. They were convinced that, if their son visited the apostolic tombs, he would be healed. The deacon agreed to take the man with him, and along the way they stopped at Nice (ancient Nicaea) at the dwelling of a recluse named Hospicius. The deacon greeted Hospicius and asked for help in gaining passage to Rome. Hospicius, however, demanded to see the other traveler. When the deacon brought the man in, Hospicius prayed for a demon to be removed, and the man was instantly healed. Astonished, the deacon cried out, "I was looking for Peter; I was looking for Paul, Lawrence, and the others who bring fame to Rome by their own blood. *Here I have found them all. Here I have discovered every one of them*" (Gregory of Tours, *Hist. franc.* 6.6, emphasis added). The deacon and his companion no longer needed to go to Rome. In the person of Hospicius, within the boundaries of Gaul itself, they had found a powerful, local substitute for Paul, Peter, and the other Roman martyrs.

Another example of this replacement comes from Lyon. According to local tradition, Epipodius and Alexander were among forty-eight martyrs

---

38. Ibid., 821.

who had died in 177 C.E. during a persecution in the area of Lyon and Vienne. Eusebius says that their bodies were cremated (*Hist. eccl.* 5.1), and Gregory of Tours tells us that Christians gathered as many of their ashes as possible and later placed them in a large church in Lyon, where they honored them annually (*Glor. mart.* 48). In the late fifth century, a preacher in Lyon elevated Epipodius and Alexander to the point of praising them over and against the martyrs from Rome:

> We possess, in fact, the glorious gift of the blessed ones whole and untainted, and, because it is possible to substitute from the entire world, within the womb of this city we hold it particularly close. We exalt the twin palm branches of triumph [Epipodius and Alexander], rivals to the apostolic city, and, since we have our own Peter and Paul, we place our two patrons in competition with that sublime see. (Eusebius "Gallicanus," *Sanct. Eph. Alex.* 4)[39]

The rhetoric is quite strong. The preacher directly challenges the primacy of Rome and the status of its martyrs by claiming that the Lyon saints were "rivals" (*aemulas*) of Paul and Peter. Epipodius and Alexander constitute the new pair of martyr-patrons that merit veneration in the city's basilica. The residents of Lyon were even competing (*certamus*) with "that sublime see."[40] They had no further need of martyrs from Rome, because their "indigenous martyrs" (*Sanct. Eph. Alex.* 1) and their city were inferior to none.

We see, therefore, divergent forces at work in the cult of Paul in Gaul. On the one hand, bishops such as Perpetuus and Gregory of Tours promoted the veneration of Paul in their region. Perpetuus dedicated a basilica to the apostles, and their relics were among those brought back to Tours by Gregory's order in the late sixth century. The number of churches named for Paul and Peter was significant, including a chapel built by Martin, the revered bishop of Tours. Rouen, Nantes, and Condat also rejoiced in the blessing of hosting the apostles. Just as the apostles sanctified Rome—particularly the areas around their tombs—so could they sanctify the churches and shrines of Gaul. Practices associated with the cult of Paul, therefore, reflected an ongoing sense of dependence on traditions originating in Rome. On the other hand, some residents of Gaul increasingly focused their veneration on local saints to the

---

39. Griffe, *Gaule chrétienne*, 3:222–23, credits this panegyric to Faustus of Riez. Cf. Raymond Van Dam, *Leadership and Community in Late Antique Gaul* (Berkeley: University of California Press, 1985), 171, who leaves the work anonymous.

40. The verb *certo* was used by Cicero to describe the competition between Romulus and Remus to name the city of Rome: Certabant, urbem Romam Remoramne vocarent (*Div.* 1.107). Just as the twin founders of Rome had struggled with each other, so now did the twin martyrs of Lyon struggle with the apostolic martyrs of Rome.

exclusion of the Roman martyrs. Martin was foremost among the objects of this devotion. This would-have-been-martyr was equal to the apostles in authority and prestige. Writers presented him as the founder and martyr-patron of the Gallic church. He replaced Paul as the model of a victorious spiritual athlete, and his tomb was considered a sacred place on par with the apostolic shrines in Rome. It was his power, not that of Paul or Peter, that healed a woman in Ternay at a shrine dedicated to the apostles. Other local figures such as Hospicius and the martyrs Epipodius and Alexander further eliminated the need for the Roman martyrs.

In the Christian discourse of late antique Gaul, Paul remained a prominent figure. In some contexts his cult was evidence of an ongoing, intimate relationship with Rome. In other contexts, the displacement of Paul's cult was evidence that such a relationship was no longer viewed as necessary.

3.3. THE PAULINE CULT IN SPAIN

3.3.1. TRADITIONS OF A PAULINE VISIT

The connection between Paul and Spain has its roots in the writings of the apostle himself. In his Epistle to the Romans, Paul expresses his desire to preach in Spain: "Because I no longer have any room for work in these regions, and because I have longed to come to you for many years, whenever I go to Spain, I hope to see you as I am passing through and to be helped along there by you after I enjoy your company for a little while.... I will go by way of you to Spain" (Rom 15:23–24, 28). Writing from Corinth in the late 50s c.e., Paul is looking forward to opening a frontier for his mission in the West. In his recent commentary on Romans, Robert Jewett has argued that the references to Spain are central to the letter as a whole. Paul had preached extensively in the East and now planned to move into new territory, but he needed help from the Roman Christians to line up the required supplies, contacts, and translators. Jewett contends that preparation for the Spanish mission, in fact, is the primary motivation for the letter. Paul wrote the epistle not just to defend himself to the Roman church but also to present himself (and perhaps set the record straight) to those from whom he needed assistance.[41] Despite the explicit references in Romans to Paul's proposed mission to Spain, it appears nowhere else in the New Testament. Some scholars, therefore, have dismissed it as an unrealized hope or simply a fiction.[42] Paul is known to have altered

---

41. Robert Jewett, *Romans: A Commentary* (Hermeneia; Minneapolis: Fortress, 2007), 74–91.

42. Pervo (*Making of Paul*, 133) labels the trip to Spain "unlikely." Allen D. Callahan

his travel plans based on changing circumstances (cf. 1 Cor 16:5–9 and 2 Cor 1:12–24), so the possibility that he might abandon his idea of going to Spain is perfectly in keeping with his attested conduct. Moreover, if the Pastoral Epistles are genuine or at least reflect authentic traditions about Paul, then it is notable that they reveal no knowledge of such a trip. Paul in the Pastorals goes East, not West. Other modern interpreters, however, have taken the Spanish mission seriously in their attempts to reconstruct Paul's life and journeys.[43] In antiquity, the clear reference to an anticipated Spanish mission was sufficient to assume that it had occurred.[44]

The first external reference to such a voyage occurs in the letter from the Roman church to the church in Corinth (*1 Clement*).[45] In describing Paul's example of faithfulness in the face of jealousy and strife, the author notes that the apostle "preached righteousness to the whole world and went to the limit of the west" (*1 Clem.* 5.1.7). This passage seems to reflect an early Roman tradition that Paul had in fact reached Spain.[46] The exact expression "the limit of the west" (τὸ τέρμα τῆς δύσεως) is not otherwise attested in ancient literature, but many authors state that Spain marked the western limit of the known world. Near the end of the first century B.C.E., Diodorus of Sicily says that the city of Gades (modern Cádiz) "is situated at the end of the inhabited world" (*Bibl. hist.* 25.10.1).[47] Writing around the turn of the eras, the geographer Strabo, who had spent time in Rome, refers to the Pillars of Heracles (the Straits of Gibraltar) and the Sacred Cape (Cape of St. Vincent) as "the most westerly point not only of Europe but of the entire inhabited world" (*Geogr.* 3.1.4 [quoted]; 2.1.1; 2.4.3; 3.1.2; 3.5.5).[48] In the first century C.E., the Roman historian Velleius Paterculus places the city of Gades "in the farthest district

("Dead Paul: The Apostle as Martyr in Philippi," in Bakirtzis and Koester, *Philippi at the Time of Paul*, 77) states that the idea of a Spanish mission is "not in the least historical." Gerd Lüdemann (*Paul: Apostle to the Gentiles: Studies in Chronology* [Philadelphia: Fortress, 1984]) does not even discuss the Spanish question.

43. The most developed of such efforts is Murphy-O'Connor, *Paul*, 328–31, 359–63. See also Robert Jewett, *A Chronology of Paul's Life* (Philadelphia: Fortress, 1979), 45–46; E. Earle Ellis, "'The End of the Earth' (Acts 1:8)," *BBR* 1 (1991): 128–32; Tajra, *Martyrdom of St. Paul*, 102–17.

44. Aligning the traditions in the Pastorals with a mission to Spain is difficult, leading most interpreters either to deny both trips or to choose one (usually the Pastorals) and deny the other.

45. On the dating of 1 Clement, see pp. 18–19 n. 7.

46. Cf. Zwierlein, *Petrus in Rom*, 21, who describes this reference to a western mission as a personal deduction by the author based on Rom 15, rather than a tradition known more widely in Rome.

47. Εἰς τὰ ἔσχατα τῆς οἰκουμένης.

48. Τὸ δυτικώτατον οὐ τῆς Εὐρώπης μόνον ἀλλὰ καὶ τῆς οἰκουμένης ἁπάσης σημεῖον.

of Spain, at the extreme end of our world" (*Hist. Rom.* 1.2.3).[49] This way of referring to Spain was still current in the late second century C.E., when Philostratus writes that "the city of Gades lies at the extreme end of Europe" (*Vit. Apoll.* 5.4; 4.47).[50] For a Roman author at the end of the first century, then, "the limit of the West" would refer to Spain.[51] This suggests that the author of *1 Clement* assumed that Paul did not die at the end of the Acts of the Apostles but had been released from imprisonment and traveled farther west to Spain.

The *Acts of Peter* (ca. 180 C.E.) contains the first explicit mention of Paul's trip to Spain, so some details of the narrative are worth repeating here. At the beginning of the story, Paul is teaching in Rome. His prison warden becomes a convert and encourages the apostle to leave the city, presumably for his own safety. Paul fasts for three days and prays for guidance on what to do next. The Lord appears to him in a vision and tells him, "Paul, get up and be a doctor for those in Spain." Paul relates this new calling to those in Rome, and they beg him to return after one year. Just then a heavenly voice interrupts their gathering and announces that Paul will die at the hands of Nero back in Rome. After preaching for several days, Paul boards a ship bound for Spain and departs (*Acta Pet.* 1–3). His mission to Spain is reiterated later in the *Acts of Peter*. When Peter lands at the port city of Puteoli, an innkeeper named Ariston expresses great joy at his arrival: "Then Ariston said (to Peter) that since Paul had left for Spain, no one from among the brothers had been able to refresh him" (*Acta Pet.* 6). Paul was now in Spain and out of the picture in Rome, so Peter steps in to bolster the local community of believers. Only after Peter's death does Paul's name reappear in the narrative, for a Christian senator named Marcellus is described as strengthening himself "until the arrival of Paul at Rome" (*Acta Pet.* 40). This is a reference to Paul's expected return from Spain to face martyrdom in Rome, as the heavenly voice had pronounced, but Paul himself does not appear again in the story.

The Muratorian Canon (or Muratorian Fragment) is an early collection of Christian writings that is probably of Roman origin. It has been alternatively dated to the second or the fourth century (the precise date is immaterial for our purposes) and specifies which books were known and considered author-

---

49. In ultimo Hispaniae tractu, in extremo nostri orbis termino … Gadis condidit.

50. Τὰ δὲ Γάδειρα κεῖται μὲν κατὰ τὸ τῆς Εὐρώπης τέρμα.

51. For further discussion, see Lona, *Der erste Clemensbrief*, 165; Angel Custudio Vega, "La venida de San Pablo a Espana y los Varones Apostólicos," *BRAH* 154 (1964): 17; Zacarías García Villada, *Historia eclesiástica de España* (3 vols.; Madrid: Compañía Iberoamericana de Publicaciones, 1929), 1:122–29; A. González Blanco, "Alusiones a España en las obras de san Juan Crisóstomo," *HAnt* 4 (1974): 352–62; Roger D. Aus, "Paul's Travel Plans to Spain and the 'Full Number of the Gentiles' of Rom XI 25," *NovT* 21.3 (1979): 242–46.

itative in that context. In the description of the Acts of the Apostles, the editor of the list notes, "Luke collected for the most excellent Theophilus the individual things that were done in his presence, as he shows clearly by leaving out the passion of Peter and the departure of Paul from the city [Rome] when he left for Spain."[52] Like the authors of *1 Clement* and the *Acts of Peter*, the editor of this text reflects an early tradition that Paul's Roman imprisonment in Acts had ended with his release. Luke's silence on events after the two-year Roman incarceration (Acts 28:30–31) has been the source of frustration and speculation for interpreters over the centuries. For the editor of the Muratorian Canon, however, this is easily explained by the fact that Luke wrote only about events that he had witnessed. The fact that the visit to Spain was left out of Acts actually confirms Luke's reliability in the rest of the work, without bringing into question the historicity of the Spanish mission itself. The editor of this text presumes that, with the help of the Roman church, Paul had indeed realized his desire to head farther west.

There are many other references to Paul's trip to Spain in the literature of the ancient Christian period. The *Acts of Xanthippe, Polyxena, and Rebecca*,[53] for example, is a third-century account of the romantic adventures of three female converts. This story is based on the premise that Paul had visited and preached in Spain (*Acta Xanth. Pol. Reb.* 7–24). Additional patristic witnesses include Jerome (*Ep.* 71.1), John Chrysostom (*Hom. Act.* 55; *Laud. Paul.* 7), Theodoret of Cyrus (*Paul. ep. comm.*, 2 Tim 4:17), and an anonymous biography of Epiphanius of Salamis (*Vit. Epiph.* 13). It is not necessary to discuss all these texts in detail. It suffices to say that many early Christian writers,

---

52. Translation based on the Latin critical text in Bruce Metzger, *The Canon of the New Testament: Its Origin, Development, and Significance* (Oxford: Clarendon, 1987), 199–201. The Muratorian Canon takes its name from Ludovico Antonio Muratori, who discovered it in Milan and published it in 1740. The traditional, second-century date has been defended by Everett Ferguson, "Canon Muratori: Date and Provenance," *StPatr* 17.2 (1982): 677–83; Charles E. Hill, "The Debate over the Muratorian Fragment and the Development of the Canon," *WTJ* 57 (1995): 437–452. Advocates for a fourth-century date include Albert C. Sundberg Jr., "Canon Muratori: A Fourth Century List," *HTR* 66 (1973): 1–41; Geoffrey Mark Hahneman, *The Muratorian Fragment and the Development of the Canon* (Oxford: Clarendon, 1992); Harry Y. Gamble, "The New Testament Canon: Recent Research and the Status Quaestionis," in *The Canon Debate* (ed. Lee Martin McDonald and James A. Sanders; Peabody, Mass.: Hendrickson, 2002), 267–94.

53. In M. R. James, ed., *Apocrypha Anecdota: A Collection of Thirteen Apocryphal Books and Fragments Now First Edited from Manuscripts* (TS 2.3; Cambridge: Cambridge University Press, 1893), 58–85. The text is set primarily in Spain, but the author reflects no knowledge of Spanish geography or customs and fails even to identify which city is the setting for the action. It was more likely produced in Rome, with Spain employed as a dramatic literary context.

informed by earlier textual or oral traditions, took Paul's voyage to Spain as a fact.[54]

Strangely, no Spanish writer of late antiquity known to us mentions this putative Pauline visit. Literary references to Paul's activities are not known in the writings of Spanish authors until the eighth century.[55] This creates a perplexing situation for the reconstruction of the earliest history of Christianity in Spain. Paul had expressed his desire to preach in Spain, and his visit there is widely spoken of by ancient Christian writers both in Rome and in the East. In addition, we know that Christianity arrived in Spain by the late second century C.E. Both Irenaeus in Gaul (*Haer.* 1.10.2) and Tertullian in North Africa (*Adv. Jud.* 7.45) attest to the existence of Christian communities in Spain in their time. Why, then, did Spanish authors not lay claim to this apostolic pedigree at an earlier date? There is no obvious answer to this question based on the available evidence. The cult of the apostle James, who has been Spain's patron saint since the medieval period, is not attested until the seventh century at the earliest.[56] Paul had no obvious rival in Spain in the earliest period, yet as it stands, we have only external literary witnesses to his alleged visit there.

3.3.2. The Vestiges of the Pauline Cult in Spain

While the Spanish literary sources for a visit are silent, there is nonetheless evidence for a Pauline cult in Spain in late antiquity (fig. 3.6). Prudentius is an important source in this regard. Writing at the end of the fourth century, this Spaniard bemoans the geographical plight of his compatriots. They are at a distinct disadvantage, because they live so far from the abundance of martyrs' tombs that existed in Rome:

54. See also Ernst Dubowy, *Klemens von Rom über die Reise Pauli nach Spanien: Historisch-kritische Untersuchung zu Klemens von Rom: 1 Kor 5,7* (BibS(F) 19.3; Freiburg im Breisgau: Herder, 1914); Luis Aguirre Prado, *San Pablo en España* (TEsp 435; Madrid: Publicaciones Españolas, 1963); González Blanco, "Alusiones a España," 352–62.

55. Pedro Castillo Maldonado, "*Angelorum Participes*: The Cult of the Saints in Late Antique Spain," in *Hispania in Late Antiquity: Current Perspectives* (ed. Kim Bowes and Michael Kulikowski; Boston: Brill, 2005), 152; Custudio Vega, "La venida de San Pablo," 9–12; Otto F. A. Meinardus, "Paul's Missionary Journey to Spain: Tradition and Folklore," *BA* 41.2 (1978): 62–63. The medieval period saw an explosion of stories related to Paul, particularly in southern Spain.

56. Louis Duchesne, "Saint Jacques en Galice," *AMidi* 12 (1900): 145–79; R. A. Fletcher, *Saint James's Catapult: The Life and Times of Diego Gelmírez of Santiago de Compostela* (Oxford: Clarendon, 1984), 54.

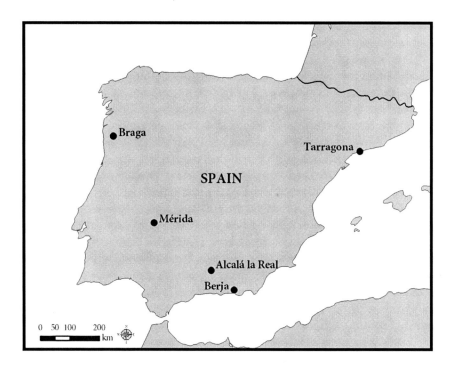

Fig. 3.6. Pauline cult sites in Spain.

O thrice and four times, yea seven times blessed the dweller of Rome, who pays honor to thee and the abode of thy bones in presence, who can kneel by them, who sprinkles the spot with his tears, bowing his breast to the ground and in a low voice pouring out his prayers. Us the Vascon Ebro separates from thee, we are far removed beyond two mountain ranges, across the Cottian heights and the snowy Pyrenees. Scarcely even have we heard report how full Rome is of buried saints, how richly her city's soil blossoms with holy tombs. Still, though we lack these blessings and cannot see the traces of blood with our own eyes, we look up to heaven on high. (Prudentius, *Perist.* 2.529–548, Thomson)

In the view of Prudentius, the landscape of Rome was sanctified by the presence of the tombs and relics of martyrs such as Paul. Spain lacked equivalent shrines in his time,[57] so its residents had to console themselves with alternatives. Some would simply "look up to heaven on high," yet elsewhere Pru-

---

57. The seventh century saw a proliferation and expansion of saints' cults to an extent more typical of other regions (Castillo Maldonado, "*Angelorum Participes*," 151–88).

dentius encouraged Spanish Christians to import and reproduce rituals of the apostolic cult on their own soil.

Prudentius dedicated poem 12 of *On the Crowns of Martyrdom* to a description of the June 29 festival of the apostles in Rome. At the opening of the poem, an uninformed visitor in the city—representing his uninformed audience—asks why Rome was in such an uproar. Prudentius responds, "Today we have the festival of the apostles' triumph coming round again, a day made famous by the blood of Paul and Peter. The same day, but recurring after a full year, saw each of them win the laurel by a splendid death" (*Perist.* 12.3–6, Thomson). He then explains to this visitor the story of Paul and Peter and their commemoration in Rome. At the end of the poem, Prudentius gives a charge to his anonymous companion and his audience: "It is enough for you to have learned all this at Rome; when you return home, remember to keep this day of two festivals as you see it here" (12.65–66, Thomson). Prudentius does not specify where "home" is in this case, but ten of the fourteen poems in *On the Crowns of Martyrdom* are directed at a Spanish audience or are about Spanish martyrs. In addition, Prudentius's use of "home" in these poems typically refers to Spain,[58] so I take it that the inhabitants of Spain are the primary audience for this poem, as well.

Prudentius describes here the astonishing scene in Rome on June 29, yet the goal of this poem is not primarily to encourage pilgrimage to that city. Rather, Prudentius intends to inspire his compatriots to copy the Roman practices in their region.[59] He wants the residents of Spain to establish their own festival in honor of Paul and Peter. In doing so, they would create local places and ritual traditions for the apostolic cult. The bones and blood may have been in Rome, but by venerating the saints, the Christians of Spain could see their own soil blossom at the sites where they bowed to pray and shed their tears. Pilgrims could visit holy places without having to cross the daunting mountains, and the cult could thrive in Spain with as much fervor as it did in Rome itself.

A fragmentary inscription now housed in Alcalá la Real suggests that Prudentius may have had some success in promoting the apostolic cult. This partial text of a liturgical calendar includes the following notation: "(Of the holy) apostles Peter and (Paul on the third) kalends of July [June 29]."[60] The inscription probably dates from the sixth century and appears to preserve the

---

58. Fux, *Les sept passions de Prudence*, 344.

59. Prudentius employs Rome throughout his work as "a model to which Spanish communities can aspire" (Roberts, *Poetry and the Cult of the Martyrs*, 36).

60. José Vives, *Inscripciones cristianas de la España romana y visigoda* (BHBB 2/18; Barcelona: Consejo Superior de Investigaciones Científicas, 1942), 335; *ILCV* 1813A.

same date for the feast that the Roman church observed. Some Christians of
the region had perhaps heeded the words of Prudentius. They adopted the
Roman festival for the cult and made it part of the annual liturgical cycle in
their city.[61]

Sarcophagus art is another medium in which we find evidence of the
apostolic cult in Spain. A white marble coffin from Berja (ancient Vergis),
but probably of Italian provenance, includes an iconographical representation of the condemnation of Paul and Peter by Nero (fig. 3.7).[62] This image is

Fig. 3.7. Berja sarcophagus showing Paul and Peter before Nero. In the Museo Arqueológico Nacional, Madrid. Courtesy of Museo Arqueológico Nacional, Madrid.

---

61. Other Spanish cities followed the example of Alcalá la Real in the Visigothic
period. See Anne-Marie Palmer, *Prudentius on the Martyrs* (Oxford: Clarendon, 1989),
261–62.

62. Giuseppe Bovini, *Sarcofagi paleocristiani della Spagna* (CACat 22; Vatican City:
Società Amici delle catacombe, 1954), 150–54, no. 25; J. M. Carriazo, "El sarcófago cristiano de Berja," *AEAA* 1 (1925): 197–218. Carriazo argues for Italian provenance (at 212),
which seems most likely. The possibility of Spanish production based on a Roman model
cannot be completely eliminated, however. J. Manjarrés Mangas and J. M. Roldán Hervás,
España Romana (218 a. de J.C.–414 de J.C.) (2nd ed.; 2 vols.; Madrid: Espasa-Calpe, 1982),
2:423–24, have argued that Roman influence can be seen as early as the fourth century on
sarcophagi being produced in workshops in Tarragona.

significant for its subject but also for its uniqueness in early Christian art. The two apostles stand side by side, identifiable by their iconographical attributes. Peter wears a long toga and holds a scroll in his left hand. He has a beard and a full head of hair. Next to him is Paul, likewise with a toga, scroll, and beard but identified by his balding head. Roman soldiers stand to either side of the apostles, and one seizes Peter's right arm. All four figures face a man seated on a throne. He has a beard and crown and extends his right arm toward the apostles. His left arm holds a long scepter, and another Roman soldier stands behind him. The seated figure is Nero,[63] and the scene parallels the traditions reflected in the Latin *Passion of the Holy Apostles Peter and Paul* and Greek *Acts of the Holy Apostles Peter and Paul*. According to the story, a sorcerer in Rome named Simon Magus[64] enjoyed the particular favor of Nero. Peter and Paul denounced him as a fraud, and a contest of power was arranged. Simon took to the air and began to fly over Rome, but by prayer the apostles struck him down to his death.[65] Nero was infuriated and ordered the apostles to appear before him. After questioning them, the emperor condemned both men to death (*Pass. Pet. Paul.* 51–60; *Acta Pet. Paul.* 72–81). This sarcophagus represents the moment at which Nero raised his hand to pronounce sentence. It is an allusion to the martyrdom of the apostles that is unparalleled in early Christian iconography,[66] yet its subject matter is clear. Peter and Paul stand before Nero, about to be sentenced to death and executed. This coffin serves as an important artifact of the proliferation of the Pauline cult in Spain. Some wealthy person seemingly went to considerable expense to bring this sarcophagus from Italy to southern Spain, where it stood as a memorial to the Roman roots of the apostolic church in the West.

References to Paul's relics in Spain are relatively rare but not unknown. The dedicatory inscription for a church built in Mérida (ancient Emerita

---

63. The representation of Nero is not typical for images of him, but the surrounding scene makes the identification clear. Bovini suggests that the artist may have drawn inspiration from images of Herod or Nebuchadnezzar. Cf. Carriazo, "Sarcófago," 211, who identifies the figured as a general magistrate or prefect.

64. This figure is traditionally linked to the Simon in Acts who attempts to buy the power to confer the Holy Spirit (Acts 8:9–24). Irenaeus of Lyon (*Haer.* 1.23) and Justin Martyr (*1 Apol.* 25) say that he was a Samaritan who came to Rome and deceived many by his magical arts.

65. Zwierlein (*Petrus in Rom*, 129–33) has argued that the tradition of a Petrine visit to Rome to defeat Simon (the "Father of Gnosis") did not appear until the second century in the context of the Roman church's struggle with gnostic heretics, the successors of Simon.

66. We have seen that iconographical references to Paul's death typically show him next to a soldier drawing his sword. Peter usually appears with his hands bound, being led off by soldiers to his death.

Augusta) in honor of Mary states, "Here are stored the relics … of the blood of our Lord, of Saint John the Baptist, of Saint S(tephen?), of Saint Paul, of Saint John the Evangelist."[67] This inscription is the earliest explicit reference to the relics of Paul in Spain.[68] His name appears here among a venerable list of Christian martyrs in a basilica that was rich in holy objects. Another possible reference appears in a letter written in 538 from Bishop Vigilius of Rome (537–555) to Bishop Profuturus of Braga (ancient Bracara Augusta, located in modern Portugal). Vigilius discusses the prayers and festival calendar of the Roman church and adds that he is sending to Profuturus relics "of the blessed apostles or martyrs" (*Profut.* 5).[69] Vigilius does not name Paul and Peter specifically, but we have already seen that Roman bishops could be generous in distributing relics of the apostles, even if only secondary relics. It is possible, then, that Vigilius sent *brandea* from the Ostian Road and the Vatican to the bishop in Braga. These would have served as tangible symbols of the translocation of the apostolic cult, now brought from its Roman source to a new outpost on the western coast of Spain.

In the earliest references to Paul's alleged mission to Spain, Rome is prominent. It is in his letter to the Romans that Paul mentions his desire to travel farther west, and the earliest attestations of this journey are in texts with strong ties to the Roman context: *1 Clement*, the *Acts of Peter*, and the Muratorian Canon. At the end of the fourth century, Prudentius employs the Roman model to promote the apostolic cult to his fellow Spaniards. Liturgical and archaeological evidence indicates that the poet may have had some success, for in late antiquity Spanish Christians embraced practices associated with the Pauline cult as a means of honoring the apostle who had left Rome to bring the Christian message to their shores.

CONCLUSION

Paul's association with Rome had a significant influence on the spread of the Pauline cult throughout the rest of Latin Europe. In the case of Milan, Bishop Ambrose emulated the architecture, veneration practices, and festivals of the ancient capital as a means of establishing his "new Rome." In Gaul, the pic-

---

67. Sunt reliquiae recondite […] de cruce D(omi)ni N(ostr)I, s(an)c(t)i Iohanni Baptiste, s(an)c(t)i S[tefani(?) …], s(an)c(t)i Pauli, s(an)c(t)i Iohanni Evangeliste (J. M. de Navascués y de Juan, "La dedicación de la iglesia de Santa María y de todas las Vírgenes de Mérida," *AEAr* 21 [1948]: 311).

68. Ibid., 349.

69. C. García Rodríguez, *El culto de los santos en la España romana y visigoda* (Madrid: C.S.I.C., 1966), 147.

ture was more complex. Some considered Paul a model martyr and sought to appropriate the sacred power of the apostles from its Roman source through constructing basilicas and other holy places, acquiring relics, and establishing festivals. In this same period, however, local saints were also rising to increasing prominence. A few authors claimed that these Gallic saints had eliminated the need for Paul as a martyr-patron. Invoking Paul was significant only as a way of emphasizing the influence and authority of these local figures. The promotion of these new patrons and their shrines directed the attention of Christians in Gaul away from the holy sites and martyrs of Rome and toward places and practices within their own region. For Spain, Paul's stated desire to go there linked him with this region from an early date in the minds of some Christians. While evidence for the Pauline cult is less abundant there than elsewhere, there are indications that Prudentius's efforts to promote a cult on the Roman model met with some success.

In all these regions, I have argued that the reception and adaptation of the Pauline cult, particularly through the establishment of sacred spaces, can be linked to attitudes toward Rome itself. The acceptance and replication of the cult reflected a recognition of the preeminence of Rome, the epicenter of the cult. Among those wishing to destabilize the Roman position, however, local figures with their own cults and cult sites were elevated as alternative martyr-patrons. Even in doing so, however, the advocates of indigenous saints exploited the cult of Paul to elevate local heroes to a status equal or even superior to that of Paul himself.

4

THE PAULINE CULT IN NORTH AFRICA

The cult of martyrs was a prominent feature of Christian piety in North Africa (a region that encompassed large portions of modern Tunisia, Algeria, and Morocco). Christians here suffered under persecutions by the Roman imperial government in the second, third, and fourth centuries, so they felt an affinity with Paul, who had likewise been victimized by a malevolent emperor. From the large coastal cities of Proconsular Africa to the small towns in outlying areas of Numidia and Mauretania (fig. 4.1), African Christians established their own sacred spaces for the Pauline cult through practices familiar to us

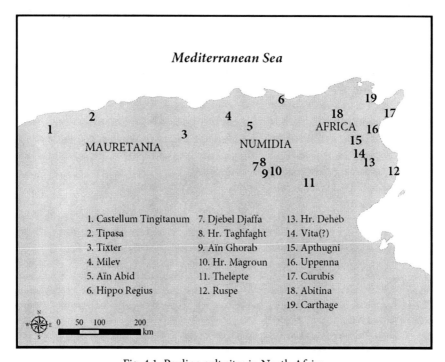

Fig. 4.1. Pauline cult sites in North Africa.

from other regions: the construction of churches and shrines, the production of literary accounts, the celebration of festivals, relic veneration, and privileged burials. An important element in the development of the North African cult, as was the case in the last chapter, was the African church's connection to the Roman church. This connection, therefore, will be central to my discussion here, particularly in the context of the Donatist controversy, where opposing sides competed over the claim to be the *true church* in the Pauline tradition.

4.1. PAUL AS MODEL MARTYR IN THE NORTH AFRICAN TRADITION

Paul never visited the shores of North Africa. Neither the New Testament accounts nor the apocryphal literature of ancient Christianity includes any reference to a Pauline mission in this region. Nonetheless, Paul's reputation and letters made an impact in North Africa, for he is an important figure in the region's earliest martyrological literature. The *Acts of the Scillitan Martyrs* dates from 180 C.E. and is a trial transcript for a group of Christians from the town of Scillium. Although we know that Augustine preached a sermon in a basilica built over their tombs (*Serm.* 155), the exact location of Scillium is still unknown.[1] These were some of the last victims of sporadic persecutions that occurred during the reign of the emperor Marcus Aurelius (161–180). Since the time of Trajan (98–117), being a Christian had technically been a crime punishable by death, but this standard was applied only selectively.[2] For reasons that are unknown, the proconsul of North Africa, Saturninus, decided to enforce this penalty on twelve Christians from Scillium. He arrested and brought them to Carthage for trial. There he demanded that they renounce their faith and offer a pinch of incense in honor of the emperor. When they refused, the proconsul attempted to dissuade them from their intractable position by urging them to consider the possible sentence.[3] The group remained resolute, however.

---

1. This basilica is also mentioned in Victor of Vita (*Hist. persec.* 1.3.9). The site was probably somewhere in Numidia, according to Roderic L. Mullen, *The Expansion of Christianity: A Gazetteer of Its First Three Centuries* (VCSup 69; Leiden: Brill, 2004), 317.

2. G. E. M. de Ste. Croix, "Why Were the Early Christians Persecuted?" *PaP* 26 (1963): 6–38; A. N. Sherwin-White, "Why Were the Early Christians Persecuted?—An Amendment," *PaP* 27 (1964): 23–27. These two authors disagree on the rationale for executing Christians in the first two centuries, but they agree on the seemingly random application of this punishment.

3. Pliny the Younger wrote to the emperor Trajan that the "inflexible obstinacy" of Christians was in itself worthy of punishment (Pliny, *Ep. Tra.* 10.96). Tertullian also stated that the "obstinate persistence" of Christians was often used as a charge against them (*Apol.*

The *Acts* account contains a verbal exchange between Saturninus and the Christians, and Paul's letters play a role at several points. When pressed repeatedly to honor the emperor, Speratus, the main spokesman for the Christians, declares, "I do not know the emperor of this age, but I serve instead that God whom no man sees nor is able to see with these eyes" (*Acta mart. Scillit.* 18–20). Here Speratus is paraphrasing a passage in the Pauline corpus, where God is described as dwelling "in unapproachable light, whom no man has ever seen or can see" (1 Tim 6:16). Facing the prospect of death, Speratus draws on Pauline language to counter the proconsul's demands. As the text reaches its climax, the importance of Paul's letters for Speratus and the other Christians comes to the forefront again:

> Speratus said, "I am a Christian." And they all agreed with him.
> Saturninus the proconsul said, "Do you want time to deliberate?"
> Speratus said, "In a just matter like this, there is no deliberation."
> Saturninus the proconsul said, "What are the things in your box?"
> Speratus said, "Books and epistles[4] of Paul, a just man."
> Saturninus the proconsul said, "Have a delay of thirty days and think it over."
> Speratus said again, "I am a Christian." And they all agreed with him. (*Acta mart. Scillit.* 10–13)

Note the progression of the narrative here, which features a distinctive chiastic structure.

A   "I am a Christian." And they all agreed with him.
    B   "Do you want time to deliberate?" "In a just matter like this, there is no deliberation."
        C   "What are the things in your box?" "Books of the epistles of Paul, a just man."
    B'   "Have a delay of thirty days and think it over."
A'   "I am a Christian." And they all agreed with him.

The frame is the repetition of the formula "I am a Christian...," which is an *inclusio* marking the beginning and end of this chiasm (A, A').[5] Saturninus

---

27). On the role of Saturninus in this story, see A. R. Birley, "Persecutors and Martyrs in Tertullian's North Africa," in *The Later Roman Empire Today: Papers Given in Honour of Professor John Mann* (ed. D. F. Clark et al.; London: Institute of Archaeology, 1993), 14–24.

4. The Latin reads *libri et epistulae*, but A. A. R. Bastiaensen has argued that this should be understood as *libri epistularum* ("books of the epistles"). See *Atti e Passioni dei Martiri* (2nd ed.; Milan: Mondadori, 1990), 410.

5. The term *chiasm* is taken from the form of the Greek letter *chi* (X). It refers to a

offers extra time for Speratus to reconsider his answer, but Speratus says that no more time is necessary (B). Later the proconsul restates his offer of additional time (B'). At the center of this chiasm is the reference to Paul (C). It functions as the turning point in the narrative, for after this exchange the proconsul immediately announces, "Speratus, Nartzalus, Cittinus, Donata, Vestia, Secunda, and the others have confessed that they live according to the Christian rite. Because they have obstinately persisted, although an opportunity was given to them to return to the custom of the Romans, it is resolved that they will be punished by the sword" (*Acta mart. Scillit.* 14). From a narrative perspective, why would Saturninus suddenly ask about the box and then move directly to condemnation? Or, from a literary perspective (and perhaps more to the point), why did the editor of the text construct a chiasm around this question and answer about Paul at this critical juncture in the narrative?

I believe that the answer lies in Paul's role in North Africa as a model martyr. In the midst of persecution, these Christians carried with them a box that contained writings from Paul.[6] From his letters they drew encouragement to persevere and face any trial. As the apostle had written, "The Spirit himself bears witness with our spirit that we are children of God ... provided we suffer with him in order that we may also be glorified with him. For I consider that the sufferings of this present time are not worth comparing with the glory that is to be revealed to us" (Rom 8:16–18). In addition to Paul's teaching, his example was a source of strength for these Christians:

> Five times I received at the hands of the Jews the forty lashes less one.
> Three times I was beaten with rods. Once I was stoned. Three times I was

---

literary device through which an author focuses the reader's attention on a single point or idea (at the center of the X) but surrounds this central point with other narrative elements that are in turn parallel to each other in concentric rings (in this case ABCB'A'). An *inclusio* is a framing device in which a word or phrase is used to bracket the opening and closing of a distinct section of a narrative. These literary techniques have been studied extensively in the New Testament and to a lesser extent in other early Christian literature, e.g., Nils Wilhelm Lund, *Chiasmus in the New Testament: A Study in Formgeschichte* (Chapel Hill: University of North Carolina Press, 1942); John W. Welch, ed., *Chiasmus in Antiquity: Structures, Analyses, Exegesis* (Hildesheim: Gerstenberg, 1981); John Breck, *The Shape of Biblical Language: Chiasmus in the Scriptures and Beyond* (Crestwood, N.Y.: St. Vladimir's Seminary Press, 1994); Ian H. Thomson, *Chiasmus in the Pauline Letters* (Sheffield: Sheffield Academic Press, 1995).

6. It is not clear which epistles they would have had, but a corpus of Pauline letters was probably circulating at a very early date. See David Trobish, *Paul's Letter Collection: Tracing the Origins* (Minneapolis: Fortress, 1994); Stanley E. Porter, "When and How Was the Pauline Canon Compiled? An Assessment of Theories," in *The Pauline Canon* (ed. Stanley E. Porter; Leiden: Brill, 2004), 95–127.

shipwrecked; a night and a day I was adrift at sea; on frequent journeys, in danger from rivers, danger from robbers, danger from my own people, danger from Gentiles, danger in the city, danger in the wilderness, danger at sea, danger from false brothers; in toil and hardship, through many a sleepless night, in hunger and thirst, often without food, in cold and exposure. (2 Cor 11:24–27)

The apostle that these North African Christians had read about had suffered much during his journeys, eventually dying for his faith. The author of this martyrdom story draws attention to the fact that the Scillitans, now faced with their own demise, were carrying some of the apostle's epistles. These brought them comfort and encouragement in their time of distress. Speratus and company did not face the proconsul and death alone, for through his letters Paul was present with them as a model and source of strength.

In death as in life, these Christians are presented as following the Pauline example. Having rejected "the custom of the Romans," they suffer death by decapitation at the order of an imperial official, just as the apostle had done. Paul is conspicuous in the *Acts of the Scillitan Martyrs* through his letters and through the martyrs' imitation of his example. The author highlights the points of connection between Paul's story and the experience of Speratus and his companions, and the brief exchange about Paul seems to seal their fate. The courage of the martyrs from Scillium was worthy of remembrance in its own right, but they were worthy of particular praise because they followed in the path of one of Christianity's greatest martyrs.

The next North African reference to Paul as a model martyr comes from Tertullian, writing around the turn of the third century C.E. In his work *On the Prescription against Heretics*, the author makes two allusions to the deaths of Paul and Peter in Rome. In the first context, Tertullian is responding to those who were asserting Paul's superiority over Peter. As part of their argument, they were seemingly claiming that Paul's death was nobler than Peter's and gave him greater status. Tertullian answers that this line of thought is foolish, for both apostles are on the same level in their spiritual status as martyrs: "Pay no attention to those who pass judgment concerning the apostles. Rightly is Peter made equal to Paul in martyrdom" (*Praescr.* 24.4). Both sides of the debate accepted the elevated status of Paul as martyr, so in this case Tertullian actually seeks to *elevate* Peter's status by comparing him with Paul. Later in the same work, Tertullian returns to the issue of Paul's martyrdom. In this context he is arguing for the continuity of the apostolic tradition, as witnessed in its ancient centers at Corinth, Philippi, Thessaloniki, and Ephesus. He finally turns his attention to Rome: "How blessed is that church to which the apostles poured out the entire doctrine with their own blood, where Peter is made equal to the passion of the Lord, where Paul is crowned by a death like that of John [the Baptist]" (*Praescr.* 36.3). The shedding of apostolic blood was central to the foundation and spread of the Christian message in Rome. Because their deaths mirrored those of Jesus and John the Baptist, Peter and Paul became model martyrs who blessed the Roman church.

Tertullian again raises the apostolic martyrs as models in *Antidote for the Scorpion's Sting*, a work in which he argues that martyrdom is not only good but is actually *commanded* by God. Those who would deny the necessity of suffering need only remember the examples of the apostles: "That Peter is beaten, that Stephen is crushed, that James is sacrificed, that Paul is dragged away—these things are written with their own blood." Even non-Christian sources confirmed the cruelty endured by the apostles in Rome: "We read the lives of the caesars. Nero was the first who stained in blood the rising faith at Rome. Then Peter is tied around the body by another when he is bound to the cross. Then Paul obtains the birth of Roman citizenship, when in that place he is born again by the nobility of martyrdom" (*Scorp.* 15). Here Tertullian links the apostles' deaths with the accounts of Nero's reign by the Roman historians Tacitus and Suetonius. According to Tacitus, the residents of Rome believed that Nero was responsible for setting the fire that destroyed a large part of the city in 64 C.E. The emperor attempted to cover up his crime by blaming the Christians. He persecuted them mercilessly, even beyond what the proponents of this "most mischievous superstition" deserved (*Ann.* 15.44). Suetonius agreed in ascribing to Nero the "torture of the Christians, a class of men following a new and mischievous superstition" (*Nero* 16). Chief among the traditional victims of Nero's rage were the apostles. In this treatise defending the merits of martyrdom, Tertullian points to Paul alongside Peter as an important example. The apostle had not wavered, even when facing an emperor as ferocious as Nero. Paul was not like those "who oppose martyr-doms, interpreting salvation as destruction" (*Scorp.* 1). Instead, he showed the way for the faithful who would follow him. Tertullian's appeals to Paul in these two texts demonstrate that, by the end of the second century, the apostle was known in the region for his courage and faithfulness to the point of death. Christians in North Africa saw Paul as a model martyr, worthy of imitation.

Paul also appears as a model in the accounts of the death of North Africa's most famous martyr, the bishop Cyprian. Cyprian was bishop of Carthage from 248 to 258 C.E., and two versions of his martyrdom were produced soon after his death. According to the *Acts of Cyprian*, the proconsul Paternus exiled Cyprian in 257 to the city of Curubis (modern Kourba, Tunisia). In 258 the bishop was back in Carthage and then summoned by the new proconsul, Galerius Maximus. When Cyprian refused to perform honorary rites for the emperor, the proconsul reluctantly sentenced him to death. In recounting the details of Cyprian's death, the anonymous author of the *Acts* makes two connections between the bishop's martyrdom and that of Paul.

First, as Cyprian approaches the place of execution, "Many cloths and handkerchiefs were placed in front of him by the brothers. Cyprian then covered his eyes by his own hand, but since he could not tie the ends of the handkerchief by himself, Julian the presbyter and Julian the subdeacon tied it for him" (*Acta Cypr.* 5.4–5). The blindfold and cloths placed before Cyprian were intended to catch his blood when he was beheaded. These would become relics carrying the full power of the saint. The cloths thrown before Cyprian are reminiscent of the shroud that covered Paul's eyes and caught the blood at his execution. This relic—reputedly returned posthumously by Paul himself to Plautilla (or Perpetua)—was supposedly stained with the apostle's blood and had healing power.[7] According to the *Acts of Cyprian*, the bishop put on a blindfold in Pauline fashion at the time of his death. It also would have been soaked in blood, along with the handkerchiefs thrown before him, making them all holy relics.

The author makes a second, more implicit connection between Cyprian and Paul at the moment that the proconsul pronounces judgment: "It is resolved that Thascius Cyprian will be punished by the sword" (*Acta Cypr.* 4). The Latin phrase used to describe Cyprian's sentence (*gladio animaduerti placet*) is identical to the phrase used at sentencing in the *Acts of the Scillitan Martyrs*. The author of the *Acts of Cyprian*, therefore, is linking Cyprian with the Scillitans and by extension with the Pauline legacy. Cyprian died by the sword, just as the Scillitan martyrs and Paul before him. While death by decapitation was not unique to these martyrs, I would argue that the author of the *Acts of Cyprian* has employed specific narrative details (the placement of handkerchiefs, death by sword) in order to set up a clear line of succession. Paul was the great first-century example of Christian martyrdom by beheading. In North Africa, this legacy was continued in the second century by the Scillitan martyrs, who were carrying Paul's letters at their trial. Finally, Cyprian took up the mantle as the great third-century example of this model of noble death.

Roughly contemporaneous with the *Acts of Cyprian* is the *Life of Cyprian* by Pontius, a deacon of Carthage who knew Cyprian personally. Pontius also draws a direct line of succession, in this case from the martyred apostles Paul and Peter to Cyprian. Pontius introduces the comparison by claiming that the former bishop had endured many trials and at last received the prize of a most glorious martyrdom: "Since his passion was thus accomplished, it came about that Cyprian, who had been an example to all good men, was also the first

---

7. This is the shroud requested from Gregory I by the empress Constantina.

example in North Africa who drenched [in blood] his priestly crown. He was the foremost [*prior*] after the apostles to undertake being such an example" (*Vit. Cypr.* 19). When the moment came for Cyprian to shed his blood, he presented a noble example to all, following the pattern of Paul and Peter. As a result, he became the foremost martyr of North Africa and the local successor to the apostolic legacy.

Just as Cyprian had followed Paul's example as a martyr, so should all Christians, according to the third-century *On the Glory of Martyrdom*. This sermon is falsely ascribed to Cyprian and may also be the work of Pontius.[8] In the midst of this lengthy treatise in praise of martyrdom, the author states,

> The apostle Paul says, "Be imitators of me, as I also am of Christ." And the same one says elsewhere, "I wish that all of you, if it were possible, should be imitators of me." The one who said this suffered, and suffered for this cause, that he might imitate the Lord. Certainly, he wished us also to suffer for this cause, that through him we might imitate Christ. (*Glor. martyr.* 28–29)

All Christians are called to imitate the example of Paul, who in turn had followed the example of Christ. The author here appeals to two passages from 1 Corinthians (6:4 and 7:7) to argue that the imitation of Christ, for Paul, pointed specifically to suffering and martyrdom. Paul's experience and model should be normative, so the path to martyrdom in the footsteps of Christ and Paul is the road for any true Christian.

A final witness to this image of Paul in North Africa comes from the late fifth-century *History of the Vandal Persecution in Africa*. Victor, bishop of Vita (possibly near modern Kairouan, Tunisia), chronicles the suffering of the pro-Nicene Christians in the region as a result of the invasion and alleged cruelties by the pro-Arian, Vandal leader Hunneric (477–484). Victor tells that at one point Hunneric closed the Nicene churches and seized for Arian worship the basilicas that housed the bodies of great North African martyrs such as Perpetua, Felicity, and the Scillitans (*Hist. persec.* 1.9). Hunneric continued to add to his crimes by interfering with the succession of bishops: "After the death of the bishop of Carthage, it then came about that it was forbidden to ordain bishops in Zeugitana and the Proconsular province (roughly the area of modern Tunisia). At that time there were 164, and the number dropped off little by little. Now it seems that there are only three, if they still survive: Vincentius of Gegi, Paul of Sinnar[9]—truly Paul by merit and by name—and

---

8. Hugo Koch, *Cyprianische Untersuchungen* (AKG 4; Bonn: Marcus & Weber, 1926), 334–57.

9. The locations of Gegi and Sinnar are unknown.

another Quintianus" (1.29). The comparison to the apostle Paul here differs from the previous examples, because the bishop of Sinnar was not yet dead, at least as far as Victor knew. In fact, he stood out specifically because he was still alive. Nonetheless, Victor focuses on the fact that this bishop was suffering as a *confessor* in the face of persecution by a cruel ruler. In doing so, this Paul followed the example of his predecessor and had earned the right to be called by the same name.[10] Even though he had not yet died, Bishop Paul's actions made him "by merit" a worthy namesake of the apostle.

These examples taken from the second through the fifth centuries demonstrate that Paul enjoyed great fame in North Africa as a model martyr. Because martyrdom played such an important role in Christian self-identity in this region, Paul's death earned him a prominent position in the literature. The authors of North Africa saw their own martyrs as heirs to this Pauline legacy. They sprinkled their accounts of the deaths of local martyrs with allusions to the stories about Paul. The Scillitan martyrs and Cyprian were like Paul in their deaths, and the bishop of Sinnar was like the apostle in his faithfulness in the face of persecution. For one author, this imitation of Paul through martyrdom was the standard for all true Christians. Although he had never visited North Africa, the apostle Paul loomed large on the Christian conceptual landscape in the region. "Born again by the nobility of martyrdom" (Tertullian, *Scorp.* 15), Paul encouraged others to follow in his footsteps.

4.2. SPECIAL CELEBRATIONS IN THE CONTEXT OF THE CULT

The annual feast of Paul and Peter had become an important date on the church's liturgical calendar at least by the time of Augustine.[11] In a sermon that probably dates from 410 and was preached in the basilica at Hippo Regius (modern Annaba, Algeria), Augustine begins, "This day has been consecrated for us by the martyrdoms of the most blessed apostles Peter and Paul. It's not some obscure martyrs we are talking about. Their sound has gone out into all the earth, and their words to the ends of the wide world. These martyrs had seen what they proclaimed; they pursued justice by confessing the truth, by

---

10. Cf. *Acta Phil.* 2–3, where Bishop Phileas of Thmuis (Egypt) appeals to Paul as an example of one who neither offered incense to the emperor nor denied the faith.

11. Guy Lapointe, *La célébration des martyrs en Afrique d'après les sermons de saint Augustin* (CCommChr 8; Montreal: Communauté chrétienne, 1972). Cyprian of Carthage tells us that a liturgical calendar for the martyrs existed in North Africa by at least the middle of the third century (*Ep.* 12.2.1; 39.3.1), but he makes no specific reference to the feast of the apostles.

dying for the truth" (*Serm.* 295.1, Hill).[12] This day was to honor "not some obscure martyrs" but those whose fame had reached the ends of the earth through their preaching and martyrdoms. Later in this same sermon, Augustine proclaims that it was the Lord who had tested Paul with chains, beatings, imprisonment, and shipwrecks and had ultimately led him to martyrdom: "He [the Lord] it was that procured his passion, he that brought him finally to this day." In response to the faithfulness of Paul and Peter and the agency of the Lord himself, "We are celebrating a feast day, consecrated for us by the blood of the apostles" (*Serm.* 295.7–8, Hill).

In another sermon preached on the annual feast day (ca. 418), Augustine calls to mind the reference to Paul's impending martyrdom in 2 Tim 4:6–8:

> Turn your attention to the apostle Paul, because it is also his feast today. [Peter and Paul] both led lives of harmony and peace, they shed their blood in companionship together, together they received the heavenly crown, they both consecrated this holy day. So turn your attention to the apostle Paul, call to mind the words which we heard a short while ago, when his letter was being read. "I," he said, "am already being sacrificed, and the time for me to cast off is at hand. I have fought the good fight, I have completed the course, I have kept the faith." ... The just judge ... will award the crown to these merits. (*Serm.* 297.5, Hill)

As the scripture reading had just reminded Augustine's audience, Paul had foreseen his violent death, yet he persevered in the course set before him. Because of his faithfulness, he was rewarded by God. Augustine then charges his own congregation to be similarly faithful, so that God might one day reward their merits, as well: "To whom will he award it? To your merits, of course. You have fought the good fight, completed the course, kept the faith; he will award the crown to these merits of yours" (*Serm.* 297.6, Hill). The festival provides an opportunity for the bishop to evoke Paul's example in exhorting his listeners to run the race in hopes of a reward. As he states plainly about the festival day, "It is on account of [the apostles'] merits that this day has become the occasion for us to celebrate their feast and imitate their holiness" (*Serm.* 299A.1, Hill).

Despite Paul's reputation and Augustine's enthusiasm, the celebration of the feast of the apostles apparently did not always draw a large crowd. On the festival in 428, the bishop bemoans the poor attendance in his basilica: "Really, we should have been celebrating the feast of such great martyrs, that is of the holy apostles Peter and Paul, with a much bigger crowd than this.

---

12. Augustine also began *Serm.* 297 and 299A–C with similar references to the significance of the birthday of the apostles.

After all, if we flock in big crowds to the celebration of the birthdays of lambs, how much more should we do so for those of the rams?" (*Serm.* 298.1, Hill). The celebrations for other martyrs (the "lambs") had drawn large numbers, so Augustine is incredulous at the poor turnout to honor the apostles themselves (the "rams"). He is so frustrated that he returns to this complaint later in the same sermon: "Don't you love Peter and Paul? It's those who are not here, of course, whom I'm addressing in you; to you, I mean, I'm grateful, because you at least have come" (*Serm.* 298.2, Hill). Augustine expected the annual feast day to be a major event in the lives of the Christians of Hippo. He took the disappointing turnout as an indication that the priorities of many Christians were not properly ordered.

Augustine's displeasure with low attendance at the basilica may have also been fueled by another factor: the competition offered by informal gatherings at shrines in honor of the martyrs. It is likely that Christians honored the apostle in this way, for North African Christians had a particularly strong affinity for this practice. They kept vigils and shared commemorative meals at tombs, memorials, or even in basilicas on the feast days of holy people, but these often did not occur under the eye of the clergy.[13] Augustine's mother, Monica, had engaged in such meals in North Africa:

> It had been my mother's custom in Africa to take meal-cakes and bread and wine to the shrines of the saints on their memorial days, but the door-keeper would not allow her to do this in Milan. When she learned that the bishop had forbidden it, she accepted his ruling with such pious submission that I was surprised to see how willingly she condemned her own practice rather than dispute his command.... She used to bring her basket full of the customary offerings of food, intending to taste a little and give the rest away. For herself she never poured more than a small cupful of wine, watered to suit her sober palate, and she drank only as much of it as was needed to do honour to the dead.... This holy bishop had forbidden such ceremonies even to those who performed them with sobriety, both for fear that to some they might be occasions for drunkenness and also because they bore so close a resemblance to the superstitious rites which the pagans held in honour of their dead. Instead of her basket full of the fruits of the earth she learned to bring to the shrines of the martyrs a heart full of prayers far purer than any of these gifts. (Augustine, *Conf.* 6.2, Pine-Coffin)

In Milan Ambrose forbade these informal meals that took place outside the purview of the bishop.[14] Even if they occurred on the proper festival days,

---

13. MacMullen, *Second Church*, 51–67.

14. Quasten, "'Vetus superstitio,'" 256: "People considered the cult of the martyrs, like

they too closely resembled the "superstitious rites" of the pagans and were "occasions for drunkenness." The bishop even posted guards at martyr shrines in Milan to prevent Christians from holding these banquets. Augustine comments that, to his mother's credit, she obediently gave up these banquets that had been standard pious practice in North Africa, even though she herself had never been guilty of any excess.

Augustine shared Ambrose's antagonism toward these meals and attacked the practice in his city. In a letter from 395, he recounts his condemnation of the drunken festival in Hippo that typically accompanied the feast of Leontius Valerius, the bishop who had ordained Augustine: "In calling it 'joy,' they try in vain to hide the term 'drunkenness' … doing something in the name of religion within the walls of the church that, if they continued to do it in their homes, it would be necessary to exclude them from what is holy and from the pearls in the church" (*Ep.* 29.2). To Augustine's horror, these shameful festivities had taken place within the basilica itself. He chastises the local Christians for casting what is holy before swine and compares them to the money changers whom Jesus had thrown out of the temple. Some asked Augustine why he was attempting to forbid these gatherings now, when others had allowed them. The exasperated bishop explains that previous leaders had permitted certain practices only as a means of easing the transition to Christianity for new converts who held strongly to their traditional feasts:

> And since they could not easily give up these most harmful yet long-standing pleasures, our predecessors decided to tolerate an aspect of their weakness for the time being by allowing them to celebrate other feast days in honor of the martyrs in place of those that they gave up. Although they no longer celebrated with a similar sacrilege, they still did so with similar unrestraint. (*Ep.* 29.9)

As these Christians heard teachings against drunkenness, they should desire to give up these meals and their "unrestraint." Augustine then declares that the time had come for people to decide for or against Christ, because only heretics continued to observe drunken feasts in their churches. Church councils

---

that of the dead, as more or less their own business, a matter of private devotion which, like the domestic cult, did not belong to the office of the priesthood, or at any rate, not to the same extent as the official cult of the Deity." At the end of the second century, Tertullian had also raised concerns about such banquets being confused with pagan rites. See Victor Saxer, *Morts, martyrs, reliques en Afrique chrétienne aux premiers siècles: Les témoignages de Tertullien, Cyprien et Augustin à la lumière de l'archéologie africaine* (ThH 55; Paris: Beauchesne, 1980), 47–52.

at Carthage in 397 and 401 officially upheld Augustine's prohibition of these unsanctioned banquets, but they continued well into the fifth century.[15]

The annual feast of the apostles prompted the "official" veneration of Paul that Augustine encouraged in his sermons. It likely also gave occasion for the unsanctioned, popular celebrations that the bishop abhorred and tried to eliminate. Like their Roman contemporaries at the Catacombs on the Appian Road, African Christians would have honored Paul with banquets at shrines throughout the region, far beyond the basilicas of the large cities. I now turn my attention to these holy sites in North Africa and to the shrines that reflect the extent of the Pauline cult.

4.3. Basilicas, Memorials, and Ties with Rome

In the year 500, Fulgentius of Ruspe (modern Kudiat Rosfa, Tunisia) went to visit Rufinianus, a North African bishop who had fled persecution to a small island near Sicily.[16] Fulgentius had planned to travel from there to Egypt, but instead, "He decided not to miss seeing the memorial of the apostles [*apostolorum memoriam*]. When the conditions of navigation were favorable, he went to Rome ... rightly called the capital of the world ... [and] piously went around to the sacred places of the martyrs" (Ferrandus, *Vit. Fulg.* 9). Fulgentius recognized Rome as the center of the apostolic cult and took advantage of the opportunity to make a pilgrimage to the city's shrines and bring back relics, as we will see later. Most other residents of North Africa, like those of Gaul and Spain, were too distant from the Roman sites for Paul and could not visit them as Fulgentius had done. Thus, they made shorter pilgrimages to basilicas and memorial shrines for the apostle in their own region.

A notation in the collection of Augustine's sermons points to a church of Paul in Carthage in the early fifth century. One of Augustine's Easter sermons bears the heading, "A sermon preached while he was living in Carthage, in the basilica of Paul of the sixth region" (*Serm.* 119). One scholar has suggested that this title is now attached to the wrong sermon,[17] but there is agreement that the bishop preached at least once in a basilica of Paul in that city. Carthage may have had at least one other basilica dedicated to the apostles Paul and

---

15. Charles Munier, ed., *Concilia Galliae a. 314–a. 506* (CCSL 148; Turnhout: Brepols, 1963), 185, no. 42; 196–97, no. 60; Rebillard, "Les chrétiens et les repas," 281–90.

16. Fulgentius later became bishop of Ruspe (507–533). Rufinianus was bishop of Victoriana in Byzancene and was listed among those present at the Council of Carthage in 484.

17. Cyrille Lambot, "La collection antique de sermons de saint Augustin," *RBén* 57 (1947): 90.

Peter.[18] Unfortunately, we have not been able to identify the precise location of either of these important churches. Basilicas for the apostles were not limited to Carthage. In 417 a church council met in the city of Thelepte (modern Medinet el-Kedima, Tunisia). The council of more than thirty bishops "gathered in the basilica of the apostles of the people of Thelepte"[19] to discuss issues related to the qualifications for members of the clergy.

A church at Aïn Ghorab reveals Roman influence on the North African cult and its architecture, for the dedicatory inscription to the apostles imitates a Roman example. The text begins as follows:

> Give way, former name; give way, what is old, to what is new.
> It is permitted to give royal(?) votives joyfully.
> This building for Peter and Paul rises again by the order of Christ.
> I ask you as one, you who are equal, to accept this one gift, though you are two.[20]

The inscriber has adapted this poem directly from an inscription that Bishop Sixtus III (432–440) had placed in the Basilica of St. Peter in Chains in Rome. A small basilica had existed before the time of Sixtus, but the Roman bishop constructed a larger edifice that incorporated the earlier church. He then dedicated it to the apostles:

> Give way, former name; give way, what is old, to what is new.
> It is permitted to give royal(?) votives joyfully.
> This building is for Peter and Paul. Now Sixtus likewise attaches his name,
> Sixtus who rejoices in the honor of the apostolic see.

---

18. Enrico Josi, "La venerazione degli apostoli Pietro e Paolo nel mondo cristiano antico," in *Saecularia Petri et Pauli* (SAC 28; Vatican City: Pontificio Istituto di Archeologia Cristiana, 1969), 177; Gabriel G. Lapeyre, "Saint Augustin et Carthage," in *Miscellanea agostiniana: Testi e studi, pubblicati a cura del-l'Ordine eremitano di s. Agostino nel XV centenario dalla morte del santo dottore* (2 vols.; Rome: Tipografia Poliglotta Vaticana, 1931), 2:95. This evidence from Carthage contradicts the theory of W. H. C. Frend that the apostolic cult did not take root in the region's major cities. See "The Memoriae Apostolorum in Roman North Africa," *JRS* 30.1 (1940): 32–49.

19. Munier, *Concilia Galliae*, 58.

20. Yvette Duval, *Loca sanctorum Africae: Le culte des martyrs en Afrique du IVe au VIIe siècle* (2 vols.; CEFR 58; Rome: École française de Rome, 1982), 1:146–48, no. 68, fig. 100; G. B. de Rossi, "Epigrafe d'una chiesa dedicata agli apostoli Pietro e Paolo," *BArC* 3.3 (1878–1879): 14–20; E. Masqueray, "Ruines anciennes de Khenchela (Mascula) à Besseriani (Ad Majores)," *RAfr* 22 (1878): 465–66; Paul Monceaux, "Enquête sur l'épigraphie chrétienne d'Afrique," *MPAIBL* 12.1 (1903): 3:195.

I ask you as one, you who are equal, to accept this one gift, though you are two.[21]

The first two lines and the fourth line from Aïn Ghorab are identical to the Roman inscription; only the third line varies. The editor has removed the name of the Roman bishop and modified the poem for the local context by inserting a reference to Christ. This North African adaptation dates from the latter part of the fifth or the sixth century.[22] As in Rome, the poem celebrates the reopening of a church that had just undergone repairs. The influence of the Roman tradition is evident. When the Christian leaders of Aïn Ghorab rededicated their basilica in honor of Peter and Paul, the model for their inscription came from an important edifice for the apostles in Rome itself.

Far more numerous than references to basilicas are references to smaller shrines identified as "memorials" (memoriae). These could take a variety of forms, such as altars, small shrines, dedicatory plaques, or reliquaries. A lintel found in Henchir Deheb (near modern Kairouan, Tunisia[23]) features a large Chi-Rho symbol and an inscription that reads, "[Memorial] of the saints Peter and Paul."[24] This stone, which is broken on both ends and originally featured a longer inscription (fig. 4.2), was found near the remains of the city's main basilica and dates from the late fourth or early fifth century. The original excavators believed that it was a dedicatory inscription for a church, but more recent scholarship suggests that it came from an altar in the baptistery. The stone reflects two stages of carving. The original phase featured only the Chi-Rho symbol and a row of decorative foliage running the length of the stone. The space along the top of the stone was blank, until the reference to a memorial of the apostles was added later. It is possible that the church acquired secondary relics of Paul and Peter, thus prompting the secondary inscription.

Other apostolic memorials in the region featured inscriptions with similar iconographical systems. At the site of Tipasa in modern Algeria, archaeologists found a gray marble stone with the inscription, "Memorial of the most blessed martyrs Peter—Chi-Rho—and Paul." Coins and lamps from the excavation at Tipasa date the inscription to the second half of the fourth century.[25]

---

21. De Rossi, "Epigrafe d'una chiesa," 15, was the first to notice the connection to the Roman antecedent.

22. De Rossi favored a sixth-century date, but Josi ("La venerazione degli apostoli," 176) has suggested that it could date from the fifth century.

23. The ancient names of a number of archaeological sites in North Africa remain unknown, so they are typically cited by their modern names.

24. [Memoria san]ctorum (Chi-Rho) Petri et Pau[li] (Duval, Loca sanctorum Africae, 1:142–43, no. 65).

25. [M]emoria beatiss[i] / [mor]um martyrum / [Pet]ri (Chi-Rho) et Pauli (ibid.,

Fig. 4.2. Lintel from Henchir Deheb marking a "[Memorial] of the saints Peter and Paul."
In the Jardin épigraphique, Tebessa, Algeria. Courtesy of École française de Rome.

Similarly, a small marble arch from Henchir Magroun features two carefully
crafted Chi-Rho symbols prominently on its face. Across the top of the arch is
an inscription of much lower quality that reads: "Memorial of lord Peter and of
Paul."[26] The Chi-Rho also appears with the names of the apostles on a fourth-
century stone coffer found near modern Aïn Abid (Algeria). On one end of
the shrine (fig. 4.3), the Chi-Rho is placed at the head of an inscription that
begins, "To the sacred spirits of the departed, of Peter, Paul, Marinus…."[27] The
invocation "to the sacred spirits of the departed" (*Dis manibus sacrum*, usually
abbreviated *DMS*) appears on thousands of Latin tombstones from the Roman
period. It invokes the "spirits" (*manes*) of the dead to ease the transition to
the underworld and may indicate that the tombs themselves were offerings to
these spirits.[28] Christians in the ancient region of Numidia, where Aïn Abid is
located, continued to employ this expression on their tombstones at least into

1:357–58, no. 169, fig. 233; Josi, "La venerazione degli apostoli," 177–78). On the possibility that the city also had a basilica dedicated to the apostles, see J. Baradaz, "La basilique
de Pierre et Paul à Tipasa de Maurétaine," in *Akten des VII. Internationalen Kongresses für
Christliche Archäologie, Trier, 5–11 September 1965* (SAC 27; Vatican City: Pontificio Istituto di Archeologia Cristiana, 1969), 341–56.

    26. Memoria domini Petri e[t] Pauli (Duval, *Loca sanctorum Africae*, 1:143–44, no.
66, fig. 97; Monceaux, "Enquête," 4:266; *ILCV* 2065. The use of the term "lord" (*dominus*) is
well attested in the region as a substitute for "saint" (*sanctus*).

    27. D M (Chi-Rho) S / Petri Pau / li Marini … (Duval, *Loca sanctorum Africae*, 1:202–
7, no. 97). The box contained a total of three dedicatory inscriptions, the other two naming
local, African figures.

    28. James B. Rives, *Religion in the Roman Empire* (Malden, Mass.: Blackwell, 2007),
19–20; Dietrich Boschung, *Antike Grabaltäre aus den Nekropolen Roms* (AcBern 10; Bern:
Stämpfli, 1987), 12. For examples of tomb inscriptions to the *manes*, see Richmond Lattimore, *Themes in Greek and Latin Epitaphs* (ISLL 28.1–2; Urbana: University of Illinois
Press, 1962), 90–95.

Fig. 4.3. Stone coffer from Aïn Abid referring to Peter and Paul. In the Musée National CIRTA, Constantine, Algeria. Courtesy of École française de Rome.

the seventh century, and here it introduces an invocation of the apostles and several others who were probably also martyrs.[29] Based on the size of the box, it could have contained some small relics or other cultic objects. A final example with the Chi-Rho comes from a stone found at Djebel Djaffa, also in ancient Numidia. There the Christogram precedes a brief inscription, "Memorial of the apostles."[30] Here again the invocation of the apostles is linked with the Chi-Rho, the symbol of triumphant Christianity that had originated in Rome with

29. Duval, *Loca sanctorum Africae*, 2:732–34. On the Christian use of *DMS* in Rome with a Chi-Rho inserted, see Northcote, *Epitaphs of the Catacombs*, 99.

30. Memoria apostoloru(m) (Duval, *Loca sanctorum Africae*, 1:165, no. 78, fig. 112; *CIL* 17:715; *ILCV* 2065).

Constantine's decisive victory on the banks of the Tiber River at the Milvian Bridge.[31]

While the inscription at Aïn Ghorab (and perhaps the Chi-Rho) might orient North African Christians toward Rome, Augustine overtly criticized and sought to undermine any local sense of deference to the cultic sites in the ancient capital. In a politically charged sermon on the feast of the apostles in 411, Augustine highlighted the Roman shrines of Paul and Peter only to decentralize their importance. Indeed, the political situation in 411 demanded some comment from the bishop on the place and fate of Rome. In the previous year, Alaric I and the Visigothic army had sacked Rome. The city was no longer the political capital of the western empire, but it had remained the spiritual capital. Many Christians had believed that no army could ever conquer Rome, because the relics of the apostles gave the city supernatural protection. As John Chrysostom once preached, "[Paul's] body fortifies that city. It is more impenetrable than any tower and countless defensive walls" (*Hom. Rom.* 32.4). On August 24, 410, the Visigoths breached the defenses and looted the city for several days. They spared many of the churches and those who fled into them for refuge,[32] but this event sent shockwaves through the Christian world. How could the martyr-patrons of Rome allow this to happen to their city? This question must have been in the minds of the congregation when Augustine stood up to preach on the apostles' birthday less than a year after the city had fallen. His audience, in fact, probably included some refugees from Rome itself.[33]

Rather than offering comfort, Augustine presented a challenge. He reminded his congregation of the fleeting nature of human suffering and invoked Paul's letter to the Romans to emphasize that current trials are insignificant compared to the future glory for Christians (Rom 8:18). This was not the common sentiment among his listeners, however:

"Peter's body lies in Rome," people are saying, "Paul's body lies in Rome …
and Rome is griefstricken, and Rome is being devastated, afflicted, crushed,

31. Eusebius recounts that Constantine had a vision of a symbol in the sky and adopted it as his own just prior to the battle of the Milvian Bridge (*Vit. Const.* 1.27–32). The Chi-Rho was used ubiquitously by Constantine, but its historical connection to Rome should not be ignored, nor should its connection to the Tiber, a symbolically important river for Christianity, according to Prudentius (*Perist.* 12.7–10).

32. In a letter to Principia concerning their mutual friend Marcella, Jerome wrote, "The barbarians conveyed both you and her to the basilica of the apostle Paul, that you might find there either a place of safety or, if not that, at least a tomb" (*Ep.* 127.13).

33. Peter J. Heather, *The Fall of the Roman Empire: A New History* (London: Macmillan, 2005), 227–29.

burnt; death stalking the streets in so many ways, by hunger, by pestilence, by the sword. Where are the memorials of the apostles?" ... They are there, they are there, but they are not in you. If only they were in you, whoever you are that are saying these things, whoever you are, foolish enough to think these things, whoever you are, called in the spirit and savoring the flesh, whoever you may be of that sort! If only the memorials of the apostles were in you, if only you really gave a thought to the apostles! Then you would see whether they were promised an earthly felicity or an eternal. (*Serm.* 296.6, Hill)

Augustine argues that the audience's fixation on these physical places was misguided. Many people were talking as if the primary legacy of Paul and Peter was the safety of Rome, guaranteed by the presence of the "memorials of the apostles." Some had indeed survived the assault by fleeing into the apostolic basilicas to find shelter, yet Rome had still fallen, and the apostles had not intervened to prevent death and suffering.

Such talk was "foolish," according to Augustine, the perspective of those who were "savoring the flesh." These people had an imperfect understanding of what it meant to honor the apostles. It was not just about going to the apostolic memorials in Rome; rather, it was about an internal change that should occur, but had not occurred, among those claiming to venerate Paul and Peter: "They are not in you." The divine promise of eternal blessing had become obscured by too much emphasis on mundane places and an "earthly felicity." Augustine did not ignore the fact that the shrines for the apostles were in Rome, nor did he wholly dispute that these locations are worthy of honor. Their power, however, lay not in a temporary blessing from seeing the sites but in the eternal and internal transformation that the apostles' example should stir in the hearts of all those "called in the spirit." They should take the apostles with them, instead of talking as if Paul and Peter were confined to their tombs in a conquered Rome.

Churches and memorials for the Pauline cult were dispersed widely across North Africa.[34] The influence of Rome on the regional Pauline cult is clearly discernible in some cases, from the voyage of Fulgentius to Rome, to the dedication of the basilica at Aïn Ghorab, to the consternation in Hippo at the sack of Rome in 410. Augustine, for his part, tried to shift the focus of his people from an external fixation on monuments to an internal pursuit of a life transformed by the apostolic teachings and example. The archaeological evidence suggests, however, that the establishment of holy places remained a central component of the Pauline cult in this region.

---

34. I have discussed here only a few illustrative examples from a much larger group of small memorials for the apostles. For more complete lists, see Frend, "Memoriae Apostolorum," 32–35; Josi, "La venerazione degli apostoli," 167–79.

4.4. Relic Veneration and Privileged Burials

The fifth-century bishop Maximus of Turin once preached, "All the martyrs must be honored with great devotion, but we must especially venerate
those whose relics we possess" (*Serm.* 12). In the case of Paul in North Africa,
the earliest reference to relics comes from Tixter in the region of Mauretania (modern Kherbet oum el-Ahdam, Algeria). A large, limestone tablet is
rounded on one end and may have served as the top of an altar (fig. 4.4). A
circle carved in the middle of the stone contains a Chi-Rho and the words
"holy memorial." Beneath, an inscription from the year 359 lists the items
that sanctified the shrine: "Some of the land [literally, the "earth"] of promise, where Christ was born, and some relics of the apostle Peter and of Paul."
Elsewhere on the stone there is also a reference to "some of the wood of the
cross."[35] These famous relics allegedly lay beneath or adjacent to the tablet
in its original context. It is striking that this church in a fairly rural location
could claim this rich cache of holy objects at such an early date. Is it possible
that pilgrims had brought back relics from journeys to Rome and Palestine?
However the items were procured,[36] the inscription illustrates that interest in
securing relics and establishing cultic locations for Paul and others was wide-
spread in North Africa by the mid-fourth century.

A limestone slab from Carthage contains a reference to relics of Paul in
that city as well (fig. 4.5). The fragment features a crown—a standard iconographical image representing the prize for martyrdom—and inside this crown
the inscription reads, "Relics of Peter and Paul. Amen." Below the crown the
name Crement is discernible.[37] The rest of the inscription, which has been
dated to the fourth or fifth century, is missing and may have identified Crement as the patron of the shrine and specified the circumstances of the arrival
of these relics. The original location of the slab is unknown, but it could have
rested either in the city's apostolic basilica or the basilica of Paul. It is an
important witness to a relic cult for Paul in Carthage. The region of Carthage
was not only the recipient of holy objects for the Pauline cult in late antiquity;
it also produced objects for the cult. The Römisch-Germanisches Museum in

---

35. Memoria sa(n)cta ... De tera promisionis ube natus est Cristus, apostoli Petri et
Pauli ... de lignu crucis (Duval, *Loca sanctorum Africae*, 1:331–37, no. 157; *CIL* 8:20600;
Monceaux, "Enquête," 317; *ILCV* 2068; now Louvre 3023).

36. It is quite possible, of course, that some of these items were of dubious provenance.

37. Reli / quias Pet / ri et Pauli / Amen / Crement [... (Duval, *Loca sanctorum Africae*,
1:5, no. 1).

Fig. 4.4. Limestone tablet from Tixter referring to "some relics of the apostle Peter and of Paul." In the Louvre, Paris. Courtesy of École française de Rome.

Fig. 4.5. Limestone tablet from Carthage with mention of apostolic relics. In the Musée national de Carthage, Tunisia. Courtesy of École française de Rome.

Cologne possesses a rare pilgrim's flask with an image of Paul (fig. 4.6).[38] The flask is African Red Slip, a type of pottery produced in the region of Carthage from the second through the sixth century c.e. and traded throughout the Mediterranean and into the northern provinces of the empire.[39] The original find location of this particular piece is, unfortunately, unknown. It has been dated on stylistic grounds to the later fourth or early fifth century and demonstrates the productive nature of the Pauline cult in and around Carthage during this period.

Shrines claiming Pauline relics were focal points for privileged burials at many sites in North Africa. A significant number of dedicatory inscriptions survive from all parts of the region, including the earliest epigraphic evidence from anywhere for a Christian burial *ad sanctos*.[40] These North African burials adjacent to apostolic relics generally fell into three broad categories: (1) a simple tomb near a holy burial or deposit of relics, either at a shrine or in a basilica; (2) a monumental tomb at a site that had relics; (3) a funerary chapel built as a tomb where relics were placed.[41] I will describe each in turn through an illustrative example.

An instance of the first category comes from Castellum Tingitanum (modern El Asnam [Orléansville], Algeria), where archaeologists unearthed a marble tablet commemorating the burial of a child. The inscription states that the mother and father laid the child (whose name is missing) to rest in 406 and "made this memorial next to the holy apostles Peter and Paul, in the name of God and Christ."[42] The language indicates that the presence of relics determined the burial site, and the wear on the stone suggests that it was part of the pavement for a floor, possibly in the city's basilica. This is not our only evidence that the fourth-century basilica at Castellum Tingitanum had strong associations with the apostles. Two ancient brick fragments found in the church honor local martyrs and invoke the names of Paul and Peter.[43] Likewise, excavators discovered in the remains of the basilica a marble tablet

---

38. Peter La Baume and J. W. Salomonson, *Römische Kleinkunst: Sammlung Karl Löffler (Katalog)* (WKRGMK 3; Cologne: Römisch-Germanisches Museum, 1976), 157–58, no. 611.

39. Paul A. Tyers, *Roman Pottery in Britain* (London: Batsford, 1996), 152–54.

40. Duval, *Loca sanctorum Africae*, 1:412–17, no. 195.

41. These categories are taken from Duval, *Loca sanctorum Africae*, 2:501.

42. … Pater et / [ ]e mater eius aput / [sancto]s apostolos Petru et / [Pauli i]n nomine Dei et Cri / [sti m]emor[ia(m) fece]runt (ibid., 1:392, no. 185, fig. 254; *CIL* 8:9715; Monceaux, "Enquête," 332; *ILCV* 2186).

43. Duval, *Loca sanctorum Africae*, 1:394–98, no. 186–187. On the date of the basilica, see Isabelle Gui, *Basiliques chrétiennes d'Afrique du nord* (rev. Noël Duval and Jean-Pierre Caillet; 2 vols.; Paris: Institut des Études Augustiniennes, 1992), 1:14.

Fig. 4.6. Pilgrim's flask with image of Paul. In the Römisch-Germanisches Museum, Cologne. Courtesy of Römisch-Germanisches Museum der Stadt Köln/Rheinisches Bildarchiv.

with the inscription, "To the blessed apostles Peter and Paul."[44] The cult of the apostles was vibrant in this particular city, and the parents buried their child "next to" (*apud*) relics of Paul and Peter, confident of the spiritual benefit from the proximity of apostolic relics.

The case of Fulgentius of Ruspe (bishop from 507 to 533) falls into the second category of burials "near the saints." Earlier (p. 167) I mentioned his pilgrimage to Rome in 500 c.e., and his biographer, Ferrandus of Carthage, records that, after his death in 533, "He was carried by the hands of priests to the church of the city, which is called Secunda, where he himself had placed relics of the apostles. There he received a glorious sepulcher" (*Vit. Fulg.* 28). According to Ferrandus, Fulgentius had adorned the local church with relics acquired on his tour of the apostolic shrines in Rome. He was rewarded for his faithful service to Ruspe with a "glorious sepulcher" and the right to be buried "near the saints." Ferrandus points out that interment in the city's basilica near the relics was a unique honor: "[Fulgentius] was clearly the first pontiff to merit being placed in this basilica, where ancient custom allowed no corpse

---

44. Duval, *Loca sanctorum Africae*, 1:392, no. 185. The current location of this stone is unknown.

to be buried—neither a member of the clergy nor a lay person" (*Vit. Fulg.*
28). Both cultural and legal restrictions traditionally strictly forbade burials
within the walls of any city, and the basilica of Ruspe was inside the walls.
By the time of Fulgentius's death, however, enforcement of these prohibitions
seems to have slackened,[45] so the beloved bishop of Ruspe could be buried in
a "glorious sepulcher" constructed for him in the midst of the basilica that he
had adorned with apostolic relics.

A basilica at Tipasa represents the third group of burials, in which relics
adorn a structure built primarily as a tomb for an individual. The three-aisle
church at Tipasa was built just outside the city walls and contained a single
tomb in the center of the nave.[46] Inside the building, but separate from this
tomb, excavators found the fragments of the marble slab discussed previously
that reads, "Memorial of the most blessed martyrs Peter—Chi-Rho—and
Paul." A prominent resident of Tipasa seems to have built the basilica as his
funerary chapel and embellished it with secondary relics of the apostles.[47] The
wealthy patron lay in the central tomb in a privileged location "near the saints"
but was not alone for long. A burgeoning cemetery soon crowded around the
outside of the church, and a rectangular funerary structure was built next to
the basilica's south wall to house several sarcophagi. Eventually, graves were
dug into the floor of the basilica itself (fig. 4.7). The exclusive burial site for the
original patron became overrun by other Christians desiring to be interred in
what they considered sacred space. As at the Pauline basilica on the Ostian
Road in Rome, the presence of relics at Tipasa created competition for privileged burial sites "near the saints."

4.5. PAUL AS A SYMBOL OF LEGITIMACY: THE "CAECILIANISTS" VERSUS THE "DONATISTS"

My discussion of the North African evidence to this point has focused on
shared elements of Pauline veneration in the region. The cult also served,
however, as a battleground for rival groups in the context of the "Donatist
controversy," the most significant ecclesiastical debate in this region in late
antiquity.[48] The roots of this fracture within the church lay in the persecu-

45. Marios Costambeys, "The Culture and Practice of Burial in and around Rome in
the Sixth Century," in Guidobaldi and Guidobaldi, *Ecclesiae urbis*, 2:721–32.

46. Baradaz, "La basilique de Pierre et Paul à Tipasa," 341–56; Gui, *Basiliques*, 1:35–37.

47. Paul-Albert Février, "Tombes privilégiées en Maurétanie et Numidie," in *L'Inhumation privilégiée du IVe au VIIIe siècle en Occident: Actes du colloque tenu à Créteil les 16–18
mars 1984* (ed. Yvette Duval and Jean-Charles Picard; Paris: de Boccard, 1986), 15.

48. The primary sources are collected in Jean-Louis Maier, *Le Dossier du Donatisme* (2
vols.; TUGAL 134–135; Berlin: Akademie, 1987–1989). See also W. H. C. Frend, *The Dona-*

Fig. 4.7. Privileged burials in and around the basilica at Tipasa (after Christern).

tions of the early fourth century, when Diocletian issued an edict ordering the demolition of churches and the burning of Christian books. The emperor then issued further edicts to suppress clergy and enforce sacrifice to the Roman gods. The punishments were severe, and the clergy found themselves in a difficult situation. If faced with the option of surrendering their lives or surrendering their books, which would they choose? Some chose the latter. When the persecution abated, a split developed within the North African church concerning the fate of these *traditores*, "those who handed over" the books. Some said that they should be forgiven, while many others thought that the *traditores* had betrayed the church and were no longer fit to hold church office or ordain other clergy.

The dispute came to a head in 311, when Caecilian was elected bishop of Carthage. Many rejected him on the grounds that one of the bishops who had

tist Church: A Movement of Protest in Roman North Africa (rev. ed.; Oxford: Clarendon, 1985); Maureen A. Tilley, trans., *Donatist Martyr Stories: The Church in Conflict in Roman North Africa* (TTH 24; Liverpool: Liverpool University Press, 1996), xiv–xvii.

consecrated him, Felix of Apthugni (modern Henchir es-Souar, Tunisia),[49] had been a *traditor*. Felix was also suspected of having conspired to prohibit aid to Christian prisoners because he feared reprisal against Christians by the secular authorities (*Pass. Dat. Saturn.* 20). If Felix was not a legitimate bishop, as some claimed, then Caecilian's ordination was invalid. With the support of many bishops of Numidia, the protestors elected Majorinus as a rival bishop. Majorinus was soon succeeded by Donatus, whose followers and successors were labeled *Donatists*. Popular sentiment strongly favored Donatus and his successors, but Caecilian and his successors enjoyed the support of the Roman church and the imperial government. For several centuries, the North African church remained divided between these competing ecclesiastical hierarchies.

Martyrdom was central to North African Christian identity in general, but it was especially so for the Donatists. They traced their movement directly to those who, like Paul and Cyprian, had faced torture or death rather than submitting to the secular government (by handing over sacred books, for example).[50] From 316 to 321, their leaders even faced persecution from a government led by a Christian emperor. In this case Constantine punished them not for their theology but because they were seen as threats to social harmony. Their movement only grew in strength. In their minds, this suffering confirmed the correctness of their position.

Laying claim to famous Christian martyrs as "their own" was a powerful tool in the polemics exchanged between the Donatists and the Caecilianists (who referred to themselves as "Catholics"[51]). Bishop Optatus of Milev (modern Mila, Algeria) represents one of the prominent voices on the Caecilianist side. Between 370 and 374 c.e., he composed six books *Against the Donatists* in which he defended the Caecilianists against charges levied by a Donatist named Parmenian. Parmenian had asserted that the Caecilianists were "betrayers" of the faith, but Optatus retorts that Paul had warned against people like Parmenian: "Concerning you the most blessed apostle Paul said, 'Some have turned aside to vain speech, desiring to be teachers of the law, but

---

49. Apthugni is probably the correct form of the city's name, not Aptunga, which is typically given in secondary literature. See Anatole Toulotte, *Géographie de l'Afrique chrétienne: Byzacène et Tripolitaine* (Montreuil-sur-Mer: Notre-Dame des Prés, 1894), 264.

50. "Paul, in his sufferings and patience, joins Jesus as a figure for Donatists to emulate" (Maureen A. Tilley, *The Bible in Christian North Africa: The Donatist World* [Minneapolis: Fortress, 1997], 155).

51. Paola Marone, "Cristianesimo e universalità nella controversia donatista," in *La natura della religione in contesto teologico: Atti del X Convegno Internazionale della Facoltà di Teologia, Pontificia Università della Santa Croce, Roma 9–10 marzo 2006* (ed. S. Sanz Sánchez; Rome: Maspero, 2008), 323–35.

understanding neither what they say nor the things about which they make assertions'" (*Adv. Donat.* 1.28.1, citing 1 Tim 1:6–7). Optatus proceeds to bolster his attack on Parmenian by appealing to sacred sites as proof that the Donatists were the true schismatics. In previous times, some Donatists had gone to live in Rome and had unsuccessfully attempted to establish a congregation in the city:

> Victor of Garba was sent first.… He was there as a son without a father, as a beginner without a master, as a disciple without a teacher, as a follower without a predecessor, as a lodger without a home, as a guest without a guest-house, as a shepherd without a flock, as a bishop without a people. For neither a flock nor a people can those few people be called, who rushed between the more than forty basilicas in Rome, but did not have a place where they could gather. Thus, they enclosed with a wooden frame a cave outside the city, where they were able to have a meeting place right away. For this reason they are called "Mountaineers." (*Adv. Donat.* 2.4.4–5)[52]

The inability to find a home among the recognized basilicas in Rome was proof of the illegitimacy of the Donatists and their bishop. They were forced to resort to a makeshift chapel in a cave outside the city.

Optatus adds another allegation that includes a direct appeal to the holy places of the Pauline cult. As the Donatist bishop, Victor of Garba also did not have access to the famous shrines of the martyrs: "Behold, in Rome are the shrines of the two apostles. Will you tell me whether he [Victor] has been able to approach them, or has offered sacrifice in those places, where, as is certain, are these shrines of the saints?" (*Adv. Donat.* 2.4.2). The Constantinian basilicas for Paul and Peter were the greatest Christian martyr monuments in the West. The Donatists were not permitted to offer sacrifice—that is, to celebrate the Eucharist—in these places, and this spatial prohibition proved that they were not true inheritors of the apostolic legacy. In the view of Optatus, this separation from the Roman tradition was indisputable evidence that the Donatists were in schism from true Christianity. The Roman legacy of Paul and Peter was *the* mark of "Catholic" Christianity in the West,[53] and the shrines in Rome were the recognized centers of the apostolic cult. The Caecilianists alone had access to these holy sites. Therefore, in North Africa it was

---

52. This reference to the Donatists in Rome as "Mountaineers" also appears in Jerome (*Chron.* 2370) and Augustine (*C. litt. Petil.* 2.108).

53. Paola Marone, "Pietro e Paolo e il loro rapporto con Roma nella letteratura antidonatista," in *Pietro e Paolo: Il loro rapporto con Roma nelle testimonianze antiche: XXIX Incontro di studiosi dell'antichità cristiana, Roma, 4–6 maggio 2000* (Rome: Institutum Patristicum Augustinianum, 2001), 471.

only their churches and monuments, not those of the Donatists, that could be legitimate centers for the Pauline cult.

Augustine was also firmly in the Caecilianist camp and set out to separate the Caecilianists from the Donatists. One of his strategies was to distinguish the true martyrs of the church, including Paul, from the false, Donatist ones:

> Precious in the sight of the Lord is the death of his just ones. Therefore the death of Peter is precious; therefore the death of Paul is precious; therefore the death of Vincent[54] is precious; therefore the death of Cyprian is precious. On what account are they precious? Because of a pure affection and a good conscience and a faith that is not false. That snake, however, sees this. That ancient serpent sees that the martyrs are honored and the temples are deserted. He carefully concocted cunning and poisonous plots against us, and because he was not able to wield influence over Christians by false gods, he created false martyrs. But oh you, catholic sprouts, compare with us a little those false martyrs with the true martyrs, and by pious faith discern that the devil is trying to cause confusion by a poisonous fraud. (*Oboed.* 16)[55]

Augustine opens with a short list of the West's most famous martyrs: Peter and Paul in Rome, Vincent in Spain, and Cyprian in North Africa. Their examples fanned the flame of the Christian faith, causing it to grow and overshadow its pagan competitors. When the devil failed to undermine Christianity by reasserting the pagan gods, he created a line of "false martyrs" in order to confuse and deceive. These pseudo-martyrs were drawing away the gullible, who mistakenly thought that they were in the line of Paul, Peter, and Cyprian. Augustine here draws a clear distinction between "us" and "them," between those who venerate the true martyrs and the Donatists. He warns his audience to shun this "poisonous fraud." Any who want to honor martyrs such as Paul should do so in the company of the true Christians, the Caecilianists.

In another sermon preached on the festival of Peter and Paul (between 403 and 406), Augustine again appeals to the apostles in order to distinguish the Caecilianists from the Donatists. Augustine had been under attack from Donatist sympathizers, and he takes the opportunity on this festival day to claim Paul and Peter for his side of the conflict. The bulk of the sermon focuses on separating true from false worshipers of God. Augustine then bases the

---

54. Vincent was a deacon of Saragossa in Spain who died during the persecution under Diocletian.

55. Augustine has in mind the Donatists in general, but probably the Circumcellion sect in particular. Members of this group reportedly jumped off cliffs in order to make themselves martyrs.

summation of his argument on the reference to Paul's impending death in
2 Tim 4:6–8:

> Today, brothers, we honor the memory of those who have sown the seed,
> through whom God exhibited what he promised to them and what he has
> promised to us through them. What did he promise them? "There remains
> for me the crown of justice, which the Lord, the righteous judge, will present
> on that day." … What will the heretics [i.e., the Donatists] read aloud against
> these things? I think that even they celebrate the birthday of the apostles.
> They indeed strive to celebrate their day, but they do not dare to sing this
> song. (*Dies nat. Pet. Paul.* 9)

The bishop reiterates the Caecilianist claim to Paul and Peter and asserts that
his congregation could look forward to receiving their own crowns at the final
judgment. The Donatist "heretics" also observe this festival day and consider
themselves heirs of the promises, but their efforts are futile. Though they may
"strive," they cannot sing the hymn of the true martyrs like Paul. The Donatists
venerate and appeal to the apostles in vain, because the great martyr-patrons
are absent from their churches. The legitimate song of praise for the apostles,
according to Augustine, rises only in the basilicas of the Caecilianists.

The Donatists, from their perspective, saw a clear parallel between their
plight and that of Peter and Paul. Like the apostles, they had suffered persecution for their beliefs at the hands of the emperor but had not relented
from their convictions. They therefore claimed Paul and Peter as their rightful martyr-patrons and sought to link their own martyrs to them. This
connection between the apostles and Donatist martyrs was made explicit in
the dedication of a church in Uppenna (modern Henshir Fraga, Tunisia). A
mosaic in the eastern apse of the basilica (fig. 4.8) reads: "Here are the names
of the martyrs: Peter, Paul, Saturninus the presbyter. Likewise Saturninus,
Bindemius, Saturninus, Donatus, Saturninus, Gududa, Paula, Clara, Lucilla,
Kortun, Iader, Cecilius, Emilius, who died and were buried on November 8."[56]
The original mosaic dates from the fourth century but was replaced in the
sixth century by the dedication in its current form. Archaeologists have suggested that the fourth-century version included only the names of the final
thirteen martyrs, beginning with the second Saturninus in the list. Only these
thirteen were believed to be buried in the basilica. The names of the apostles
and the presbyter Saturninus were added in the later mosaic as part of a reno-

---

56. Duval, *Loca sanctorum Africae*, 1:63–67, no. 29; Monceaux, "Enquête," 334–35.
Frend's reproduction in "Memoriae Apostolorum," 33, contains two errors. The burial date
of *VI idus nobembres* is misprinted as *IIII idus nobembres*, and the final word *ominibus* (for
hominibus) is given as *omnibus*.

Fig. 4.8. Mosaic from Uppenna with a list of martyrs that includes Peter and Paul.
In the Musée d'Enfidaville, Tunisia. Courtesy of École française de Rome.

vation project. The later addition is the key to understanding how this mosaic functioned for the Donatists. A few words are in order, therefore, about the background to "Saturninus the presbyter."

The *Acts of the Abitinian Martyrs*[57] tells the story of the presbyter Saturninus and a group of Christians from Abitina, a village near Carthage (modern Chahoud el-Batin, Tunisia). According to the story, they were arrested in 304 during the persecution under Diocletian on the charge of performing the Christian liturgy. They were sent to Carthage, where the proconsul Anulinus questioned and tortured them. He then threw them into prison and expected them to die there. Family members and friends came at night to bring food and drink, but they were rebuffed and beaten not by Roman soldiers but by agents of Bishop Mensurius and the deacon (and later bishop) Caecilian.

---

57. This is the common name for this account, although the Latin title is *Passio ss. Dativi, Saturnini presb. et aliorum.*

Mensurius and Caecilian perhaps sought to avoid inciting the proconsul any further,[58] but for the author of the *Acts of the Abitinian Martyrs*, this was further evidence of the depravity of Mensurius, a *traditor*: "Mensurius, the so-called bishop of Carthage, polluted by the recent handing over of scripture … raged against the martyrs with the same resolve with which he had handed over the divine laws, thus adding to his transgressions even more shameful acts" (*Pass. Dat. Saturn.* 20, Tilley). By his treacherous actions, Mensurius declared himself an enemy of the true church. He had betrayed the martyrs and was outside the succession of its rightful leaders. Saturninus, on the other hand, followed the example of faithfulness set by the apostles themselves. The condemnation of Mensurius and Caecilian in this story clearly marks it as a Donatist text, with Saturninus as the Donatist hero.

The significance of the sixth-century addition to the Uppenna mosaic becomes clearer in light of the *Acts of the Abitinian Martyrs*. Saturninus stands alongside the apostles as the heir to their legacy. Paul and Peter were the greatest Christian martyrs in the West, and Saturninus was the leader of some of the greatest Donatist martyrs.[59] By extension, the thirteen local martyrs buried in the church also shared in this apostolic lineage. They were connected to Saturninus because they, like the Abitinian martyrs, had given their lives to defend the true (Donatist) faith in North Africa. They represented the continuation of the Donatist line of martyrs that went back through Saturninus to Paul and Peter. This line of succession gave the Uppenna basilica legitimacy as a holy site. As the author of the *Acts of the Abitinian Martyrs* had commented, "One must flee and curse the whole corrupt congregation of all the polluted people and all must seek the glorious lineage of the blessed martyrs, which is the one, holy, and true church, from which the martyrs arise and whose divine mysteries the martyrs observe" (*Pass. Dat. Saturn.* 23, Tilley).[60] For the Donatists at Uppenna, the true veneration of Paul took place in their church, where the "glorious lineage" of the apostles and other true martyrs was honored,

---

58. The emperor Licinius had passed a law stating that anyone feeding those condemned to starvation would receive the same sentence (Tilley, *Donatist Martyr Stories*, 25–26).

59. Also among the Abitinian martyrs was a lector named Emeritus (*Pass. Dat. Saturn.* 11–12). The name Emeritus is linked to the site of the apostolic basilica at Aïn Ghorab, as well as to a "memorial of the apostles" at Henchir Taghfaght (near Khenchela, Algeria). See Duval, *Loca sanctorum Africae*, 1:151–54, no. 70; 1:163–64, no. 77. However, Duval considers the identification of this Emeritus with the Abitinian lector "very problematic" (1:164; 2:686–87).

60. On the role of this text as a catalyst for the schism in the North African church, see Alan Dearn, "The Abitinian Martyrs and the Outbreak of the Donatist Schism," *JEH* 55.1 (2004): 1–18.

not in the churches of the illegitimate Caecilianist bishops and their "corrupt congregation."

The cult of Paul took on a particularly polemical edge in the debate between the Caecilianists and the Donatists.[61] The Caecilianists argued that only they could claim Paul, because they were still in communion with the Roman church. They alone could worship in any of the Roman basilicas and could celebrate the Eucharist at the apostolic shrines. Their churches in North Africa, therefore, were also the legitimate places for Pauline veneration on the annual feast days of the apostles. The Donatists countered that legitimacy came through an unbroken succession of faithful bishops and martyrs that went back directly to the apostles and was not dependent on the approval of Rome or the emperor. They saw themselves as standing in this line. Paul belonged to them, and they invoked his name as an endorsement of their martyrs and their basilica in Uppenna.

Conclusion

In a region that placed a heavy emphasis on the martyr tradition, the apostle Paul was an important figure in popular piety. The Christians of North Africa revered him for his courage in the face of persecution and considered him a model martyr. Thus, when authors set out to recount the deaths of prominent local martyrs, they employed language and imagery that linked those martyrdoms with that of Paul. In addition to crafting these literary references, Christians created a regional Pauline cult through the observance of special feast days, the construction of basilicas and memorials, and the procurement of relics, some of which became the focal point for privileged burials. In some cases, these practices explicitly reflected or mimicked those that occurred in Rome, yet the North Africans also made Paul their own, a prominent figure among their most revered Christian martyrs. Because of the popularity of his cult, Paul became important political capital in the lengthy dispute between the Donatists and the Caecilianists. Both sides venerated him, but both sides also claimed him for themselves and asserted that they were the legitimate heirs of his legacy. The Pauline cult in North Africa, therefore, became as much a source of division as it was a source of Christian unity.

---

61. Both sides also cited the Pauline writings as prooftexts in their literary war of words. See W. H. C. Frend, "The Donatist Church and St. Paul," in *Le epistole paoline nei manichei, i donatisti e il primo Agostino* (2nd ed.; Rome: Istituto Patristico Augustinianum, 2000), 91–133.

Conclusion

Ancient Christians in the West created an expansive cult for Paul as martyr. It developed around particular locations that were designated holy places for the apostle and were often marked with shrines, from simple memorials to large basilicas. These places then served as focal points for other practices that contributed to the cult: producing stories about Paul's life and death, venerating cultic objects, traveling on pilgrimage, burying the dead "near the saints," celebrating festival days and meals, and claiming patronage relationships with the apostle.

The city of Rome was the primary center for this cult. Paul's martyrdom site and tomb were believed to lie next to the Ostian Road, where cultic practices arose by the time of Caius and then expanded greatly in the fourth century within basilicas built with imperial money. Nearby, the Appian Road featured a site at which Christians honored Paul together with Peter by the mid-third century. At the Catacombs, pilgrims and clients scratched their appeals to the martyr-patrons into a stucco wall and feasted in a special dining room. Constantine's basilica there for the apostles further monumentalized the site as part of the cult. From its Roman center the cult spread to other places in the West. Ambrose promoted it in Milan as part of his effort to establish his city as a legitimate successor to Rome. In Gaul, Spain, and North Africa, Christians imported holy objects and established churches, memorials, and festival days in honor of Paul. They viewed him as a model of faithfulness and linked their own martyrs to him as a means of raising the status of these local figures. The practices in these other areas drew heavily upon Roman examples, even in those cases in which the Pauline cult was actively subverted or disputed as a sign of separation from Rome.

This study represents the first book to incorporate the various forms of evidence for Pauline veneration into an integrated narrative of the apostle's cult. As such, it offers an important contribution to scholarly conversations about Pauline reception, the cult of the saints, and the history of the early church. While I have focused on the cult in the late antique Latin West, this is only part of a much larger story. There was also a vibrant Pauline cult in the East during the same period, the story of which remains largely untold.

Of course, the Pauline cult also expanded to other regions in the centuries following the period that I have studied. The religious topography of (the other) Augustine's Canterbury in the seventh century, for example, featured Paul prominently and drew explicitly on Roman models. These other manifestations of the cult fall outside the purview of my current study, but they are significant and worthy of scholarly attention. As the Bollandist Hippolyte Delehaye once observed, "The complete history of the cult of a saint has only rarely been attempted with success. Most of the time, scholars who work in this area of study feel the need to narrow the field of their investigation. The number of these partial contributions that will some day be part of a larger synthesis is considerable."[1] I hope that my own "partial contribution" to the study of the Pauline cult will induce others to take up the task of expanding the story geographically and chronologically, or perhaps of exploring the stories of other important martyr cults.

---

1. Hippolyte Delehaye, "Loca sanctorum," *AnBoll* 48 (1930): 24–25.

Bibliography

Primary Sources

1 Clement (Πρὸς Κορινθίους). Pages 33–131 in *The Apostolic Fathers: Greek Texts and English Translations.* Edited by Michael W. Holmes. 3rd ed. Grand Rapids: Baker, 2007.

Acta Cypriani. Pages 193–231 in *Atti e Passioni dei Martiri.* Edited by A. A. R. Bastiaensen. Milan: Mondadori, 1987.

Acta martyrum Scillitanorum. Pages 97–105 in *Atti e Passioni dei Martiri.* Edited by A. A. R. Bastiaensen. Milan: Mondadori, 1987.

Acta Petri. Pages 45–77 in *Acta Apostolorum apocrypha post Constantinum Tischendorf.* Edited by R. A. Lipsius and M. Bonnet. Leipzig: Mendelssohn, 1891. Repr., Hildesheim: Olms, 1972.

Acta Petri et Pauli. Pages 178–222 in *Acta Apostolorum apocrypha post Constantinum Tischendorf.* Edited by R. A. Lipsius and M. Bonnet. Leipzig: Mendelssohn, 1891. Repr., Hildesheim: Olms, 1972.

Acta Phileae. Pages 247–337 in *Atti e Passioni dei Martiri.* Edited by A. A. R. Bastiaensen. Milan: Mondadori, 1987.

Acta Thomae. Pages 447–511 in *The Apocryphal New Testament: A Collection of Apocryphal Christian Literature in an English Translation.* Translated by J. K. Elliott. Oxford: Oxford University Press, 1993.

Acta Xanthippae et Polyxenae et Rebeccae. Pages 58–85 in *Apocrypha Anecdota: A Collection of Thirteen Apocryphal Books and Fragments Now First Edited from Manuscripts.* Edited by M. R. James. TS 2.3. Cambridge: Cambridge University Press, 1893.

Acts of Sharbil. Pages 41–62 in *Ancient Syriac Documents Relative to the Earliest Establishment of Christianity in Edessa and the Neighbouring Countries.* Translated by William Cureton. London: Williams & Norgate, 1864.

Ambrose of Milan. *De excessu fratris sui Satyri.* Pages 207–325 in vol. 7 of *Sancti Ambrosii Opera.* Edited by O. Faller. CSEL 73.7. Vienna: Hoelder-Pichler-Tempsky, 1955.

———. *De virginitate.* PL 16:187–232.

———. *Epistulae.* PL 16:875–1288.

———. *Hymni.* Edited by Jacques Fontaine. Paris: Cerf, 1992.

Ammianus Marcellinus. *Res gestae.* Translated by John C. Rolfe. Rev. ed. 3 vols. LCL. Cambridge: Harvard University Press, 1971–1972.

Arator. *De actibus apostolorum.* In *Arator's On the Acts of the Apostles.* Translated by Richard J. Schrader. Atlanta: Scholars Press, 1987.

Augustine of Hippo. *Confessionum libri XIII.* In *Saint Augustine: Confessions.* Translated by R. S. Pine-Coffin. New York: Penguin, 1961.

———. *De oboedientia.* In "Nouveaux sermons de saint Augustin pour la conversion des païens et des donatistes (III)." Edited by François Dolbeau. *REAug* 38 (1992): 50–79.

———. *Sermo sancti Augustini habitus ad populum in die natalico apostolorum sanctorum Petri et Pauli.* In "Nouveaux sermons de saint Augustin pour la conversion des païens et des donatistes (VI)." Edited by François Dolbeau. *REAug* 39 (1993): 411–23.

———. *The Works of Saint Augustine: A Translation for the 21st Century.* Translated by Edmund Hill. Edited by John E. Rotelle. Brooklyn: New City Press, 1990–.

Basil of Seleucia. *Miracula Theclae.* In *Vie et miracles de Sainte Thècle.* Edited by Gilbert Dagron. SHG 62. Brussels: Société des Bollandistes, 1978.

Bede. *De temporum ratione (Chronica maiora).* Pages 223–354 in vol. 3 of *Chronica minora saec. IV. V. VI. VII.* Edited by T. Mommsen. MGH.AA 13. Berlin: Weidmann, 1898.

Bordeaux Pilgrim. *Itinerary from Bordeaux to Jerusalem.* Edited by Aubrey Stewart and Charles William Wilson. London: Committee of the Palestine Exploration Fund, 1887.

Chronicon paschale. PG 92:70–1145.

Cicero. *De re publica; De legibus.* Translated by Clinto Walker Keyes. LCL. Cambridge: Harvard University Press, 1961.

———. *De senectute, De amicitia, De divinatione.* Translated by W. A. Falconer. LCL. Cambridge: Harvard University Press, 1959.

Clercq, Charles de, ed. *Concilia Galliae a. 511–a. 695.* CCSL 148A. Turnhout: Brepols, 1963.

Codex Theodosianus. Edited by T. Mommsen and Paulus M. Meyer. The Roman Law Library. Online: http://ancientrome.ru/ius/library/codex/theod/index.htm.

Constitutiones apostolicae. In *Les constitutions apostoliques.* Edited by Marcel Metzger. 3 vols. SC 320, 329, 336. Paris: Cerf, 1985–1987.

Cyprian of Carthage. *Epistulae.* In *Saint Cyprien correspondence.* Edited by Louis Bayard. 2 vols. Paris: Belles Lettres, 1945.

Cyril of Jerusalem. *Catecheses.* Pages 87–168 in *Cyril of Jerusalem.* Translated by Edward Yarnold. ECF. New York: Routledge, 2000.

Damasus of Rome. *Epigrammata*. In *Epigrammata Damasiana*. Edited by Antonio Ferrua. SSAC 2. Vatican City: Pontificio Istituto di Archeologia Cristiana, 1942.

De locis sanctis martyrum quae sunt foris civitatis Romae. Pages 106–31 in vol. 2 of *Codice topografico della città di Roma*. Edited by Roberto Valenti and Giuseppe Zucchetti. 4 vols. FSI 88. Rome: Tip. del Senato, 1940–1953.

Depositio martyrum. Pages 71–72 in vol. 1 of *Chronica minora saec. IV. V. VI. VII*. Edited by T. Mommsen. MGH.AA 9. Berlin: Weidmann, 1892.

Dinamius Patricius. *Vita Maximi*. PL 80:31–40.

Diodorus of Sicily. *Bibliotheca historica*. Edited by I. Bekker, L. Dindorf, and F. Vogel. 5 vols. Leipzig: Teubner, 1888–1906.

Egeria. *Itinerarium*. In *Journal de voyage (Itinéraire)*. Edited by Pierre Maraval. SC 296. Paris: Cerf, 1982.

Ehrman, Bart D., trans. *The Apostolic Fathers*. 2 vols. LCL. Cambridge: Harvard University Press, 2003.

Elliott, J. K. *The Apocryphal New Testament: A Collection of Apocryphal Christian Literature in an English Translation*. Oxford: Oxford University Press, 1993.

Eusebius "Gallicanus." *Homily 55: De sanctis martyribus Ephypodio et Alexandro*. Pages 639–44 in *Collectio homiliarum; Sermones extravagantes*. Edited by F. Glorie. CCSL 101. Turnhout: Brepols, 1970.

Eusebius of Caesarea. *Historia ecclesiastica*. In *Eusebius' Ecclesiastical History*. Translated by C. F. Cruse. Peabody, Mass.: Hendrickson, 1998.

———. *Theophania*. In Early Church Fathers—Additional Texts. Translated by Samuel Lee. Online: http://www.ccel.org/ccel/pearse/morefathers/files/index.htm#Theophania.

———. *Vita Constantini*. Edited by Bruno Bleckmann. FontC 83. Turnhout: Brepols, 2007.

Faustus of Riez. *De sancte Maxime*. In vol. 6 of *Maxima bibliotheca veterurn patrum et antiquorum scriptorum ecclesiasticorum*. Lyons: Anisson, 1677.

Ferrandus of Carthage. *Vita sancti Fulgentii*. In *Vie de saint Fulgence de Ruspe*. Edited by Gabriel G. Lapeyre. Paris: Lethielleux, 1929.

Flodard of Reims. *Flodoardi historia remensis ecclesiae*. Translated by M. Lejeune. Reims: L'Académie impériale de Reims, 1854.

Gregory I. *Gregorii I Papae Registrum Epistolarum*. Edited by Paul Ewald and Ludo Hartmann. 2 vols. MGH.Ep 1–2. Berlin: Weidmann, 1893.

———. *The Letters of Gregory the Great*. Translated by John R. C. Martyn. 3 vols. MST 40. Toronto: Pontifical Institute of Mediaeval Studies, 2004.

Gregory of Nazianzus. *Oration 4 (Against Julian)*. PG 35:531–663.

Gregory of Tours. *De gloria martyrum*. In *Gregory of Tours: Glory of the Mar-

tyrs. Translated by Raymond Van Dam. TTHLS 3. Liverpool: Liverpool University Press, 1988.

———. *Historia francorum.* Books 1–6 in *Histoire des Francs Livres I–VI: Texte du manuscrit de Corbie.* Edited by Henri Omont. Paris: Picard, 1886. Books 7–10 in *Histoire des Francs Livres VII–X: Texte du manuscrit de Bruxelles.* Edited by Gaston Collon. Paris: Picard, 1893.

———. *Vita Martini.* Pages 200–303 in *Saints and Their Miracles in Late Antique Gaul.* Translated by Raymond Van Dam. Princeton: Princeton University Press, 1993.

———. *Vita patrum.* In *Gregory of Tours: Life of the Fathers.* Translated by Edward James. TTHLS 1. Liverpool: Liverpool University Press, 1991.

Günther, Otto, ed. *Epistulae imperatorum pontificum aliorum inde ab a. CCCLXVII usque ad a. DLIII datae: Inde ab a. CCCLXVII usqve ad a. DLIII datae.* CSEL 35.1.2. Leipzig: Tempsky, 1895.

Hilary of Poitiers. *Fragmenta historica.* Edited by Alfred Feder. CSEL 65. Vienna: Tempsky, 1916.

———. *Liber contra Constantium.* In *Contre Constance.* Edited by André Rocher. SC 334. Paris: Cerf, 1987.

Hormisdas of Rome. *Epistulae.* In *Epistolae romanorum pontificum genuinae et quae ad eos scriptae sunt: A S. Hilaro usque ad Pelagium II.* Edited by Andreas Thiel. 2nd ed. Hildesheim: Olms, 2004.

Irenaeus of Lyon. *Adversus haereses.* In *Against the Heresies.* Translated by Dominic J. Unger and John J. Dillon. ACW 55. New York: Paulist, 1992.

Jerome. *Adversus Vigilantium.* PL 23:337–52.

———. *Chronicle.* In Early Church Fathers—Additional Texts. Edited by Roger Pearse. Online: http://www.ccel.org/ccel/pearse/morefathers/files/jerome_chronicle_00_eintro.htm.

———. *Commentariorum in Epistulam ad Gatatas libri III.* PL 26:307–438.

———. *Commentariorum in Ezechielem libri XVI.* PL 25:15–497.

———. *De viris illustribus.* In *On Illustrious Men.* Translated by Thomas P. Halton. FC 100. Washington, D.C.: Catholic University of America Press, 1999.

———. *Epistulae.* Edited by I. Hilberg. 3 vols. CSEL 54–56. Vienna: Tempsky, 1910–1918.

———. *Tractatus sive homiliae in psalmos.* Pages 3–352 in *Tractatus sive homiliae in psalmos; In Marci evangelium; Alia varia argumenta.* Edited by G. Morin, B. Capelle, and J. Fraipont. CCSL 78. Turnhout: Brepols, 1958.

John Chrysostom. *Contra Judaeos et gentiles quod Christus sit deus.* PG 48:813–39.

———. *De laudibus sancti Pauli apostoli.* PG 50:473–513.

———. *Homilia in martyres.* PG 50:661–65.

———. *Homiliae in Acta apostolorum.* PG 60:13–391.

———. *Homiliae in epistulam ad Ephesios.* PG 62:5–177.

———. *Homiliae in epistulam ad Romanos.* PG 60:395–680.

———. *Homiliae in Genesim.* PG 53–54.

Julian. *Contra Galileos.* Edited by Emanuele Masaracchia. TCU 9. Rome: Ateneo, 1990.

Justin Martyr. *Apologia I.* Pages 23–72 in *The First and Second Apologies.* Translated by Leslie William Barnard. ACW 56. New York: Paulist, 1997.

Lactantius. *De mortibus persecutorum.* Edited by Alfons Städele. FontC 43. Turnhout: Brepols, 2003.

Layton, Bentley. *The Gnostic Scriptures: A New Translation with Annotations and Introductions.* Garden City, N.Y.: Doubleday, 1987.

Leo I. *Sermones.* In *Sermons of St. Leo the Great.* Translated by Jane P. Freeland and Agnes J. Conway. FC 93. Washington, D.C.: Catholic University of America Press, 1996.

Liber Pontificalis. In *The Book of Pontiffs (Liber Pontificalis): The Ancient Biographies of the First Ninety Roman Bishops.* Translated by Raymond Davis. TTHLS 5. Liverpool: Liverpool University Press, 1989.

———. In *Le Liber pontificalis: Texte, introduction et commentaire.* Edited by Louis Duchesne and Cyrille Vogel. 2nd ed. 3 vols. BEFAR. Paris: de Boccard, 1955–1957.

Livy. *Ab urbe condita.* Edited by Robert Maxwell Ogilvie. 6 vols. OCT. Oxford: Clarendon, 1974–1999.

Lucian of Samosata. *De luctu.* Pages 111–31 in vol. 4 of *Lucian.* Translated by A. M. Harmon. LCL. Cambridge: Harvard University Press, 1969.

Maier, Jean-Louis. *Le Dossier du Donatisme.* 2 vols. TUGAL 134–135. Berlin: Akademie, 1987–1989.

Marcus Cornelius Fronto. *The Correspondence of Marcus Cornelius Fronto.* Translated by C. R. Haines. 2 vols. LCL. Cambridge: Harvard University Press, 1957–1962.

Martial. *Epigrammata.* Translated by D. R. Shackleton Bailey. 3 vols. LCL. Cambridge: Harvard University Press, 1993.

Martyrdom and Ascension of Isaiah. In *Ascensio Isaiae.* Edited by Paolo Bettiolo and Enrico Norelli. 2 vols. CCSA 7–8. Turnhout: Brepols, 1995.

Martyrium Ignatii. Pages 254–65 in vol. 1 of *Opera patrum apostolicorum.* Edited by Francis Xavier Funk. 5th ed. 3 vols. Tübingen: Laupp, 1878.

Martyrium Perpetuae et Felicitatis. Pages 107–47 in *Atti e Passioni dei Martiri.* Edited by A. A. R. Bastiaensen. Milan: Mondadori, 1987.

Martyrium Polycarpi. Pages 298–333 in *The Apostolic Fathers: Greek Texts and English Translations.* Edited by Michael W. Holmes. Grand Rapids: Baker, 1999.

Martyrium sancti Pauli apostoli (Acta Pauli). Pages 104–17 in *Acta Apostolorum apocrypha post Constantinum Tischendorf.* Edited by R. A. Lipsius and M. Bonnet. Leipzig: Mendelssohn, 1891. Repr., Hildesheim: Olms, 1972.

Martyrologium Hieronymianum. Edited by G. B. de Rossi and L. Duchesne. Brussels: Société des Bollandistes, 1971.

Maximus of Turin. *Sermones.* In *Maximi episcopi Taurinensis: Collectionem sermonum antiquam nonnullis sermonibus extravagantibus adiectis.* Edited by Almut Mutzenbecher. CCSL 23. Turnhout: Brepols, 1962.

Mirabiliana (The Marvels of Roman Churches, A.D. 1375). Pages 121–52 in *Mirabilia urbis Romae: The Marvels of Rome, or A Picture of the Golden City: An English Version of the Medieval Guide-Book with a Supplement of Illustrative Matter and Notes.* London: Ellis & Elvey, 1889.

Miraculum sancti Anastasii martyris. AnBoll 11 (1892): 233–41.

Munier, Charles, ed. *Concilia Galliae a. 314–a. 506.* CCSL 148. Turnhout: Brepols, 1963.

Muratorian Canon. Pages 191–201 in *The Canon of the New Testament: Its Origin, Development, and Significance.* Translated by Bruce M. Metzger. Oxford: Clarendon, 1987.

Optatus of Milev. *Adversus Donatistas.* In *Traité contre les donatistes.* Edited by Mireille Labrousse. 2 vols. SC 412–413. Paris: Cerf, 1995–1996.

Ovid. *Fasti.* In *Les fastes.* Edited by Robert Schilling. 2 vols. CUFr. Paris: Belles Lettres, 1992–1993.

Passio sancti Pauli apostoli. Pages 23–44 in *Acta Apostolorum apocrypha post Constantinum Tischendorf.* Edited by R. A. Lipsius and M. Bonnet. Leipzig: Mendelssohn, 1891. Repr., Hildesheim: Olms, 1972.

Passio sanctorum apostolorum Petri et Pauli. Pages 119–77 in *Acta Apostolorum apocrypha post Constantinum Tischendorf.* Edited by R. A. Lipsius and M. Bonnet. Leipzig: Mendelssohn, 1891. Repr., Hildesheim: Olms, 1972.

Passio Sebastiani. PL 17:1021–56.

Passio ss. Dativi, Saturnini presb. et aliorum (Acts of the Abitinian Martyrs). Pages 27–49 in *Donatist Martyr Stories: The Church in Conflict in Roman North Africa.* Translated by Maureen A. Tilley. TTH 24. Liverpool: Liverpool University Press, 1996.

Paulinus of Milan. *Vita Ambrosii.* PL 14:27–46.

Paulinus of Nola. *Carmina.* In *The Poems of St. Paulinus of Nola.* Translated by P. G. Walsh. ACW 40. New York: Newman, 1975.

——. *Epistulae.* In *Letters of St. Paulinus of Nola.* Translated by P. G. Walsh. 2 vols. ACW 35–36. Westminster, Md.: Newman, 1966.

——. *Sancti Pontii Meropii Paulini Nolani.* Edited by Wilhelm Hartel. CSEL 29b. Vienna: Österreichischen Akademie der Wissenschaften, 1999.

Philostorgius. *Historia ecclesiastica*. In *Philostorgius: Church History*. Translated by Philip R. Amidon. SBLWGRW 23. Leiden: Brill, 2007.

Philostratus. *Vita Apollonii*. In *Philostratus in Honour of Apollonius of Tyana*. Translated by J. S. Phillimore. 2 vols. Oxford: Clarendon, 1912.

Pliny the Younger. *Epistulae ad Trajanum*. In *The Letters of Pliny: A Historical and Social Commentary*. Translated by A. N. Sherwin-White. Oxford: Clarendon, 1966.

Plutarch. *Vitae parallelae*. Translated by Bernadotte Perrin. 11 vols. LCL. Cambridge: Harvard University Press, 1914–1926.

Pontius of Carthage. *Vita Cypriani*. Pages 4–48 in *Vita di Cipriano; Vita di Ambrogio; Vita di Agostino*. Edited by A. A. R. Bastiaensen. Milan: Fondazione Lorenzo Valla, 1975.

Procopius of Caesarea. *Opera omnia*. Edited by Jakob Haury and Gerhard Wirth. 4 vols. Munich: Saur, 2001.

Prosper of Aquitaine. *Epitoma chronicon*. Pages 385–485 in vol. 1 of *Chronica minora saec. IV. V. VI. VII.* Edited by T. Mommsen. MGH.AA 9. Berlin: Weidmann, 1892.

Prudentius. *Peristephanon (De coronis martyrum)*. Pages 98–345 in vol. 2 of *Prudentius*. Translated by H. J. Thomson. 2 vols. LCL. Cambridge: Harvard University Press, 1953.

Pseudo-Cyprian. *De gloria martyrii*. Pages 26–52 in *S. Thasci Caecili Cypriani Opera omnia*. Edited by Wilhelm Hartel. CSEL 3.3. Vienna: Gerold, 1871.

Pseudo-Ignatius. *Epistula ad Tarsenses*. Pages 95–105 in vol. 2 of *Opera patrum apostolicorum*. Edited by Francis Xavier Funk. 3 vols. Tübingen: Laupp, 1881.

Rossi, G. B. de, Angelo Silvagni, and Antonio Ferrua, eds. *Inscriptiones Christianae urbis Romae septimo saeculo antiquiores*. Rome: Ex Officina Libraria Doct. Befani, 1922–.

Rufinus of Aquileia. *Historia ecclesiastica*. In *The Church History of Rufinus of Aquileia: Books 10 and 11*. Translated by Philip R. Amidon. New York: Oxford University Press, 1997.

Sacramentarium Leonianum (Sacramentarium Veronense). Edited by L. C. Mohlberg. RED.F 1. Rome: Herder, 1966.

Seneca. *De brevitate vitae (Epistulae morales)*. Pages 286–354 in vol. 2 of *Moral Essays*. Translated by John W. Basore. 3 vols. LCL. Cambridge: Harvard University Press, 1935.

Shepherd of Hermas. Pages 442–685 in *The Apostolic Fathers: Greek Texts and English Translations*. Edited by Michael W. Holmes. 3rd ed. Grand Rapids: Baker, 2007.

Socrates Scholasticus. *Historia ecclesiastica*. In *Histoire ecclésiastique*. Edited by G. C. Hansen. 4 vols. SC 477, 493, 505, 506. Paris: Cerf, 2004–2007.

Sozomen Scholasticus. *Historia ecclesiastica*. In *Histoire ecclésiastique*. Translated by André-Jean Festugière. Edited by J. Bidez-Hansen. 4 vols. SC 306, 418, 495, 516. Paris: Cerf, 1983–2008.

Strabo. *Geographica*. Edited by Franciscus Sbordone. 3 vols. SGL. Rome: Typis Publicae Officinae Polygraphicae, 1963.

Suetonius. *Vita neronis (De vita caesarum)*. Pages 85–198 in vol. 2 of *Suetonius*. Translated by J. C. Rolfe. 2 vols. LCL. Cambridge: Harvard University Press, 1964.

Sulpicius Severus. *Chronica*. In *Sulpice Sévère: Chroniques*. Edited by Ghislaine de Senneville-Grave. SC 441. Paris: Cerf, 1999.

———. *Dialogi*. In *Gallus: Dialogues sur les "vertus" de saint Martin*. Edited by Jacques Fontaine. SC 510. Paris: Cerf, 2006.

———. *Vita Martini*. In *Vie de Saint Martin*. Edited by Jacques Fontaine. 3 vols. SC 133–135. Paris: Cerf, 1967.

Symmachus. *Relationes*. In *Prefect and Emperor: The Relationes of Symmachus, A.D. 384*. Translated by R. H. Barrow. Oxford: Clarendon, 1973.

Tacitus. *Annales*. Translated by John Jackson. 4 vols. LCL. Cambridge: Harvard University Press, 1931–1937.

Tertullian. *Opera I*. Edited by E. Dekkers. CCSL 1. Turnhout: Brepols, 1953.

———. *Opera II*. Edited by A. Gerlo. CCSL 2. Turnhout: Brepols, 1954.

Theodore of Mopsuestia: Commentaries on the Minor Epistles of Paul. Translated with an introduction by Rowan A. Greer. SBLWGRW 26. Atlanta: Society of Biblical Literature, 2010.

Theodoret of Cyrus. *Commentary on the Letters of St. Paul*. Translated by Robert C. Hill. 2 vols. Brookline: Holy Cross Orthodox Press, 2001.

———. *Historia ecclesiastica*. PG 82:879–1278.

———. *In quatuordecim sancti Pauli epistolas commentarius*. PG 82:31–878.

Tilley, Maureen A., trans. *Donatist Martyr Stories: The Church in Conflict in Roman North Africa*. TTH 24. Liverpool: Liverpool University Press, 1996.

Velleius Paterculus. *Historiae romanae*. In *Ad M. Vinicium consulem libri duo*. Edited by Maria Elefante. BWeid 3. Hildesheim: Olms, 2009.

Venantius Fortunatus. *Carmina*. In *Venance Fortunat: Poèmes*. Edited by Marc Reydellet. 2 vols. Paris: Belles Lettres, 1994.

Victor of Vita. *Historia persecutionis Africanae provinciae*. In *Histoire de la persécution vandale en Afrique*. Edited by Serge Lancel. CUFr.L. Paris: Belles Lettres, 2002.

Victricius of Rouen. *De laude sanctorum*. Edited by R. Demeulenaere. CCSL 64. Turnhout: Brepols, 1991.

Vigilius of Rome. *Epistula Vigilii papae ad Profuturum episcopum*. PL 84:829–32.

Virgil. *Aeneid.* Translated by Sarah Ruden. New Haven: Yale University Press, 2008.

Vita patrum Iurensium. Edited by François Martine. SC 142. Paris: Cerf, 1968.

Vita sancti Epiphanii. PG 41:23–115.

Vita sancti Leonis papae. Pages 17–18 in *AASS* April 2.11. Antwerp, 1675.

Vives, José. *Inscripciones cristianas de la España romana y visigoda.* BHBB 2/18. Barcelona: Consejo Superior de Investigaciones Científicas, 1942.

Walpole, A. S., ed. *Early Latin Hymns.* Hildesheim: Olms, 1966.

Weidemann, Margarete, ed. *Geschichte des Bistums Le Mans von der Spätantike bis zur Karolingerzeit: Actus pontificum Cenomannis in urbe degentium und Gesta Aldrici.* 3 vols. Mainz: Römisch-Germanisches Zentralmuseum, 2002.

SECONDARY SOURCES

Aguirre Prado, Luis. *San Pablo en España.* TEsp 435. Madrid: Publicaciones Españolas, 1963.

Apollonj-Ghetti, B. M. "Le basiliche cimiteriali degli apostoli Pietro e Paolo a Roma." Pages 7–34 in *Saecularia Petri et Pauli.* SAC 28. Vatican City: Pontificio Istituto di Archeologia Cristiana, 1969.

Arnaud, Pascal. *Les routes de la navigation antique: Itinéraires en Méditerranée.* Paris: Errance, 2005.

Aune, David E. *Revelation 6–16.* WBC 52B. Nashville: Thomas Nelson, 1998.

Aus, Roger D. "Paul's Travel Plans to Spain and the 'Full Number of the Gentiles' of Rom XI 25." *NovT* 21 (1979): 232–62.

Bakirtzis, Charalambos. "Byzantine Ampullae from Thessaloniki." Pages 140–50 in *The Blessings of Pilgrimage.* Edited by Robert Ousterhout. Urbana: University of Illinois Press, 1990.

———. "Paul and Philippi: The Archaeological Evidence." Pages 37–48 in *Philippi at the Time of Paul and after His Death.* Edited by Charalambos Bakirtzis and Helmut Koester. Harrisburg, Pa.: Trinity Press International, 1998.

Baradaz, J. "La basilique de Pierre et Paul à Tipasa de Maurétaine." Pages 341–56 in *Akten des VII. Internationalen Kongresses für Christliche Archäologie, Trier, 5–11 September 1965.* SAC 27. Vatican City: Pontificio Istituto di Archeologia Cristiana, 1969.

Bardy, Gustave. "Pèlerinages à Rome vers la fin du IVe siècle." *AnBoll* 67 (1949): 224–35.

Barnes, A. S. *The Martyrdom of St. Peter and St. Paul.* London: Oxford University Press, 1933.

Barrett, Charles K. "The End of Acts." Pages 545–55 in vol. 3 of *Geschichte-*

Tradition-Reflexion: Festschrift für Martin Hengel zum 70. Geburtstag. Edited by Hubert Cancik, Hermann Lichtenberger, and Peter Schäfer. 3 vols. Tübingen: Mohr Siebeck, 1996.

Bastiaensen, A. A. R. "Augustin commentateur de saint Paul et l'Ambrosiaster." *SacEr* 36 (1996): 37–65.

Beaujard, Brigitte. "Cités, évêques et martyrs en Gaule à la fin de l'époque romaine." Pages 175–91 in *Les fonctions des saints dans le monde occidental (IIIe–XIIIe siècle): actes du colloque.* Rome: École française de Rome, 1991.

Bekker, Henk. "Potamiaena: Some Observations about Martyrdom and Gender in Ancient Alexandria." Pages 331–50 in *The Wisdom of Egypt.* Edited by A. Hilhorst and G. H. van Kooten. Leiden: Brill, 2005.

Belayche, Nicole. "Les pèlerinages dans le monde romain antique." Pages 136–54 in *Histoire des pèlerinages non chrétiens: Entre magique et sacré, le chemin des dieux.* Edited by J. Chélini and H. Branthomme. Paris: Hachette, 1982.

Belloni, Paolo. *Sulla grandezza e disposizione della primitiva basilica ostiense stabilita dalla sua absida rinvenuta nell'anno.* Rome: Tip. Forense, 1853.

Belvederi, Giulio. *Le tombe apostoliche nell'età paleocristiana.* CACat 12. Vatican City: Pontificio Istituto di Archeologia Cristiana, 1948.

Benedict XVI. "Pauline Year Proclamation." *Basilica Papale San Paolo Fuori le Mura Press Office* 28 June 2007. Online: http://www.annopaolino.org/interno.asp?id=2&lang=eng.

Bentley, James. *Restless Bones: The Story of Relics.* London: Constable, 1985.

Bernand, Etienne. "Pèlerins dans l'Égypte grecque et romain." Pages 49–63 in vol. 1 of *Mélanges Pierre Lévêque.* 8 vols. Paris: Belles Lettres, 1988–1995.

Betz, Hans Dieter. "Hero Worship and Christian Beliefs: Observations from the History of Religion on Philostratus's *Heroikos.*" Pages 25–47 in *Philostratus's* Heroikos: *Religion and Cultural Identity in the Third Century C.E.* Edited by Ellen Bradshaw Aitken and Jennifer K. Berenson Maclean. SBLWGRW 6. Atlanta: Society of Biblical Literature, 2004.

Birley, A. R. "Persecutors and Martyrs in Tertullian's North Africa." Pages 37–68 in *The Later Roman Empire Today: Papers Given in Honour of Professor John Mann.* Edited by D. F. Clark, M. M. Roxan, and J. J. Wilkes. London: Institute of Archaeology, 1993.

Bisconti, Fabrizio. "La Memoria Apostolorum." Pages 63–66 in *Pietro e Paolo: La storia, il culto, la memoria nei primi secoli.* Edited by Angela Donati. Milan: Electa, 2000.

———. "La sapienza, la concordia, il martirio: La figura di Paolo nell'immaginario iconografico della tarda antichità." Pages 163–76 in *San Paolo in Vaticano: La figura e la parola dell'Apostolo delle Genti nelle raccolte pontificie.* Edited by Umberto Utro. Todi: Tau Editrice, 2009.

Bisconti, Fabrizio, and Danilo Mazzoleni. *The Christian Catacombs of Rome: History, Decoration, Inscriptions.* Regensburg: Schnell & Steiner, 1999.

Blanco, A. González. "Alusiones a España en las obras de San Juan Crisóstomo." *HAnt* 4 (1974): 345–68.

Blázquez, José Maria. "Die Rolle der Kirche in Hispanien im 4. und 5. Jahrhundert." *KLIO.BAG* 63 (1981): 649–60.

Bodel, John. "From Columbaria to Catacombs: Collective Burial in Pagan and Christian Rome." Pages 177–243 in *Commemorating the Dead: Texts and Artifacts in Context: Studies of Roman, Jewish, and Christian Burials.* Edited by Laurie Brink and Deborah A. Green. Berlin: de Gruyter, 2008.

Bollok, J. "The Description of Paul in the *Acta Pauli.*" Pages 1–15 in *The Apocryphal Acts of Paul and Thecla.* Edited by Jan N. Bremmer. Kampen: Kok Pharos, 1996.

Bolyki, J. "Events after the Martyrdom: Missionary Transformation of an Apocalyptical Metaphor in *Martyrium Pauli.*" Pages 92–106 in *The Apocryphal Acts of Paul and Thecla.* Edited by Jan N. Bremmer. Kampen: Kok Pharos, 1996.

Boschung, Dietrich. *Antike Grabaltäre aus den Nekropolen Roms.* AcBern 10. Bern: Stämpfli, 1987.

Bosio, Antonio. *Roma sotterranea.* Rome: Facciotti, 1632.

Boulet, Noële Maurice-Denis. "À propos des fouilles de Saint-Pierre." *RSR* 34 (1947): 385–406.

Bovini, Giuseppe. *Sarcofagi paleocristiani della Spagna.* CACat 22. Vatican City: Società Amici delle catacombe, 1954.

Bozóky, Edina. *La politique des reliques de Constantin à Saint Louis: Protection collective et légitimation du pouvoir.* Paris: Beauchesne, 2006.

Brandenburg, Hugo. *Ancient Churches of Rome from the Fourth to the Seventh Century: The Dawn of Christian Architecture in the West.* Translated by Andreas Kropp. BAnT 8. Turnhout: Brepols, 2005.

———. "Die Architektur der Basilika San Paolo fuori le mura: Das Apostelgrab als Zentrum der Liturgie und des Märtyrerkultes." *MDAI(R)* 112 (2005/2006): 237–75.

———. "Die Basilica S. Paolo fuori le mura, der Apostel-Hymnus des Prudentius (Peristeph. XII) und die architektonische Ausstattung des Baues." Pages 1525–78 in vol. 3 of *Ecclesiae urbis: Atti del Congresso internazionale di studi sulle Chiese di Roma (IV–X secolo), Roma, 4–10 settembre 2000.* Edited by Federico Guidobaldi and Alessandra Guiglia Guidobaldi. 3 vols. Vatican City: Pontificio Istituto di Archeologia Cristiana, 2002.

Braune, Sarah. *Convivium funebre: Gestaltung und Funktion römischer Grabtriklinien als Räume für sepulkrale Bankettfeiern.* Hildesheim: Olms, 2008.

Breck, John. *The Shape of Biblical Language: Chiasmus in the Scriptures and Beyond.* Crestwood, N.Y.: St. Vladimir's Seminary Press, 1994.

Brenk, Beat. "Der Kultort, seine Zugänglichkeit und seine Besucher." Pages 69–122 in vol. 1 of *Akten des XII. Internationalen Kongresses für Christliche Archäologie: Bonn 22.–28. September, 1991.* Edited by Ernst Dassmann and Josef Engemann. 3 vols. Münster: Aschendorffsche Verlagsbuchhandlung, 1995–1997.

Brink, Laurie, and Deborah Green, eds. *Commemorating the Dead: Texts and Artifacts in Context: Studies of Roman, Jewish, and Christian Burials.* New York: de Gruyter, 2008.

Brown, Peter R. L. *The Cult of the Saints: Its Rise and Function in Latin Christianity.* Chicago: University of Chicago Press, 1981.

———. *Relics and Social Status in the Age of Gregory of Tours.* Reading: University of Reading, 1977.

Buschmann, Gerd. *Das Martyrium des Polykarp.* KAV 6. Göttingen: Vandenhoeck & Ruprecht, 1998.

Callahan, Allen D. "Dead Paul: The Apostle as Martyr in Philippi." Pages 67–84 in *Philippi at the Time of Paul and after His Death.* Edited by Charalambos Bakirtzis and Helmut Koester. Harrisburg, Pa.: Trinity Press International, 1998.

Campenhausen, Hans von. "Bearbeitungen und Interpolationen des Polykarpmartyriums." Pages 253–301 in *Aus der Frühzeit des Christentums: Studien zur Kirchengeschichte des ersten und zweiten Jahrhunderts.* Tübingen: Mohr Siebeck, 1963.

———. *The Fathers of the Latin Church.* Translated by Manfred Hoffman. London: Black, 1964.

Capocci, V. "Sulla tradizione del martirio di S. Paolo alle Acque Salvie." Pages 11–19 in vol. 2 of *Atti dello VIII congresso internazionale di studi bizantini, Palermo 3–10 aprile 1951.* 2 vols. Rome: Associazione nazionale per gli studi bizantini, 1953.

Carcopino, Jérôme. *De Pythagores aux Apôtres: études sur la conversion du monde romain.* Paris: Flammarion, 1956.

Carletti, Carlo, ed. *Damaso e i martiri di Roma: Anno Damasi saeculari XVI.* Translated by Antonio Ferrua. Vatican City: Pontificia Commissione di Archeologia Sacra, 1985.

Carriazo, J. M. "El sarcófago cristiano de Berja." *AEAA* 1 (1925): 197–218.

Carroll, Maureen. *Spirits of the Dead: Roman Funerary Commemoration in Western Europe.* Oxford: Oxford University Press, 2006.

Cartlidge, David R., and J. K. Elliott. *Art and the Christian Apocrypha.* London: Routledge, 2001.

Caseau, Béatrice, Jean-Claude Cheynet, and Vincent Déroche, eds. *Pèleri-*

nages et lieux saints dans l'antiquité et le moyen âge: Mélanges offerts à Pierre Maraval. Paris: Association des amis du Centre d'histoire et civilisation de Byzance, 2006.

Castelli, Elizabeth A. *Martyrdom and Memory: Early Christian Culture Making.* New York: Columbia University Press, 2004.

Castillo Maldonado, Pedro. "*Angelorum Participes*: The Cult of the Saints in Late Antique Spain." Pages 151–88 in *Hispania in Late Antiquity: Current Perspectives.* Edited by Kim Bowes and Michael Kulikowski. Boston: Brill, 2005.

Cecchelli, Carlo. "Note sopra il culto delle reliquie nell'Africa romana." *APARA.R* 15 (1939–1940): 125–34.

Chadwick, Henry. "Pope Damasus and the Peculiar Claim of Rome to St. Peter and St. Paul." Pages 313–18 in *Neotestamentica et Patristica: Eine Freundesgabe, Herrn Professor Dr. Oscar Cullmann zu seinem 60. Geburtstag überreicht.* NovTSup 6. Leiden: Brill, 1962.

———. "St Peter and St Paul in Rome: The Problem of the *Memoria Apostolorum ad Catacumbas*." *JTS* NS 8 (1957): 31–52.

Champlin, Edward. *Nero.* Cambridge: Harvard University Press, 2005.

Chastagnol, André. *Les fastes de la préfecture de Rome au Bas-Empire.* EPros 2. Paris: Nouvelles Éditions Latines, 1962.

———. "Sur quelques documents relatifs à la basilique de Saint-Paul-hors-les-murs." Pages 421–38 in *Mélanges d'archéologie et d'histoire offerts à André Piganiol.* Edited by Raymond Chevallier. Paris: SEVPEN, 1966.

Chiesa, Gemma Sena, and Fabrizio Slavazzi. "La capsella argentea di San Nazaro: Primi risultati di una nuova indagine." *AnTard* 7 (1999): 187–204.

Chioffi, Laura. *Mummificazione e imbalsamazione a Roma ed in altri luoghi del mondo romano.* Rome: Quasar, 1998.

Christern, J. "Basilika und Memorie der Heiligen Salsa in Tipasa." *BAA* 3 (1968): 193–258.

Chueca, Pilar Riesco. *Pasionario Hispánico.* Seville: Universidad de Sevilla, 1995.

Clark, Gillian. "Translating Relics: Victricius of Rouen and Fourth-Century Debate." *EMEur* 10.2 (2001): 161–76.

———. "Victricius of Rouen: Praising the Saints." *JECS* 7.3 (1999): 365–99.

Clarysse, Willy. "The Coptic Martyr Cult." Pages 377–95 in *Martyrium in Multidisciplinary Perspective.* Edited by M. Lamberigts and P. Van Deun. BETL 117. Leuven: Peeters, 1995.

Congar, Yves M.J. "S. Paul et l'autorité de l'église romaine d'après la tradition." Pages 491–516 in vol. 1 of *Studiorum Paulinorum Congressus Internationalis Catholicus 1961: Simul Secundus Congressus Internationalis Catholicus de Re Biblica: Completo undevicesimo saeculo post S. Pauli in urbem adventum*. 2 vols. AnBib 17–18. Rome: Pontificio Instituto Biblico, 1963.

Cooper, Kate. "The Martyr, the *Matrona* and the Bishop: The Matron Lucina and the Politics of Martyr Cult in Fifth- and Sixth-Century Rome." *EMEur* 8.3 (1999): 297–317.

Cooper, Stephen A. *Marius Victorinus' Commentary on Galatians: Introduction, Translation, and Notes*. Oxford: Oxford University Press, 2005.

Correnti, Venerando. "Relazione dello studio compiuto su tre gruppi di resti scheletrici umani già rinvenuti sotto la confessione della Basilica Vaticana." Pages 83–160 in *Le reliquie di Pietro sotto la Confessione della Basilica vaticana: Una messa a punto*. Edited by Margherita Guarducci. Rome: Coletti, 1967.

Costambeys, Marios. "The Culture and Practice of Burial in and around Rome in the Sixth Century." Pages 721–32 in vol. 2 of *Ecclesiae urbis: Atti del Congresso internazionale di studi sulle Chiese di Roma (IV–X secolo), Roma, 4–10 settembre 2000*. Edited by Federico Guidobaldi and Alessandra Guiglia Guidobaldi. 3 vols. Vatican City: Pontificio Istituto di Archeologia Cristiana, 2002.

Cullmann, Oscar. *Peter: Disciple, Apostle, Martyr*. 2nd ed. Translated by Floyd V. Filson. London: SCM, 1962.

Custudio Vega, Angel. "La venida de San Pablo a España y los Varones Apostólicos." *BRAH* 154 (1964): 7–78.

Davis, Stephen J. *The Cult of Saint Thecla: A Tradition of Women's Piety in Late Antiquity*. OECS. Oxford: Oxford University Press, 2001.

Dearn, Alan. "The Abitinian Martyrs and the Outbreak of the Donatist Schism." *JEH* 55.1 (2004): 1–18.

Dehandschutter, Boudewijn. "The Martyrium Polycarpi: A Century of Research." *ANRW* 27.1:497–502.

———. "Research on the Martyrdom of Polycarp: 1990–2005." Pages 85–92 in *Polycarpiana: Studies on Martyrdom and Persecution in Early Christianity: Collected Essays*. Edited by J. Leemans. BETL 205. Leuven: Peeters, 2007.

———. "Some Notes on 1 Clement 5, 4–7." *IP* 19 (1989): 83–89.

Deichmann, Friedrich Wilhelm. *Archeologia cristiana*. SAEB 63. Rome: "L'Erma" di Bretschneider, 1993.

———. "Märtyrerbasilika, Martyrion, Memoria und Altargrab." *MDAI(R)* 77 (1970): 144–69.

———, ed. *Repertorium der christlich-antiken Sarkophage*. 4 vols. Wiesbaden: Steiner, 1967–2003.

Delehaye, Hippolyte. "Loca sanctorum." *AnBoll* 48 (1930): 5–64.

———. *Les origines du culte des martyrs*. 2nd ed. SHG 20. Brussels: Société des Bollandistes, 1933.

————. *Sanctus: Essai sur le culte des saints dans l'antiquité.* SHG 17. Brussels: Société des Bollandistes, 1927.

————. "Tusco et Basso cons." Pages 201–7 in *Mélanges Paul Thomas.* Bruges: Sainte Catherine, 1930.

Della Portella, Ivana, Mark Smith, and Richard Pierce. *Subterranean Rome.* Venice: Arsenale, 2002.

Den Boeft, Jan, and Jan Bremmer. "Notiunculae Martyrologicae IV." Review of A. A. R. Bastiaensen, ed., *Atti e Passioni dei Martiri. VC* 45.2 (1991): 105–22.

Deniaux, Elizabeth. *Clientèles et pouvoir à l'époque de Cicéron.* CEFR 182. Rome: École française de Rome, 1993.

Denzey, Nicola. *The Bone Gatherers: The Lost Worlds of Early Christian Women.* Boston: Beacon, 2007.

Dillon, Matthew. *Pilgrims and Pilgrimage in Ancient Greece.* New York: Routledge, 1997.

Dix, Gregory. *The Shape of the Liturgy.* London: Dacre, 1945.

Docci, Marina. *San Paolo fuori le mura: Dalle origini alla basilica delle 'origini.'* Rome: Gangemi, 2006.

Dölger, F. J. *Ichthys: Das Fischsymbol in frühchristlicher Zeit.* 5 vols. Münster: Aschendorffschen Verlagsbuchhandlung, 1922–1943.

Donati, Angela, ed. *Pietro e Paolo: La storia, il culto, la memoria nei primi secoli.* Milan: Electa, 2000.

Donati, Natascia, and Patrizia Stefanetti. *Dies natalis: I calendari romani e gli anniversari dei culti.* Rome: Quasar, 2006.

Douglas, E. M. "Iuno Sospita of Lanuvium." *JRS* 3.1 (1913): 61–72.

Dresken-Weiland, Jutta. *Sarkophagbestattungen des 4.–6. Jahrhunderts im Westen des römischen Reiches.* RQ.S 55. Rome: Herder, 2003.

Dubowy, Ernst. *Klemens von Rom über die Reise Pauli nach Spanien: historisch-kritische Untersuchung zu Klemens von Rom: 1 Kor 5,7.* BibS(F) 19.3. Freiburg im Breisgau: Herder, 1914.

Duchesne, Louis. *Fastes épiscopaux de l'ancienne Gaule.* 3 vols. Paris: Fontemoing, 1900–1915.

————. *Origines du culte chrétien: Etude sur la liturgie latine avant Charlemagne.* 5th ed. Paris: Albert Fontemoing, 1909.

————. "Saint Jacques en Galice." *AMidi* 12 (1900): 145–79.

Duncan-Flowers, Maggie. "A Pilgrim's Ampulla from the Shrine of St. John the Evangelist at Ephesus." Pages 125–39 in *The Blessings of Pilgrimage.* Edited by Robert Ousterhout. Urbana: University of Illinois Press, 1990.

Dunn, Geoffrey D. "Peter and Paul in Rome: The Perspective of the North African Church." Pages 405–13 in *Pietro e Paolo: Il loro rapporto con Roma nelle testimonianze antiche: XXIX Incontro di studiosi dell'antichità cristiana, Roma, 4–6 maggio 2000*. Rome: Institutum Patristicum Augustinianum, 2001.

Dunn, Peter. "L'image de Paul dans les *Actes de Paul.*" *FoiVie* 34.4 (1995): 75–85.

Duval, Noël. "L'espace liturgique dans les églises paléochrétiennes." *MD* 193.1 (1993): 7–29.

Duval, Yvette. *Auprès des saints corps et âme: L'inhumation "ad sanctos" dans la chrétienté d'Orient et d'Occident du IIIe au VIIe siècle.* Paris: Études Augustiniennes, 1988.

———. *Loca sanctorum Africae: le culte des martyrs en Afrique du IVe au VIIe siècle.* 2 vols. CEFR 58. Rome: École française de Rome, 1982.

———. "Sanctorum sepulcris sociari." Pages 333–51 in *Les fonctions des saints dans le monde occidental (IIIe–XIIIe siècle): Actes du colloque.* Rome: École française de Rome, 1991.

Ellis, E. Earle. " 'The End of the Earth' (Acts 1:8)." *BBR* 1 (1991): 123–32.

Elsner, Jaś. *Art and the Roman Viewer: The Transformation of Art from the Pagan World to Christianity.* Cambridge: Cambridge University Press, 1997.

———. "Inventing Christian Rome: The Role of Early Christian Art." Pages 71–99 in *Rome the Cosmopolis.* Edited by Catharine Edwards and Greg Woolf. Cambridge: Cambridge University Press, 2003.

Elsner, Jaś, and Ian Rutherford, eds. *Pilgrimage in Graeco-Roman and Early Christian Antiquity: Seeing the Gods.* Oxford: Oxford University Press, 2005.

Erbes, Carl. *Die Todestage der Apostel Paulus und Petrus und ihre römischen Denkmäler.* Leipzig: Hinrichs, 1899.

Ewig, Eugen. "Le culte de Saint Martin à son époque franque." *RHEF* 47 (1961): 1–18.

———. "Der Petrus- und Apostelkult im spätrömischen und fränkischen Gallien." *ZKG* 71 (1960): 215–51.

Fears, J. R. "The Cult of Jupiter and Roman Imperial Ideology." *ANRW* 17.1:3–141.

Feeney, Denis. *Caesar's Calendar: Ancient Times and the Beginnings of History.* Berkeley: University of California Press, 2007.

Feissel, Denis, ed. *Recueil des inscriptions chrétiennes de Macédoine du IIIe au VIe siècle.* Athens: École française d'Athènes, 1983.

Ferguson, Everett. "Canon Muratori: Date and Provenance." *StPatr* 17.2 (1982): 677–83.

Ferrari, Guy. *Early Roman Monasteries.* Vatican City: Pontificio Istituto di Archeologia Cristiana, 1957.

Ferrari, Guy, and Charles R. Morey. *The Gold-Glass Collection of the Vatican Library: With Additional Catalogues of Other Gold-Glass Collections.* CMSBAV. Vatican City: Biblioteca Apostolica Vaticana, 1959.

Ferrua, Antonio. *La basilica e la catacomba di S. Sebastiano.* CatRI 3. Vatican City: Pontificia Commissione di Archeologia Sacra, 1990.

———. "Nuove iscrizioni della via Ostiense." *Epig.* 21 (1959): 97–116.

———. "Riliggendo i graffiti di S. Sebastiano." Pages 297–314 in *Scritti vari di epigrafia e antichità cristiane.* Bari: Edipuglia, 1991.

Février, Paul-Albert. "À propos du repas funéraire: Culte et sociabilité." *CAr* 26 (1977): 29–46.

———. "Le culte des morts dans les communautés chrétiennes durant le IIIe siècle." Pages 211–74 in vol. 1 of *Atti del IX Congresso internazionale di archeologia cristiana, Roma, 21–27 settembre 1975.* 2 vols. SAC 32. Vatican City: Pontificio Istituto di Archeologia Cristiana, 1978.

———. "Tombes privilégiées en Maurétanie et Numidie." Pages 13–24 in *L'inhumation privilégiée du IVe au VIIIe siècle en Occident: Actes du colloque tenu à Créteil les 16–18 mars 1984.* Edited by Yvette Duval and Jean-Charles Picard. Paris: de Boccard, 1986.

Fichtenau, Heinrich. "Zum Reliquienwesen im früheren Mittelalter." *MIÖG* 60 (1952): 60–89.

Filippi, Giorgio. "La basilica di San Paolo fuori le mura." Pages 59–62 in *Pietro e Paolo: La storia, il culto, la memoria nei primi secoli.* Edited by Angela Donati. Milan: Electa, 2000.

———. "Die Ergebnisse der neuen Ausgrabungen am Grab des Apostels Paulus: Reliquienkult und Eucharistie im Presbyterium der Paulsbasilika." *MDAI(R)* 112 (2005/2006): 277–92.

———. *Indice della raccolta epigrafica di San Paolo Fuori le Mura.* ISS 3. Vatican City: Monumenti Musei e Gallerie Pontificie, 1998.

———. "La tomba di San Paolo alla luce delle recent ricerche." Pages 1–12, 99–106 in *Il culto di San Paolo nelle chiese cristiane e nella tradizione Maltese.* Edited by J. Azzopardi. Rabat, Malta: Wignacourt Museum, 2006.

———. "La tomba di San Paolo e le fasi della basilica tra il IV e VII secolo: Primi risultati di indagini archeologiche e ricerche d'archivio." *BMusPont* 24 (2004): 187–224.

———. "La tomba di San Paolo: I dati archeologici del 2006 e il taccuino Moreschi del 1850." *BMusPont* 26 (2007–2008): 321–52.

———. "Un decennio di ricerche e studi nella basilica Ostiense." Pages 29–43 in *San Paolo in Vaticano: La figura e la parola dell'Apostolo delle Genti nelle raccolte pontificie.* Edited by Umberto Utro. Todi: Tau Editrice, 2009.

Filippi, Giorgio, and Sible de Blaauw. "San Paolo fuori le mura: La disposizione liturgica fino a Gregorio Magno." *MNHIR* 59 (2002): 5–26.

Fitzgerald, John T. "Christian Friendship: John, Paul, and the Philippians." *Int* 61.3 (2007): 284–96.

———, ed. *Greco-Roman Perspectives on Friendship*. Atlanta: Scholars Press, 1997.

———. "Theodore of Mopsuestia on Paul's Letter to Philemon." Pages 333–63 in *Philemon in Perspective: Interpreting a Pauline Letter*. Edited by D. Francois Tolmie. BZNW169. Berlin: de Gruyter, 2010.

Fletcher, R. A. *Saint James's Catapult: The Life and Times of Diego Gelmírez of Santiago de Compostela*. Oxford: Clarendon, 1984.

Frend, W. H. C. *The Donatist Church: A Movement of Protest in Roman North Africa*. Rev. ed. Oxford: Clarendon, 1985.

———. "The Donatist Church and St. Paul." Pages 91–133 in *Le epistole paoline nei manichei, i donatisti e il primo Agostino*. 2nd ed. Rome: Istituto Patristico Augustinianum, 2000.

———. "The Early Christian Church in Carthage." Pages 21–40 in vol. 3 of *Excavations at Carthage Conducted by the University of Michigan*. 7 vols. Ann Arbor: Kelsey Museum of Archaeology, 1975–1978.

———. *The Early Church*. Minneapolis: Fortress, 1982.

———. "The Failure of the Persecutions in the Roman Empire." Pages 263–87 in *Studies in Ancient Society*. Edited by M. I. Finley. London: Routledge & Kegan Paul, 1974.

———. *Martyrdom and Persecution in the Early Church*. Oxford: Blackwell, 1965.

———. "The Memoriae Apostolorum in Roman North Africa." *JRS* 30.1 (1940): 32–49.

Friedman, Mark. "Jewish Pilgrimage after the Destruction of the Second Temple." Pages 136–46 in *City of the Great King: Jerusalem from David to the Present*. Edited by Nitza Rosovsky. Cambridge: Harvard University Press, 1996.

Fuchs, Rüdiger. *Unerwartete Unterschiede: Müssen wir unsere Ansichten über "die" Pastoralbriefe revidieren?* Wuppertal: Brockhaus, 2003.

Fux, Pierre-Yves. *Les sept passions de Prudence: Peristephanon 2, 5, 9, 11–14*. Par. 46. Fribourg: Éditions Universitaires, 2003.

Gagé, Jean. "Membra Christi et la déposition des reliques sous l'autel." *RAr* 29 (1929): 137–53.

Gaiffier, Baudouin de. "La lecture des actes des martyrs." *AnBoll* 72 (1954): 134–66.

———. "La lecture des passions des martyrs à Rome." *AnBoll* 87 (1969): 63–78.

Gamble, Harry Y. "The New Testament Canon: Recent Research and the Status Quaestionis." Pages 267–94 in *The Canon Debate*. Edited by Lee Martin McDonald and James A. Sanders. Peabody, Mass.: Hendrickson, 2002.

García Rodriguez, C. *El culto de los santos en la España romana y visigoda*. Madrid: C.S.I.C., 1966.

García Villada, Zacarías. *Historia eclesiástica de España*. 3 vols. Madrid: Compañía Ibero-americana de Publicaciones, 1929.

García Villoslada, Ricardo. *La Iglesia en la España romana y visigoda (siglos I–VIII)*. Vol. 1 of *Historia de la Iglesia en España*. BAC 16. Madrid: EDICA, 1979.

Garrucci, Raffaele. *Storia della arte cristiana nei primi otto secoli della chiesa*. Prato: Guasti, 1872.

Gauthier, Nancy, Jean-Charles Picard, and Noël Duval, eds. *Topographie chrétienne des cités de la Gaule, des origines au milieu du VIIIe siècle*. 14 vols. Paris: de Boccard, 1986–2007.

Geary, Patrick J. *Furta Sacra: Thefts of Relics in the Central Middle Ages*. Rev. ed. Princeton: Princeton University Press, 1990.

Geerlings, W. "Untersuchung zum Paulusverständnis des Ambrosisaster." PhD diss., University of Tübingen, 1980.

Gerke, Friedrich. *Die christlichen Sarkophage der vorkonstantinischen Zeit*. StSKG 11. Berlin: de Gruyter, 1940.

González Blanco, A. "Alusiones a España en las obras de san Juan Crisóstomo." *HAnt* 4 (1974): 345–68.

Grabar, André. *Martyrium: Recherches sur le culte des reliques et l'art chrétien antique*. Paris: Collège de France, 1946.

Green, Bernard. *Christianity in Ancient Rome: The First Three Centuries*. New York: T&T Clark, 2010.

Grant, Robert M. "The Description of Paul in the Acts of Paul and Thecla." *VC* 36 (1982): 1–4.

Gregory, Timothy E. "The Survival of Paganism in Christian Greece: A Critical Essay." *AJP* 107 (1986): 229–42.

Griffe, Élie. *La Gaule chrétienne à l'époque romaine*. 3 vols. Paris: Picard, 1947–1965.

Grig, Lucy. *Making Martyrs in Late Antiquity*. London: Duckworth, 2004.

Grisar, Hartmann. *Analecta romana*. Rome: Desclée Lefebvre, 1899.

Grossi-Gondi, F. "Il Refrigerium celebrato in onore dei SS. Apostoli Pietro e Paolo nel sec. IV *ad Catacumbas*." *RQ* 29 (1915): 221–68.

Guarducci, Margherita. *Pietro ritrovato: Il martirio, la tomba, le reliquie*. 2nd ed. Milan: Mondadori, 1970.

———. *The Tomb of St. Peter*. New York: Hawthorn, 1960.

Gui, Isabelle. *Basiliques chrétiennes d'Afrique du nord*. Revised by Noël Duval and Jean-Pierre Caillet. 2 vols. Paris: Institut des Études Augustiniennes, 1992.

Guignebert, Charles. *La primauté de Pierre et la venue de Pierre à Rome*. Paris: Nourry, 1909.

Gustafsson, Gabriella. Evocatio deorum: *Historical and Mythical Interpretations of Ritualised Conquests in the Expansion of Ancient Rome*. AAU.HR 16. Stockholm: Elanders Gotab, 2000.

Hahn, Cynthia. "Loca Sancta Souvenirs: Sealing the Pilgrim's Experience." Pages 85–96 in *The Blessings of Pilgrimage*. Edited by Robert Ousterhout. Urbana: University of Illinois Press, 1990.

Hahneman, Geoffrey Mark. *The Muratorian Fragment and the Development of the Canon*. Oxford: Clarendon, 1992.

Hanson, R. P. C. *The Search for the Christian Doctrine of God*. Edinburgh: T&T Clark, 1988.

Harden, Donald B. *Glass of the Caesars*. Milan: Olivetti, 1987.

Harnack, Adolf von. *Einführung in die alte Kirchengeschichte: Das Schreiben der römischen Kirche an die Korinthische aus der Zeit Domitians (I. Clemensbrief)*. Leipzig: Hinrich, 1929.

Hartney, Aideen M. *Gruesome Deaths and Celibate Lives: Christian Martyrs and Ascetics*. Bristol: Bristol Phoenix, 2005.

Hartog, Paul A. *Polycarp and the New Testament*. WUNT 2/134. Tübingen: Mohr Siebeck, 2002.

Hasenclever, Adolf. *Der altchristliche Gräberschmuck: Ein Beitrag zur christlichen Archäologie*. Braunschweig: Schwetschke & Sohn, 1886.

Head, Thomas. "The Cult of the Saints and Their Relics." *On-line Reference Book for Medieval Studies*. Online: http://www.the-orb.net/encyclop/religion/hagiography/cult.htm.

Heather, Peter J. *The Fall of the Roman Empire: A New History*. London: Macmillan, 2005.

Hemer, Colin J. *The Book of Acts in the Setting of Hellenistic History*. Edited by Conrad H. Gempf. WUNT 49. Tübingen: Mohr Siebeck, 1989.

Hershbell, Jackson P. "Philostratus's *Heroikos* and Early Christianity: Heroes, Saints, and Martyrs." Pages 169–79 in *Philostratus's* Heroikos: *Religion and Cultural Identity in the Third Century C.E.* Edited by Ellen Bradshaw Aitken and Jennifer K. Berenson Maclean. SBLWGRW 6. Atlanta: Society of Biblical Literature, 2004.

Herzer, Jens. "Rearranging the 'House of God': A New Perspective on the Pastoral Epistles." Pages 547–66 in *Empsychoi Logoi: Religious Innovations in Antiquity: Studies in Honour of Pieter Willem van der Horst*. Edited by Alberdina Houtman, Albert de Jong, and Magda Misset-van de Weg. Leiden: Brill, 2008.

Hilhorst, A. "Tertullian on the Acts of Paul." Pages 150–63 in *The Apocryphal*

Acts of Paul and Thecla. Edited by Jan N. Bremmer. Kampen: Kok Pharos, 1996.

Hill, Charles E. "The Debate over the Muratorian Fragment and the Development of the Canon." *WTJ* 57 (1995): 437–52.

Holloway, R. Ross. *Constantine and Rome*. New Haven: Yale University Press, 2004.

Hunt, E. D. *Holy Land Pilgrimage in the Later Roman Empire, AD 312–460*. Oxford: Clarendon, 1982.

Hunter, David G. "Vigilantius of Calagurris and Victricius of Rouen: Ascetics, Relics, and Clerics in Late Roman Gaul." *JECS* 7.3 (1999): 401–30.

Huskinson, J. M. *Concordia Apostolorum: Christian Propaganda at Rome in the Fourth and Fifth Centuries*. BARIS 148. Oxford: British Archaeological Reports, 1982.

Janssens, Jos. "Le tombe e gli edifici funerari dei papi dell'antichità." Pages 221–63 in vol. 3 of *Ecclesiae urbis: Atti del Congresso internazionale di studi sulle Chiese di Roma (IV–X secolo), Roma, 4–10 settembre 2000*. Edited by Federico Guidobaldi and Alessandra Guiglia Guidobaldi. SAC 59. 3 vols. Vatican City: Pontificio Istituto di Archeologia Cristiana, 2002.

Jastrzebowska, Elisabeth (Elżbieta). "Les scènes de banquet dans les peintures et sculptures chrétiennes des IIIe et IVe siècles." *RechAug* 14 (1979): 3–90.

———. *Untersuchungen zum christlichen Totenmahl aufgrund der Monumente des 3. und 4. Jahrhunderts unter der Basilika des Hl. Sebastian in Rom*. EHS.A 2. Frankfurt am Main: Lang, 1981.

Jensen, Robin M. "Dining with the Dead: From the *Mensa* to the Altar in Christian Late Antiquity." Pages 107–44 in *Commemorating the Dead: Texts and Artifacts in Context: Studies of Roman, Jewish, and Christian Burials*. Edited by Laurie Brink and Deborah A. Green. Berlin: de Gruyter, 2008.

Jewett, Robert. *A Chronology of Paul's Life*. Philadelphia: Fortress, 1979.

———. *Romans: A Commentary*. Hermeneia. Minneapolis: Fortress, 2007.

Jones, H. Stuart. "The Memoria Apostolorum on the Via Appia." *JTS* OS 18 (1926): 30–39.

Josi, Enrico. "La venerazione degli apostoli Pietro e Paolo nel mondo cristiano antico." Pages 149–98 in *Saecularia Petri et Pauli*. SAC 28. Vatican City: Pontificio Istituto di Archeologia Cristiana, 1969.

Kant, Laurence. "The Interpretation of Religious Symbols in the Graeco-Roman World: A Case Study of Early Christian Fish Symbolism." PhD diss., Yale University, 1993.

Keating, John F. *The Agapé and the Eucharist in the Early Church: Studies in the History of the Christian Love-Feasts*. London: Methuen, 1901.

Kerkeslager, Allen. "Jewish Pilgrimage and Jewish Identity in Hellenistic and Early Roman Egypt." Pages 99–225 in *Pilgrimage and Holy Space in Late Antique Egypt*. Edited by David Frankfurter. Leiden: Brill, 1998.

Kilde, Jeanne Halgren. *Sacred Power, Sacred Space: An Introduction to Christian Architecture and Worship*. New York: Oxford University Press, 2008.

Kirsch, J. P. "Der Ort des Martyriums des Hl. Paulus." *RQ* 2 (1888): 233–47.

Kirschbaum, Engelbert. *The Tombs of St Peter and St Paul*. Translated by John Murray. New York: St. Martin's, 1957.

Kjaergaard, Jørgen. "From 'Memoria Apostolorum' to Basilica Apostolorum: On the Early Christian Cult-Centre on the Via Appia." *ARID* 13 (1984): 59–76.

Kloppenborg, John S. "*Evocatio Deorum* and the Date of Mark." *JBL* 124 (2005): 419–50.

Koch, Hugo. *Cyprianische Untersuchungen*. AKG 4. Bonn: Marcus & Weber, 1926.

Koester, Helmut. "On Heroes, Tombs, and Early Christianity: An Epilogue." Pages 257–64 in *Flavius Philostratus: Heroikos*. Translated by Jennifer K. Berenson Maclean and Ellen Bradshaw Aitken. SBLWGRW 1. Atlanta: Society of Biblical Literature, 2001.

Konstan, David. *Friendship in the Classical World*. Cambridge: Cambridge University Press, 1997.

Kötting, Bernhard. *Der frühchristliche Reliquienkult und die Bestattung im Kirchengebäude*. Cologne: Westdeutscher, 1965.

———. *Peregrinatio Religiosa: Wallfahrten in der Antike und das Pilgerwesen in der alten Kirche*. 2nd ed. Münster: Antiquariat Th. Stenderhoff, 1980.

Koukouli-Chrysantaki, Chaido. "Colonia Iulia Augusta Philippensis." Pages 5–36 in *Philippi at the Time of Paul and after His Death*. Edited by Charalambos Bakirtzis and Helmut Koester. Harrisburg, Pa.: Trinity Press International, 1998.

Krautheimer, Richard. *Corpus basilicarum christianarum Romae*. 5 vols. Vatican City: Pontificio Istituto di Archeologia Cristiana, 1937–1977.

———. *Early Christian and Byzantine Architecture*. 4th ed. New York: Penguin, 1986.

———. "Intorno alla fondazione di SPFLM." *APARA.R* 53–54 (1980–1982): 213–20.

———. "Mensa-Coemeterium-Martyrium." *CAr* 11 (1960): 15–40.

———. *Rome: Profile of a City, 312–1308*. Princeton: Princeton University Press, 1980.

Künzl, Ernst, and Gerhard Koeppel. *Souvenirs und Devotionalien: Zeugnisse des geschäftlichen, religiösen und kulturellen Tourismus im antiken Römerreich*. Mainz am Rhein: von Zabern, 2002.

La Baume, Peter, and J. W. Salomonson. *Römische Kleinkunst: Sammlung Karl Löffler (Katalog)*. WKRGMK 3. Cologne: Römisch-Germanisches Museum, 1976.

La Piana, George. "The Tombs of Peter and Paul ad Catacumbas." *HTR* 14 (1921): 53–94.

Lafferty, Maura K. "Translating Faith from Greek to Latin: *Romanitas* and *Christianitas* in Late Fourth-Century Rome and Milan." *JECS* 11.1 (2003): 21–62.

Lambot, Cyrille. "La collection antique de sermons de saint Augustin." *RBén* 57 (1947): 89–108.

———. "Les sermons de saint Augustin pour les fêtes de martyrs." *RBén* 79 (1969): 82–97.

Lampe, Peter. *From Paul to Valentinus: Christians at Rome in the First Two Centuries*. Translated by Michael Steinhauser. Minneapolis: Fortress, 2003.

———. "Paul, Patrons, and Clients." Pages 488–523 in *Paul in the Graeco-Roman World: A Handbook*. Edited by J. Paul Sampley. Harrisburg, Pa.: Trinity Press International, 2003.

Lanciani, R. A. "Delle scoperte fatte nel 1838 e 1850 presso il sepolcro di Paolo Apostolo." *NBArC* 23 (1917): 7–27.

———. *Pagan and Christian Rome*. Boston: Houghton and Mifflin, 1899.

———. *Wanderings through Ancient Roman Churches*. Boston: Houghton Mifflin, 1924.

Lange, Ulrike. *Ikonographisches Register für das Repertorium der christlich-antiken Sarkophage*. CArch 2. Dettelbach: J. H. Röll, 1996.

Lapeyre, Gabriel G. "Saint Augustin et Carthage." Pages in 91–148 in *Miscellanea agostiniana: Testi e studi, pubblicati a cura del-l'Ordine eremitano di s. Agostino nel XV centenario dalla morte del santo dottore*. Rome: Tipografia Poliglotta Vaticana, 1931.

Lapointe, Guy. *La célébration des martyrs en Afrique d'après les sermons de saint Augustin*. CCommChr. Montreal: Communauté chrétienne, 1972.

Lassus, Jean. *Sanctuaires chrétiens de Syrie*. BAH 42. Paris: Geuthner, 1947.

Lattimore, Richmond. *Themes in Greek and Latin Epitaphs*. ISLL 28.1–2. Urbana: University of Illinois Press, 1962.

Le Blant, E. *Les sarcophages chrétiens de la Gaule*. Paris: Imprimerie Nationale, 1886.

Leclercq, Henri. *L'Afrique chrétienne*. BEHEc. 2 vols. Paris: V. Lecoffre, 1904.

Lemerle, Paul. *Philippes et la Macédoine orientale à l'époque chrétienne et byzantine: Recherches d'histoire et d'archéologie*. BEFAR 158. Paris: de Boccard, 1945.

Levine, Lee I. "Bet Še'arim in Its Patriarchal Context." Pages 197–225 in "*The

Words of a Wise Man's Mouth Are Gracious" (Qoh 10,12): Festschrift for Günter Stemberger on the Occasion of His 65th Birthday. Edited by Mauro Perani. Berlin: de Gruyter, 2005.

Lewis, Suzanne. "Function and Symbolic Form in the Basilica Apostolorum at Milan." *JSAH* 28.2 (1969): 83–98.

Leyerle, Blake. "Pilgrim Eulogiae and Domestic Rituals." *AfRG* 10 (2008): 223–37.

Lietzmann, Hans. *Petrus und Paulus in Rom.* 2nd ed. Berlin: de Gruyter, 1927.

———. "The Tomb of the Apostles ad Catacumbas." *HTR* 16.2 (1923): 147–62.

Lightfoot, J. B. *S. Clement of Rome: The Two Epistles to the Corinthians.* London: Macmillan, 1869.

Lindemann, Andreas. *Die Clemensbriefe.* HNT 17. Tübingen: Mohr Siebeck, 1992.

———. *Paulus im ältesten Christentum: Das Bild des Apostels und die Rezeption der paulinischen Theologie in der frühchristlichen Literatur bis Marcion.* Tübingen: Mohr Siebeck, 1979.

Liverani, Paolo. "La basilica di San Pietro in Vaticano." Pages 55–58 in *Pietro e Paolo: La storia, il culto, la memoria nei primi secoli.* Edited by Angela Donati. Milan: Electa, 2000.

Lloyd, Joan Barclay. "Krautheimer and S. Paolo fuori le mura: Architectural, Urban, and Liturgical Planning in Late Fourth-Century Rome." Pages 11–24 in vol. 1 of *Ecclesiae urbis: Atti del Congresso internazionale di studi sulle Chiese di Roma (IV–X secolo), Roma, 4–10 settembre 2000.* Edited by Federico Guidobaldi and Alessandra Guiglia Guidobaldi. 3 vols. Vatican City: Pontificio Istituto di Archeologia Cristiana, 2002.

Logan, Alastair. "When and by Whom Was the Roman Basilica Apostolorum Built?" *JOUHS* 5 (2007): 1–14.

Lohse, Bernhard. "Beobachtungen zum Paulus-Kommentar des Marius Victorinus und zur Wiederentdeckung des Paulus in der lateinischen Theologie des vierten Jahrhunderts." Pages 351–66 in *Kerygma und Logos.* Edited by A. M. Ritter. Göttingen: Vandenhoeck & Ruprecht, 1979.

Lona, Horacio E. *Der erste Clemensbrief.* KAV 2. Göttingen: Vandenhoeck & Ruprecht, 1998.

Longenecker, Richard N. "The Acts of the Apostles." Pages 207–573 in vol. 9 of *The Expositor's Bible Commentary.* Edited by F. E. Gabelein. 12 vols. Grand Rapids: Zondervan, 1976–1992.

Lønstrup, Gitte. "Constructing Myths: The Foundation of *Roma Christiana* on 29 June." *ARID* 33 (2008): 27–64.

Lüdemann, Gerd. *Paul: Apostle to the Gentiles: Studies in Chronology.* Philadelphia: Fortress, 1984.

Luiselli, Bruno. "In margine al problema della traslazione delle ossa di Pietro e Paolo." *MEFRA* 98.2 (1986): 843–54.

Lund, Nils Wilhelm. *Chiasmus in the New Testament: A Study in Formgeschichte.* Chapel Hill: University of North Carolina Press, 1942.

Lunn-Rockliffe, Sophie. *Ambrosiaster's Political Theology.* Oxford: Oxford University Press, 2007.

MacDonald, Dennis R. *The Legend and the Apostle: The Battle for Paul in Story and Canon.* Philadelphia: Westminister, 1983.

MacGregor, Neil. *Seeing Salvation: Images of Christ in Art.* New Haven: Yale University Press, 2000.

MacMullen, Ramsay. "Christian Ancestor Worship in Rome." *JBL* 129 (2010): 597–613.

———. *Christianizing the Roman Empire (A.D. 100–400).* New Haven: Yale University Press, 1984.

———. *The Second Church: Popular Christianity A.D. 200–400.* SBLWGRW-Sup 1. Atlanta: Society of Biblical Literature; Leiden: Brill, 2009.

Magness, Jodi. "The Arch of Titus and the Fate of the God of Israel." *JJS* 59.2 (2008): 201–17.

Malbon, Elizabeth Struthers. *The Iconography of the Sarcophagus of Junius Bassus.* Princeton: Princeton University Press, 1990.

Mancinelli, Fabrizio. *The Catacombs of Rome and the Origins of Christianity.* Translated by Carol Wasserman. Florence: Scala, 1981.

Mancini, Gioacchino, and Benedetto Pesci. *San Sebastiano fuori le mura.* New ed. CRoI 48. Rome: Marietti, 1958.

Manjarrés Mangas, J., and J. M. Roldán Hervás. *España Romana (218 a. de J.C.–414 de J.C.).* 2nd ed. 2 vols. Madrid: Espasa-Calpe, 1982.

Maraval, Pierre. *Lieux saints et pèlerinages d'Orient: Histoire et géographie des origines à la conquête arabe.* 2nd ed. Paris: Cerf, 2004.

Marichal, Robert. "La date des graffiti de la basilique de Saint-Sébastien à Rome." *NC* 5 (1953): 119–20.

———. "La date des graffiti de la Triclia de Saint-Sébastien et leur place dans l'histoire de l'écriture latine." *RevScRel* 36 (1962): 111–54.

———. "Les dates des graffiti de Saint-Sébastien." *CRAI* 97 (1953): 60–68.

Markus, R. A. "How on Earth Could Places Become Holy? Origins of the Christian Idea of Holy Places." *JECS* 2 (1994): 257–71.

Marone, Paola. "Cristianesimo e universalità nella controversia donatista." Pages 323–35 in *La natura della religione in contesto teologico: Atti del X Convegno Internazionale della Facoltà di Teologia, Pontificia Università della Santa Croce, Roma 9–10 marzo 2006.* Edited by S. Sanz Sánchez. Rome: Maspero, 2008.

————. "Pietro e Paolo e il loro rapporto con Roma nella letteratura antidonatista." Pages 457–72 in *Pietro e Paolo: Il loro rapporto con Roma nelle testimonianze antiche: XXIX Incontro di studiosi dell'antichità cristiana, Roma, 4–6 maggio 2000*. Rome: Institutum Patristicum Augustinianum, 2001.

Marshall, I. Howard. *A Critical and Exegetical Commentary on the Pastoral Epistles*. ICC. Edinburgh: T&T Clark, 1999.

Masqueray, E. "Ruines anciennes de Khenchela (Mascula) à Besseriani (Ad Majores)." *RAfr* 22 (1878): 444–72.

Matthews, John F. *Western Aristocracies and Imperial Court, A.D. 364–425*. Oxford: Clarendon, 1975.

Mazzoleni, Danilo. "Papa Damaso e l'archeologia cristiana." Pages 5–14 in *Saecularia Damasiana: Atti del Convegno internazionale per il XVI centenario della morte di papa Damaso I (1984)*. Vatican City: Pontificio Istituto di Archeologia Cristiana, 1986.

McLynn, Neil B. *Ambrose of Milan: Church and Court in a Christian Capital*. TCH 22. Berkeley: University of California Press, 1994.

Meeks, Wayne A., and John T. Fitzgerald, eds. *The Writings of St. Paul*. 2nd ed. New York: Norton, 2007.

Meinardus, Otto F. A. "Paul's Missionary Journey to Spain: Tradition and Folklore." *BA* 41.2 (1978): 61–63.

Merdinger, Jane E. *Rome and the African Church in the Time of Augustine*. New Haven: Yale University Press, 1997.

Metzger, Bruce M. *A Textual Commentary on the Greek New Testament*. 2nd ed. Stuttgart: Deutsche Bibelgesellschaft, 1994.

Meyer, Hugo. *Antinoos: Die archäologischen Denkmäler unter Einbeziehung des numismatischen und epigraphischen Materials sowie der literarischen Nachrichten: Ein Beitrag zur Kunst- und Kulturgeschichte der hadrianischfrühantoninischen Zeit*. Munich: Fink, 1991.

Mitchell, Margaret M. *The Heavenly Trumpet: John Chrysostom and the Art of Pauline Interpretation*. Tübingen: Mohr Siebeck, 2000.

Mohlberg, Leo Kunibert. "Historisch-kritische Bemerkungen zum Ursprung der sogenannten 'Memoria Apostolorum' an der Appischen Strasse." Pages 52–74 in *Colligere Fragmenta: Festschrift Alban Dold zum 70. Geburtstag am 7.7.1952*. Beuron in Hohenzollern: Beuroner Kunstverlag, 1952.

Mohrmann, Christine. "À propos de deux mots controversés de la latinité chrétienne: Tropaeum-Nomen." *VC* 8.1 (1954): 154–73.

Monaca, Mariangela. "Pietro e Paolo a Roma nel *De praescriptione haereticorum* di Tertulliano." Pages 431–44 in *Pietro e Paolo: Il loro rapporto con Roma nelle testimonianze antiche: XXIX Incontro di studiosi dell'antichità cristiana, Roma, 4–6 maggio 2000*. Rome: Institutum Patristicum Augustinianum, 2001.

Monceaux, Paul. "Enquête sur l'épigraphie chrétienne d'Afrique." *MPAIBL* 12.1 (1903): 161–340.

Moorhead, John. *Ambrose: Church and Society in the Late Roman World.* New York: Addison-Wesley Longman, 1999.

Morey, Charles R. "The Silver Casket of San Nazaro in Milan." *AJA* 23.2 (1919): 101–25.

Moss, Candida R. "On the Dating of Polycarp: Rethinking the Place of the Martyrdom of Polycarp in the History of Christianity." *EC* 1 (2010): 539–74.

———. *The Other Christs: Imitating Jesus in Ancient Christian Ideologies of Martyrdom.* New York: Oxford University Press, 2010.

Motte, André. "Pèlerinages de la Grèce antique." Pages 94–135 in *Histoire des pèlerinages non chrétiens: Entre magique et sacré, le chemin des dieux.* Edited by J. Chélini and H. Branthomme. Paris: Hachette, 1982.

Mullen, Roderic L. *The Expansion of Christianity: A Gazetteer of Its First Three Centuries.* VCSup 69. Leiden: Brill, 2004.

Munck, Johannes. *Petrus und Paulus in der Offenbarung Johannis.* Copenhagen: Rosenkilde & Bagger, 1950.

Murphy-O'Connor, Jerome. *Paul: A Critical Life.* Oxford: Clarendon, 1996.

Navascués y de Juan, J. M. de. "La dedicación de la iglesia de Santa María y de todas las Vírgenes de Mérida." *AEAr* 21 (1948): 309–59.

Neyrey, Jerome. *The Passion according to Luke: A Redaction Study of Luke's Soteriology.* New York: Paulist, 1985.

Niquet, Heike. *Monumenta virtutum titulique: Senatorische Selbstdarstellung im spätantiken Rom im Spiegel der epigraphischen Denkmäler.* Stuttgart: Steiner, 2000.

Northcote, J. Spencer. *Epitaphs of the Catacombs: Or Christian Inscriptions in Rome during the First Four Centuries.* London: Longmans, Green, 1878.

Noy, David. "Rabbi Aqiba Comes to Rome: A Jewish Pilgrimage in Reverse?" Pages 373–85 in *Pilgrimage in Graeco-Roman and Early Christian Antiquity: Seeing the Gods.* Edited by Jaś Elsner and Ian Rutherford. Oxford: Oxford University Press, 2005.

Odahl, Charles M. *Constantine and the Christian Empire.* London: Routledge, 2004.

Orselli, Alba M. *L'idea e il culto del santo patrono cittadino nella letteratura latina cristiana.* StRicNS 12. Bologna: Zanichelli, 1965.

Ousterhout, Robert, ed. *The Blessings of Pilgrimage.* Urbana: University of Illinois Press, 1990.

Painter, K. "Frammenti di coppa." Pages 279–81 in *Vetri dei Cesari*. Edited by Donald B. Harden. Exposition Catalog: Milan, 1988.

Palmer, Anne-Marie. *Prudentius on the Martyrs*. Oxford: Clarendon, 1989.

Parrot, André. *Le "Refrigerium" dans l'au delà*. Paris: Librairie Leroux, 1937.

Pavia, Carlo. *Guida delle catacombe romane: dai "tituli" all'ipogeo di via Dino Compagni*. Rome: Gangemi, 2000.

Pelekanidis, Stylianos. "Kultprobleme im Apostel-Paulus Octogon von Philippi im Zusammenhang mit einem älteren Heroenkult." Pages 393–97 in vol. 2 of *Atti del IX Congresso internazionale di archeologia cristiana, Roma, 21–27 settembre 1975*. SAC 32. 2 vols. Vatican City: Pontificio Istituto di Archeologia Cristiana, 1978.

Pelekanidou, Elli. "Ἡ κατὰ τὴν παράδοση φυλακὴ τοῦ Ἀποστόλου Παύλου στοὺς Φιλίππους [Concerning the Traditional Prison of the Apostle Paul at Philippi]." Pages 427–35 in Ἡ Καβάλα καὶ ἡ περιοχὴ τῆς [*Kavala and Its Surroundings*]. Thessaloniki: Institute for Balkan Studies, 1980.

Peretto, Elio. *Clemente Romano: Lettera ai Corinzi*. Bologna: Dehoniane, 1999.

Pervo, Richard I. *Acts: A Commentary*. Hermeneia. Minneapolis: Fortress, 2009.

———. *The Making of Paul: Constructions of the Apostle in Early Christianity*. Minneapolis: Fortress, 2010.

Petersen, Joan. *The "Dialogues" of Gregory the Great in Their Late Antique Cultural Background*. Toronto: Pontifical Institute of Mediaeval Studies, 1984.

———. "Did Gregory Know Greek?" Pages 121–34 in *The Orthodox Churches and the West*. Edited by Derek Baker. Oxford: Blackwell, 1976.

Pfister, F. "Die zweimalige römische Gefangenschaft und die spanische Reise des Apostels Paulus." *ZNW* 14 (1913): 216–21.

Picard, Jean-Charles. "Le Quadriportique de Saint-Paul-hors-les-murs à Rome." *MEFRA* 87.1 (1975): 377–95.

Pietri, Charles. "Concordia Apostolorum et renovatio urbis (Culte des martyrs et propagande pontificale)." *MEFR* 73 (1961): 275–322.

———. "Damase évêque de Rome." Pages 29–58 in *Saecularia Damasiana: Atti del Convegno internazionale per il XVI centenario della morte di papa Damaso I (1984)*. Vatican City: Pontificio Istituto di Archeologia Cristiana, 1986.

———. "L'évolution du culte des saints aux premiers siècles chrétiens: Du témoin à l'intercesseur." Pages 15–36 in *Les fonctions des saints dans le monde occidental (IIIe–XIIIe siècle)*. CEFR 149. Rome: École française de Rome, 1991.

———. *Roma christiana: Recherches sur l'Église de Rome, son organisation, sa politique, son idéologie de Miltiade à Sixte III (311–440)*. 2 vols. BEFAR 224. Rome: École française de Rome, 1976.

Pietri, Luce. "Culte des saints de religiosité politique dans la Gaule du Ve et du VIe siècle." Pages 353–69 in *Les fonctions des saints dans le monde occidental (IIIe–XIIIe siècle): Actes du colloque.* Rome: École française de Rome, 1991.

———. *La ville de Tours du IVe au VIe siècle: Naissance d'une cité chrétienne.* CEFR 69. Rome: École française de Rome, 1983.

Porter, Stanley E. "When and How Was the Pauline Canon Compiled? An Assessment of Theories." Pages 95–127 in *The Pauline Canon.* Edited by Stanley E. Porter. Leiden: Brill, 2004.

Poupon, Gérard. "Les 'Actes de Pierre' et leur remaniement." *ANRW* 25.6:4363–83.

Prandi, Adriano. *La Memoria apostolorum in catacumbas.* RSCr 2. Vatican City: Pontificio Istituto di Archeologia Cristiana, 1936.

Quasten, Johannes. " 'Vetus superstitio et nova religio': The Problem of *refrigerium* in the Ancient Church of North Africa." *HTR* 33 (1940): 153–66.

Quentin, Enrico. "Tusco et Basso consulibus." *APARA.R* 5 (1926): 145–47.

Rebillard, Éric. "Les chrétiens et les repas pour les fêtes des morts (IVe–Ve siècles)." Pages 281–90 in *Bestattungsrituale und Totenkult in der römischen Kaiserzeit.* Edited by Jörg Rüpke and John Scheid. Stuttgart: Steiner, 2010.

Reekmans, Louis. "L'implantation monumentale chrétienne dans le paysage urbain de Rome de 300 à 850." Pages 861–915 in *Actes du XIe congrès international d'archéologie chrétienne: Lyon, Vienne, Grenoble, Genève et Aoste (21–28 septembre 1986).* CEFR 123. Rome: École française de Rome, 1989.

Rensberger, David K. "As the Apostle Teaches: The Development of the Use of Paul's Letters in Second-Century Christianity." PhD diss., Yale University, 1981.

Reynier, Chantal. *Saint Paul sur les routes du monde romain.* Paris: Cerf, 2009.

Rives, James B. *Religion in the Roman Empire.* Malden, Mass.: Blackwell, 2007.

Roberts, Michael J. *Poetry and the Cult of the Martyrs: The* Liber Peristephanon *of Prudentius.* RLLTC. Ann Arbor: University of Michigan Press, 1993.

Ronchey, Silvia. *Indagine sul Martirio di San Policarpo: Critica storica e fortuna agiografica di un caso Giudiziario in Asia Minore.* NSS 6. Rome: Istituto Storico Italiano per il Medio Evo, 1990.

Rordorf, Willy. "The Relation between the *Acts of Peter* and the *Acts of Paul*: State of the Question." Pages 178–91 in *The Apocryphal Acts of Peter: Magic, Miracles and Gnosticism.* Edited by Jan N. Bremmer. Leuven: Peeters, 1998.

Rossi, G. B de. "Epigrafe d'una chiesa dedicata agli apostoli Pietro e Paolo." *BArC* 3.3 (1878–1879): 14–20.

———. "I carmi de s. Damaso." *BArC* 4.3.1 (1884–1885): 7–29.

———. "I monumenti antichi cristiani." *BArC* 2 (1863): 115–59.

———. "Recenti scoperte nella chiesa alle Acque Salvie dedicata alla memoria del martirio dell'apostolo Paolo." *BArC* 7 (1869): 83–92.

———. *Roma sotterranea*. Edited by J. Spencer Northcote and W. R. Brownlow. London: Longmans, Green, Reader & Dyer, 1869.

Rush, Alfred C. *Death and Burial in Christian Antiquity*. Washington, D.C.: Catholic University of America Press, 1941.

Rutgers, Leonard Victor. *Subterranean Rome: In Search of the Roots of Christianity in the Catacombs of the Eternal City*. Leuven: Peeters, 2000.

Rutherford, Ian. "'To the Land of Zeus.' Patterns of Pilgrimage in Aelius Aristides." *AevumAnt* 12 (1999): 133–48.

———. "Tourism and the Sacred: Pausanius and the Traditions of Greek Pilgrimage." Pages 40–52 in *Pausanias: Travel and Imagination in Roman Greece*. Edited by Susan E. Alcock, John F. Cherry, and Jaś Elsner. Oxford: Oxford University Press, 2001.

Saggiorato, Annarosa. *I sarcofagi paleocristiani con scene di Passione*. Edited by Giuseppe Bovini. SAC(B) 1. Bologna: R. Pàtron, 1968.

Sághy, Marianne. "*Scinditur in partes populus*: Pope Damasus and the Martyrs of Rome." *EMEur* 9.3 (2000): 273–87.

Saller, Richard P. *Personal Patronage under the Early Empire*. Cambridge: Cambridge University Press, 1982.

Salzman, Michele Renee. *On Roman Time: The Codex-Calendar of 354 and the Rhythms of Urban Life in Late Antiquity*. TCH 17. Berkeley: University of California Press, 1990.

Sansterre, Jean-Marie. *Les moines grecs et orientaux à Rome aux époques byzantine et carolingienne*. Brussels: Académie Royale de Belgique, 1982.

Santis, Paola de. "Elementi di corredo nei sepolcri delle catacombe romane: L'esempio della regione di Leone e dalla galleria Bb nella catacombi di Commodilla." *VetChr* 31.1 (1994): 23–51.

Savio, Fedele. *La Lombardia*. Vol. 1 of *Gli antichi vescovi d'Italia dalle origine al 1300*. Florence: Libreria Editrice Fiorentina, 1913.

Saxer, Victor. *Morts, martyrs, reliques en Afrique chrétienne aux premiers siècles: les témoignages de Tertullien, Cyprien et Augustin à la lumière de l'archéologie africaine*. ThH 55. Paris: Beauchesne, 1980.

Schneider, Alfons Maria. "Die Memoria Apostolorum an der Via Appia." *NAWG.PHK* 3 (1951): 1–15.

Seeley, David. *The Noble Death: Graeco-Roman Martyrology and Paul's Concept of Salvation*. JSNTSup 28. Sheffield: JSOT, 1990.

Sherwin-White, A. N. "Why Were the Early Christians Persecuted?—An Amendment." *PaP* 27 (1964): 23–27.

Simon, Marcel. "L'apôtre Paul dans le symbolisme funéraire chrétien, à propos d'un fragment de sarcophagi avec barque et scène de pêche." *MEFR* 50 (1933): 156–82.

———. "Les Pèlerinages dans l'antiquité chrétienne." Pages 97–115 in *Pèlerinages de l'antiquité biblique et classique à l'occident medieval.* Edited by F. Raphaël. Paris: Librairie Orientaliste Paul Geuthner, 1973.

Skedros, James C. "The *Heroikos* and Popular Christianity in the Third Century C.E." Pages 181–93 in *Philostratus's Heroikos: Religion and Cultural Identity in the Third Century C.E.* Edited by Ellen Bradshaw Aitken and Jennifer K. Berenson Maclean. SBLWGRW 6. Atlanta: Society of Biblical Literature, 2004.

———. *Saint Demetrios of Thessaloniki: Civic Patron and Divine Protector, 4th–7th Centuries CE.* HTS 47. Harrisburg, Pa.: Trinity Press International, 1999.

Smelik, K. A. D. "Aliquanta ipsius sancti Thomae." *VC* 28 (1974): 290–94.

Smith, Dennis E. *From Symposium to Eucharist: The Banquet in the Early Christian World.* Minneapolis: Fortress, 2003.

Snyder, Glenn E. "Remembering the *Acts of Paul.*" PhD diss., Harvard University, 2010.

Snyder, Graydon F. *Ante Pacem: Archaeological Evidence of Church Life before Constantine.* Rev. ed. Macon, Ga.: Mercer University Press, 2003.

Sotomayor, Manuel. *Sarcófagos romano-cristianos de España: Estudio iconográfico.* BTGran 16. Granada: Facultad de Teología, 1975.

Spera, Lucrezia. "Aquae Salvias, Massa." Pages 147–48 in vol. 1 of *Lexicon topographicum urbis Romae: Suburbium.* Edited by Adriano La Regina. 5 vols. Rome: Quasar, 2001–2006.

———. "Christianization of Space along the Via Appia: Changing Landscape in the Suburbs of Rome." *AJA* 107.1 (2003): 23–43.

———. "Riti funerari e culto dei morti nella tarda antichità." *Aug* 45 (2005): 5–34.

Spicq, Ceslas. *Saint Paul: Les Épîtres pastorales.* EBib. 2 vols. Paris: Gabalda, 1969.

Stafford, Cardinal James Francis. "Decree of Special Indulgences." *Basilica Papale San Paolo Fuori le Mura Press Office* 10 May 2008. Online: http://www.annopaolino.org/Indulgenza%20ING.pdf.

Ste. Croix, G. E. M. de. *Christian Persecution, Martyrdom, and Orthodoxy.* Edited by Michael Whitby and Joseph Streeter. Oxford: Oxford University Press, 2006.

———. "Why Were the Early Christians Persecuted?" *PaP* 26 (1963): 6–38.

Stöckhert, Luise. *Die Petrus- und Paulusmartyrien auf Filaretes Bronzetür von St. Peter in Rom: Eine Vorform des Panoramas als kirchenpolitische Aussage.* EHS.K. Frankfurt am Main: Lang, 1997.

Stopani, Renato. *Le vie di pellegrinaggio del Medioeveo: Gli itinerari per Roma, Gerusalemme, Compostella.* Florence: Le Lettere, 1991.

Straw, Carole. *Gregory the Great: Perfection in Imperfection.* Berkeley: University of California Press, 1988.

Stuiber, Alfred. *Refrigerium Interim: Die Vorstellungen vom Zwischenzustand und die frühchristliche Grabeskunst.* Theophaneia 11. Bonn: Hanstein, 1957.

Styger, Paul. "Gli Apostoli Pietro e Paolo ad Catacumbas sulla via Appia." *RQ* 29.3 (1915): 149–205.

———. "Il monumento apostolico della via Appia." *APARA.D* 2.13 (1918): 1–115.

———. "Scavi a San Sebastiano." *RQ* 29.2 (1915): 73–110.

Sundberg, Albert C., Jr. "Canon Muratori: A Fourth Century List." *HTR* 66 (1973): 1–41.

Tajra, H. W. *The Martyrdom of St. Paul: Historical and Judicial Context, Traditions, and Legends.* Tübingen: Mohr Siebeck, 1994.

Talbert, Charles H. *Literary Patterns, Theological Themes, and the Genre of Luke-Acts.* SBLMS 20. Missoula, Mont.: Scholars Press, 1974.

Tanner, Norman P. *Decrees of the Ecumenical Councils.* 2 vols. Washington, D.C.: Georgetown University Press, 1990.

Testini, Pasquale. *Le catacombe e gli antichi cimiteri cristiani in Roma.* Bologna: Cappelli Editore, 1966.

———. "L'iconografia degli apostoli Pietro e Paolo nelle cosiddette 'arti minori.'" Pages 241–323 in *Saecularia Petri et Pauli.* Vatican City: Pontificio Istituto di Archeologia Cristiana, 1969.

Thacker, Alan, and Richard Sharpe, eds. *Local Saints and Local Churches in the Early Medieval West.* Oxford: Oxford University Press, 2002.

Thomas, Christine M. *The Acts of Peter, Gospel Literature, and the Ancient Novel: Rewriting the Past.* Oxford: Oxford University Press, 2003.

Thomson, Ian H. *Chiasmus in the Pauline Letters.* Sheffied: Sheffield Academic Press, 1995.

Thümmel, Hans G. *Die Memorien für Petrus und Paulus in Rom.* Berlin: de Gruyter, 1999.

Tillemont, Louis-Sébastien Le Nain de. *Mémoires pour servir à l'histoire ecclésiastique des six premiers siècles.* 2nd ed. 16 vols. Paris: Charles Robustel, 1701–1712.

Tilley, Maureen A. *The Bible in Christian North Africa: The Donatist World.* Minneapolis: Fortress, 1997.

Tolles, Delight. "The Banquet-Libations of the Greeks." PhD diss., Bryn Mawr College, 1943.

Tolotti, Francesco. "Le confessioni succedutesi sul sepolcro di S. Paolo." *RivAC* 59.1–2 (1983): 87–149.

———. *Memorie degli apostoli in Catacumbas: Rilievo critico della Memoria e della Basilica Apostolorum al III miglio della Via Appia.* CACat 19. Vatican City: Società "Amici delle catacomb," 1953.

Torp, Hjalmar. "The Vatican Excavations and the Cult of Saint Peter." *AcAr* 24 (1953): 27–66.

Toulotte, Anatole. *Géographie de l'Afrique chrétienne: Byzacène et Tripolitaine.* Montreuil-sur-Mer: Notre-Dame des Prés, 1894.

Towner, Philip H. *The Letters to Timothy and Titus.* NICNT. Grand Rapids: Eerdmans, 2006.

Toynbee, J. M. C. "The Shrine of St. Peter and Its Setting." *JRS* 43 (1953): 1–26.

Trobish, David. *Paul's Letter Collection: Tracing the Origins.* Minneapolis: Fortress, 1994.

Trout, Dennis. "Damasus and the Invention of Early Christian Rome." *JMEMS* 33.3 (2003): 517–36.

———. "Saints, Identity, and the City." Pages 165–87 in *Late Ancient Christianity.* Edited by Virginia Burrus. Minneapolis: Augsburg Fortress, 2005.

Tsafrir, Yoram. "Jewish Pilgrimage in the Roman and Byzantine Periods." Pages 369–76 in vol. 1 of *Akten des XII. Internationalen Kongresses für christliche Archäologie, Bonn 22.–28. September, 1991.* Edited by Ernst Dassmann and Josef Engemann. 3 vols. Münster: Aschendorffsche Verlagsbuchhandlung, 1995–1997.

Tyers, Paul A. *Roman Pottery in Britain.* London: Batsford, 1996.

Urbain, August. *Ein Martyrologium der christlichen Gemeinde zu Rom am Anfang des V. Jahrhunderts.* Edited by Oscar von Gebhardt and Adolf von Harnack. TUGAL 21. Leipzig: Hinrichs, 1901.

Urner, Hans. *Die ausserbiblische Lesung im christlichen Gottesdienst.* Berlin: Evangelische Verlagsanstalt, 1952.

Utro, Umberto. "I sarcofagi paleocristiani dal complesso di S. Paolo fuori le mura." Pages 47–66 in *San Paolo in Vaticano: La figura e la parola dell'Apostolo delle Genti nelle raccolte pontificie.* Edited by Umberto Utro. Todi: Tau Editrice, 2009.

Valantasis, Richard, ed. *Religions of Late Antiquity in Practice.* Princeton: Princeton University Press, 2000.

Van Dam, Raymond. *Leadership and Community in Late Antique Gaul.* Berkeley: University of California Press, 1985.

———. *Saints and Their Miracles in Late Antique Gaul.* Princeton: Princeton University Press, 1993.

Vieillard-Troiekouroff, May. *Les monuments religieux de la Gaule d'après les oeuvres de Grégoire de Tours.* Paris: Champion, 1976.

Villa, E. "Un autografo di Sant'Ambrogio." *Ambr* 30 (1954): 65–68.

Vives, José. "Las actas de los Varones Apostólicos." Pages 33–43 in vol. 1 of *Miscellanea liturgica in honorem L. Cuniberti Mohlberg*. 2 vols. BEL.H 22. Rome: Ed. Liturgiche, 1948.

Vogel, Cyrille. "Prière ou intercession? Une ambiguïté dans le culte paléochrétien des martyrs." Pages 284–89 in *Communio sanctorum: Mélanges offerts à Jean-Jacques von Allmen*. Edited by B. Bobrinskoy. Geneva: Labor et Fides, 1982.

Volp, Ulrich. *Tod und Ritual in den christlichen Gemeinden der Antike*. VCSup 65. Leiden: Brill, 2002.

Vopel, Hermann. *Die altchristlichen Goldgläser: Ein Beitrag zur altchristlichen Kunst- und Kulturgeschichte*. Freiburg: Mohr Siebeck, 1899.

Waal, Anton de. "Zu Wilperts *Domus Petri*." RQ 26 (1912): 123–32.

Wallace-Hadrill, Andrew. *Patronage in Ancient Society*. LNSAS 1. London: Routledge, 1989.

Walsh, J. E. *The Bones of St. Peter*. New York: Doubleday, 1982.

Ward-Perkins, J. B. "Memoria, Martyr's Tomb and Martyr's Church." *JTS* 17 (1966): 20–37.

Weiss, Zeev. "Social Aspects of Burial in Beth She'arim: Archeological Finds and Talmudic Sources." Pages 357–71 in *The Galilee in Late Antiquity*. Edited by Lee I. Levine. New York: Jewish Theological Seminary of America, 1992.

Welborn, Laurence L. "The Preface to 1 Clement: The Rhetorical Situation and the Traditional Date." Pages 197–216 in *Encounters with Hellenism: Studies on the First Letter of Clement*. Edited by Cilliers Breytenbach and Laurence L. Welborn. Leiden: Brill, 2004.

Welch, John W., ed. *Chiasmus in Antiquity: Structures, Analyses, Exegesis*. Hildesheim: Gerstenberg, 1981.

White, Benjamin L. " 'Imago Pauli': Memory, Tradition, and Discourses on the 'Real' Paul in the Second Century." PhD diss., The University of North Carolina at Chapel Hill, 2010.

White, L. Michael. "Paul and *Pater Familias*." Pages 457–87 in *Paul in the Graeco-Roman World: A Handbook*. Edited by J. Paul Sampley. Harrisburg, Pa.: Trinity Press International, 2003.

Wilpert, Joseph (Josef). "*Domus Petri*." RQ 26 (1912): 117–22.

———. *Fractio Panis: Die älteste Darstellung des eucharistischen Opfers in der "Capella Graeca."* Freiburg im Breisgau: Herder, 1895.

———. *I sarcofagi cristiani antichi*. MAC. 2 vols. Rome: Pontificio Istituto di Archeologia Cristiana, 1929–1932.

Wilson, Stephen, ed. *Saints and Their Cults: Studies in Religious Sociology, Folklore and History*. Cambridge: Cambridge University Press, 1983.

Witherington, Ben, III. *The Acts of the Apostles: A Socio-rhetorical Commentary*. Grand Rapids: Eerdmans, 1998.

Wolski, Wanda, and Ion Berciu, "Contribution au problème des tombes romaines à dispositif pour les libations funéraires." *Latomus* 32.2 (1973): 370–79.

Yasin, Ann Marie. "Funerary Monuments and Collective Identity: From Roman Family to Christian Community." *ArtB* 87.3 (2005): 433–57.

———. *Saints and Church Spaces in the Late Antique Mediterranean: Architecture, Cult, and Community*. Cambridge: Cambridge University Press, 2009.

Zahn, Theodor. *Geschichte des neutestamentlichen Kanons*. 2 vols. Erlangen and Leipzig: Deichert, 1890–1892.

Zahrnt, M. "Antinoopolis in Ägypten: Die hadrianische Gründung und ihre Privilegien in der neueren Forschung." *ANRW* 10.1:669–706.

Zovatto, P. L. "L'urnetta argentea di S. Ambrogio nell'ambito della rinascenza teodosiana." *CrArte* 13–14 (1956): 2–14.

Zwierlein, Otto. *Petrus in Rom: Die literarischen Zeugnisse*. Berlin: de Gruyter, 2009.

Scriptural Citations

Primary Source Citations

Subject Index

Abitinian Martyrs (North Africa), 184–86

Achaia. *See* Greece

ad sanctos. See privileged burials

Aelia Secundula (mother honored with meals), 75–84

Aemiliana (relative of Felix III and Petronia), 48

Aeneas (hero), 31–32

Agiulf (deacon of Tours), 130–32

Agnes (martyr), 90, 138

Aïn Abid (North Africa), 170–71

Aïn Ghorab (North Africa), 168–69, 172–73

Alaric I (king of the Visigoths), 172

Alba Longa (predecessor to Rome), 31–32, 53

Alcalá la Real (Spain), 150–51

Allobroges (ancient Celtic tribe of Gaul), 133

Altar of Peace (Rome), 24

Ambrose (bishop of Milan), 8–9, 23 n. 19, 54, 94, 117–24, 131, 153, 165–66, 187

Ambrosian Basilica (Milan), 131

Ambrosiaster (commentator on Pauline epistles), 28 n. 28

Ammianus Marcellinus (Roman historian), 105 n. 86

Ammonius (Egyptian monk, pilgrim to Rome), 90

Amulius (king of Alba Longa), 32–33

Andrew (apostle), 51 n. 86, 133, 140

Angers (Gaul), 132, 142

Antinous (hero), 75–77

Antioch (Syria), 102–3, 107

Antonius (pilgrim to Catacombs), 85–86

Anulinus (proconsul), 184

apostolic residence in Rome, 98–100

Appian (Roman historian), 125

Aquae Salvias (Rome), 63–69

Arator (commentator on Acts of the Apostles), 23 n. 19

Arcadius (emperor), 27

Arch of Titus (Rome), 104 n. 85

Aricia (valley near Lake Nemi), 76

Ariston (innkeeper at Puteoli), 146

Arles (Gaul), 134, 136

Armenia, 48 n. 75

Athanasius (bishop of Alexandria), 90

Attila (ruler of the Huns), 88

Augustine (bishop of Canterbury), 188

Augustine (bishop of Hippo Regius), 6, 9, 23 n. 19, 43 n. 62, 118 n. 2, 119 n. 4, 131, 156, 163–67, 172–73, 181 n. 52, 182–83

Augustus (emperor), 23 n. 19

Aurelian Way (Rome), 96 n. 65

Byzantium (city on the Bosporus), 102
Caecilian (bishop of Carthage), 179–80, 184–85
Caecilianists, 180–86
Caius (ecclesiastical historian), 21–22, 24, 34, 46, 55, 89, 187
calendars
   liturgical, 4 n. 9, 9, 22, 95–97, 129, 150–51, 153, 163
   Roman civil, 9 n. 18, 23 n. 21
Camillus (Roman general), 103
Campania (region of Italy), 53
Canterbury (Britain), 188
Capua (region of Italy), 53
Carthage (North Africa), 5, 104, 156, 160–62, 167–68, 174–76, 179–80, 184
Cassius (child buried at the Catacombs), 92
Cassius Dio (Roman historian), 125
Castellum Tingitanum (North Africa), 176–77
Castor and Pollux (gods), 33 n. 43
Catacombs (St. Sebastian), 11, 54 n. 93, 71–114, 167, 187
Catholics, as term used by Caecilianists, 180–182
Celerinus (inscriber at Catacombs), 72
cemeteries, 22, 53, 71–72, 122–24
   of Callistus (Rome), 77–78, 96, 105 n. 88
cemetery art, 77–79
cenotaphs, 93
chains of the apostles. See Paul, chains of ; Peter, chains of
Chalcedon (Asia Minor), 125
Charles Borromeo (archbishop of Milan), 121
chiasm, 157–58

Chi-Rho/Christogram, 169–72, 174, 178
Chrysanthus (martyr), 130
Church of Santa Maria in Scala Coeli (Rome), 68
Church of the Holy Apostles (Constantinople), 102
Cilicia (Asia Minor), 64–66
Circumcellions, 182 n. 55
citizenship, 97, 101, 103, 104–5, 109, 111–13, 160
Clement (bishop or secretary of Rome), 18 n. 6
clients. See patronage
Clovis I (Frankish king), 134
Codex Sinaiticus (manuscript), 125–26
Condat Abbey (Gaul), 133–34, 143
confessors, 2, 141, 163
Constantina (empress), 50, 57, 60–61, 111, 161 n. 7
Constantine (emperor), 2, 8, 24–28, 34, 38, 77, 89–90, 102, 114, 122, 123 n. 7, 172, 180, 187
Constantinople, 29, 50, 51 n. 86, 59, 102–3
Constantius (bishop of Milan), 50–51 n. 85
Constantius Chlorus (emperor), 102 n. 81, 118 n. 1
Corinth (Greece), 18–19, 144, 159
Cornelius (bishop of Rome), 109–10
Corsica, 127
Council of Carthage
   (397), 167
   (401), 167
   (484), 167 n. 16
Council of Constantinople (381), 103
Council of Nicea
   (325), 102

CPSIA information can be obtained at www.ICGtesting.com
Printed in the USA
BVOW03s0824271213

340256BV00001B/34/P